Biblical Healing and Deliverance

Biblical Healing and Deliverance

A Guide to Experiencing Freedom from Sins of the Past, Destructive Beliefs, Emotional and Spiritual Pain, Curses and Oppression

Chester and Betsy Kylstra

Chosen
Grand Rapids, Michigan

Published in the USA in 2005 by Chosen Books
a division of Baker Publishing Group
P.O. Box 6287, Grand Rapids, MI 49516-6287
www.chosenbooks.com

Originally published under the title *An Integrated Approach to Biblical Healing Ministry* by Sovereign World Limited of Tonbridge, Kent, England

Third printing, August 2007

Printed in the United States of America

Library of Congress Cataloging-in-Publication Data
Kylstra, Chester.
    [Integrated approach to biblical healing ministry]
    Biblical healing and deliverance: a guide to experiencing freedom from sins of the past, destructive beliefs, emotional and spiritual pain, curses and oppression / Chester and Betsy Kylstra.
        p. cm.
    Originally published: Integrated approach to biblical healing ministry. Tonbridge, Kent, England : Sovereign World, c2003.
    Includes bibliographical references and index.
    ISBN 0-8007-9403-6 (pbk.)
    1. Spiritual healing.   I. Kylstra, Betsy. II. Title.

BT732.5.K95 2005
234'.131—dc22
                                                                    2005048457

Contents

Index of Figures

Index of Tables

Acknowledgments

Very little that is worthwhile has ever been done totally solo. The people who have given love, inspiration, and physical and financial help are usually not in front of the camera helping to collect the prize but are off to the side cheering or praising the Lord in their hearts. We had much support as we wrote and produced the first and second editions of our earlier book *Restoring the Foundations*. It has been the same as we prepared *Biblical Healing and Deliverance* for release.

Chris and Jan Mungeam of Sovereign World have been major encouragers. We are pleased to join our vision with theirs to take Christian books into third-world nations. Tim Pettingale has provided steady support and wise counsel as the book moved through the publishing process.

We also want to acknowledge the dedicated and committed friends and colaborers of the Healing House Network. Together we are taking the message and actuality of God's healing to the world. Thanks for traveling with us.

We are also grateful to our office staff, including Susan Hedman and Jeannie Mack, for keeping the "home fires burning" while we are traveling and "hiding out" writing books.

We again want to acknowledge and bless all of the pastors, churches and network leaders that are helping us spread the Restoring the Foundations integrated approach to biblical healing ministry message and ministry.

We are grateful to Bishop Bill Hamon and Christian International Ministries for their continuing love and support, and for providing a home base for us even as we travel.

The Christian International Family Church intercessory team assigned to us as we travel internationally has helped keep the enemy at bay and the details covered. Thank you very much.

Without your help, we could not have brought this effort to completion.

Foreword

The ministry brought forth through *Biblical Healing and Deliverance* helps individuals return to their true foundations: the foundations of their soul, mind and spirit. As they go through ministry for the four problem areas, they receive enlightenment, healing, deliverance and restoration. My wife and I were greatly blessed by going through this ministry. These truths and ministries were such a blessing and so restorational that I requested that all of my Christian International Board of Governors receive the ministry. We also challenged all 500 ministers in the Christian International Ministries Network to go through the restoration process and then establish it in their church as an ongoing ministry.

The truths presented in this book are not theories but proven, divine biblical principles and practices that bring transformation and restoration. During the 49 years of my ministry, I have been exposed to almost every ministry available in the Body of Christ. I can truly say that *Biblical Healing and Deliverance* expresses the most balanced and workable ministry in this area that I have ever witnessed or experienced. This book and its application in the ministry the Kylstras have developed are being used by the Holy Spirit to take the spots and wrinkles out of Christ's Church.

I have worked with Chester and Betsy Kylstra for many years. Their "10 Ms" are in proper order in their personal lives. The evidence of the fruit of their ministry can be seen in the hundreds of transformed Christian lives, the many rescued marriages and restored ministers. We thank you and bless you, Chester and Betsy, for your commitment to God to bring such truths of ministry to Christ's corporate Church.

Dr. Bill Hamon,
founder and president,
Christian International Ministries Network

Preface

We are pleased and excited to release *Biblical Healing and Deliverance*. It represents the continuation of a strong directive from the Lord to "spread the word" of the revelation of the power and effectiveness of the Restoring the Foundations ministry to as many in the Body of Christ as possible. The time is short, and He *is* coming back for a Bride without spot or wrinkle.[1]

This book represents another very important step in "spreading the word." It is a new venture in expressing the Restoring the Foundations (RTF) ministry. The first and second editions of *Restoring the Foundations*, released in 1996 and 2000, were the initial phases. They are published by Proclaiming His Word Publishing. But now Sovereign World wants to take the revelation of *Biblical Healing and Deliverance* worldwide. This book has been written to be a suitable vehicle for this mission. Our zeal to share the revelation in this book with the entire Body of Christ has increased with this opportunity. It is with much excitement that we anticipate seeing it translated into other languages.

This book represents many years of our personal healing and training by the Holy Spirit. Even as He was healing us from our own hurts and bondages, He was training us to minister to and train others. Restoring the Foundations integrated approach to biblical healing ministry expresses this very effective approach to ministry.

God has given us a revelation of His intense desire to see His people healed, delivered and set free. This desire is so great that He took a professional secular counselor/teacher (Betsy) and a professional aerospace, software engineer/teacher (Chester), and gradually developed a healing/deliverance ministry team responsive to His Holy Spirit. He has given us a desire to share this knowledge through Restoring the Foundations ministry by training, equipping and activating others. This book is one of the vehicles to be used for sharing these basic understandings, with biblical support for the concepts and principles.

This book covers the basic, *foundational, restorational* tasks that need to be accomplished in every saint's life as God the Holy Spirit does His work of sanctification.[2] This *foundational ministry* provides a good base upon which other, more specific kinds of ministry, discipleship and equipping can be built.

We think of this process as Restoring the Foundations ministry. It is an integrated approach to biblical healing ministry that deals with the four *foundational* problem areas of:

1. Sins of the fathers and resulting curses,

2. Ungodly beliefs,

3. Soul/spirit hurts, and

4. Demonic oppression.

The key phrase, *an integrated approach to biblical healing ministry*, means ministry to *all* of these areas in concert, under the direction and power of the Holy Spirit. When this is done, there is deeper and more lasting healing and deliverance than when there is ministry to only one, two or even three of these areas during the same time period.

This *restoration* process, which is going on in each saint's life, also coincides with the *restoration* of the Church. It fits in with, and is a part of, the *restoration* of the apostles and prophets.[3] Restoring the Foundations (RTF) ministry (and other similar healing ministry approaches) has been brought forth by God over the last twenty years to bring *foundational* healing and freedom to the Church. He particularly wants His five-fold ministers[4] healed and free so that they can fulfill their part in preparing the Bride for the coming of the Lord and the *restoration* of all things.[5]

Three levels of *foundations* are being restored today: the foundation of each saint, the foundation of the local church and the foundation of Christ's Church universal. As each individual saint is restored, all three of these foundations are being restored, healed, strengthened, enabled and equipped. As a result, the entire temple is being restored, thus preparing the way for the return of the Lord.[6]

Putting It into Practice

The biblical understandings and concepts as expressed in our original book *Restoring the Foundations* and in this book must be translated into practice in order to be effective. We have developed several teaching/training/apprenticeship programs for the local church and para-church ministries. These programs equip RTF lay ministers, cell/small-group leaders, and other five-fold ministers.[7] We are grateful for the anointing and the abundant fruit coming forth in all of these areas.

A Note of Caution Regarding the Testimonies

A note of caution is in order before we launch into the main portion of the book. Although we received permission to use the personal testimonies of the people portrayed in the ministry illustrations, we have changed their names to protect their identity. If you think you recognize someone by the events of the story, please remember that we have ministered to hundreds of people with similar problems. As Paul writes in 1 Corinthians 10:13, "There hath no temptation taken hold of you but such as is common to man. But God is faithful . . ." (KJ21).

Many people have shared how significant the Restoring the Foundations ministry has been to them and its impact on their lives. Recently a man commented, "Next to the Bible, *Restoring the Foundations* is the most valuable book I own." Needless to say, it is tremendously satisfying to us to help others through our books.

May God bless you and bring you to a new level of revelation of His healing grace as you read and study this book.

Chester and Betsy Kylstra
January 2003

1

What Is the Integrated Approach?

Therefore, having these promises, beloved,
let us cleanse ourselves from all defilement of flesh and spirit,
perfecting holiness in the fear of God.
2 Corinthians 7:1, NASB

Many people in the world are trapped and wounded, and believe they are helpless. We were once among that group. By the grace of God, we were given a revelation of significant keys of the Kingdom that enabled first us and then many others to receive God's restorative healing, deliverance and freedom.[1] This book reveals the keys needed to unlock the chains that bind our lives and block and hinder our Christian growth. These keys are the revelation of how to minister to four problem areas that are in all of our lives and the importance of ministering to all of these problem areas simultaneously. When we minister to (1) sins of the fathers and resulting curses, (2) ungodly beliefs, (3) soul/spirit hurts and (4) demonic oppression as a unit, we call this an integrated approach to biblical healing ministry.

God has shown us that each of these four areas are connected to and strengthened by each of the other three. If we ignore any one of these problem areas when we are ministering to someone, we leave an open door for the enemy to undermine the entire healing process.

A. Four Problem Areas

Let's take a brief look at these four problem areas.

1. Sins of the fathers and resulting curses (SOFCs)

This problem area is rooted in the second commandment (Exodus 20:3–6), in which the sin of idolatry results in the curse of "visiting the iniquity of the fathers upon the children unto the third and fourth generation" (KJ21). In order to get free of this curse, God provides a pattern of confession that we can follow, first mentioned in Leviticus 26:40. We confess our ancestors' sin as well as our own sin (1 John 1:9), forgive as needed (Matthew 6:14–15) and appropriate Christ's finished work on the cross to break curses (Galatians 3:13) and recover the "legal ground" from the enemy (Colossians 2:14).

2. Ungodly beliefs (UGBs)

Our minds are full of untruths and half-truths inherited from our ancestors (i.e., our parents, grandparents) and formed from the hurtful circumstances and experiences of our own lives. These ungodly beliefs (UGBs) need to be changed into godly beliefs (GBs) (Romans 12:2). This is accomplished through a carefully structured procedure of repentance for believing lies, renouncing those lies and receiving God's truth to renew our minds. This procedure also recovers "legal ground" as we break our agreements with demons.

3. Soul/spirit hurts (SSHs)

Jesus came to heal the brokenhearted (Luke 4:18). As we "wait upon the Lord" with "listening prayer," He is eager to come and heal the hurts of our soul and spirit. He does this by showing us the original causes of our hurts. Then, after we take care of necessary forgiveness, releasing and renouncing, He heals what He has revealed. All "legal ground" given to the enemy from our sinful responses to the hurts, as well as the inherited legal ground, is recovered as a part of the ministry.

4. Demonic oppression (DO)

After ministering to the above three problem areas, it is now relatively easy to disassemble and destroy the demonic oppression structures (Mark 16:17) and eliminate them from our lives, since they have lost their "legal ground." It is a delight to help others gain this freedom.

Completing the Restoring the Foundations integrated approach to biblical healing ministry in these four problem areas brings integrated healing into our lives. This can be a major life-changing occurrence. We experience the transforming power of God's grace as His purpose is accomplished and we are conformed more and more into the image of His dear Son, Jesus the Christ.[2] This further opens the door for intimate fellowship with God and His empowerment, making it possible for us to live the "overcoming" Christian life.[3]

In the following chapters, we present the four problem areas in greater detail so that you may be better equipped both to receive ministry and to minister more effectively to others. Before we look at these, however, let's look at several foundational truths that undergird this integrated approach to biblical healing ministry. We also will give the first installment of Sandy's story, a story of God's healing in one woman's life that we will weave throughout this book.

B. Foundational Truths

The Restoring the Foundations integrated approach to biblical healing ministry is based on the central truths of the Christian faith. Both the minister and the ministry receiver need to understand and apply the truths regarding the cross, God's law, hearing God's voice and God's weapons.[4]

1. The cross

At the heart of Christianity is the cross of Jesus Christ. At the heart of our faith is the cross. At the heart of all effective Christian ministry stands the cross.[5]

The cross is the source of God's greatest provision for us. The cross represents the exchanged life, in which we give Jesus all that we are in exchange for Himself and all that He has done for us. Because of the substitutionary atonement in which Jesus became sin for us and on our behalf, we now have a pathway back to righteousness. Through the cross, Jesus Christ gives us the provisions for a victorious life: forgiveness of sin, victory over the power of sin, victory over Satan and his demons, power over sickness and disease and triumph over death itself. The cross provides the basis for reconciliation with Jesus and with our Abba Father. Because of the cross, we can live an abundant, joyful life on earth, as well as experience the glorious knowledge of eternal life.

In the cross, we see God's expansive love reaching out to us. This gives us hope to reach back toward Him, to begin to seek His healing for our pain. Through the cross, where God's wrath toward our sin was satisfied and our punishment borne, we can now repent and be totally forgiven and thoroughly cleansed. Because of the cross, where Jesus became a curse for us, we can now break the power of the curses (judgment) in our lives and be free of the sins of the fathers and resulting curses. By the cross, Jesus demonstrated that He is the way, the truth and the life.[6] He is the standard of truth, allowing us to recognize and leave behind our ungodly beliefs and move toward His godly beliefs. Because Jesus bore our grief and sorrow on the cross, we can now legitimately release all of our pain and hurt to Him, expecting His healing of our soul/spirit hurts. At the cross, where Jesus defeated Satan, we can now receive the authority He has provided for us to be victorious over Satan and all the hordes of hell. As believers, we can cast out demons and remove demonic oppression from our lives.

The cross is central to our freedom. In the Restoring the Foundations integrated approach to biblical healing ministry, we appropriate the cross in all of its fullness into our lives. We receive it, apply it to our lives, possess its reality and victory and are empowered to move forward in faith. Then we are in the position to help others by bringing the power of the cross into their lives for their healing and deliverance.

2. God's law

As ministers, it is most important that we understand several things about God's law. We need to know that there are consequences when we, or the people to whom we are ministering, violate or are disobedient to God's law. It is precisely because God's judgment is released when His law is violated that He sent Jesus Christ to provide a way out of the judgment. Our job is to learn how to appropriate God's provision and then help others to be set free.

First, let's remember Jesus' attitude toward the law. Jesus said:

> "Think not that I am come to destroy the Law or the Prophets. I am not come to destroy, but to fulfill. For verily I say unto you, till heaven and earth pass away, not one jot or one tittle shall in any wise pass from the law till all be fulfilled."
>
> Matthew 5:17–18, KJ21

Then He turns to "us" and says:

> "Whosoever therefore shall break one of these least commandments and shall teach men so, he shall be called the least in the Kingdom of Heaven; but whosoever shall do and teach them, the same shall be called great in the Kingdom of Heaven."
>
> Matthew 5:19, KJ21

So here in Matthew and in many other passages, as in Luke 24:44 and Luke 16:17, Jesus demonstrates His honor and respect for the law. He clearly expects us to do the same.

Results of violating God's law

When we (and our ancestors) violate the law of God, several consequences occur. First, automatic repercussions are activated. We can look at the law of gravity as a natural example. Stepping off of a building causes one to fall. Gravity is working day and night. It is working for both the saved and unsaved. It is impartial. Every one of God's laws is impartial and always active. When we sin, a chain reaction is put into motion that has negative consequences for everyone it touches.

A second consequence is that pain is almost always created. In fact, most people come for ministry because they are in pain. They are experiencing turmoil, confusion, torment, guilt, shame, anger; the list goes on and on. Pain drives us to God.

Another very important consequence is spiritual separation from God. As Isaiah 59:2 (NIV) states:

> But your iniquities have separated
>   you from your God;
> your sins have hidden his face from you,
>   so that he will not hear.

A fourth unfortunate consequence is that we give legal opportunity for demonic oppression. Paul expressed this clearly when he wrote in Ephesians 4:26–27: "Be ye angry, and sin not: let not the sun go down on your wrath, neither give place to the devil" (KJ21).

God's solution

As Christians, we have two advantages over the rest of the world regarding the violation of God's law:

1. We have a remedy when we violate God's law, and
2. We can ask the Holy Spirit for grace and empowerment to avoid breaking God's law in the future.

The place to receive help is at the cross. We have already discussed the awesome provision of the cross. The ability to receive God's healing and freedom is centered on God's provision at the cross. Here the consequences of *all* of the violations of God's law were poured out on one man, Jesus Christ. Being saved from God's judgment occurs only when we meet His conditions. We appropriate by faith the provision He made for us at the cross. The cross made it possible for us to "enter into" God's promises of healing and deliverance.

One important, representative passage is God's conditional promise found in 1 John: "If we confess our sins, He is faithful and just to forgive us our sins, and to cleanse us from all unrighteousness" (1 John 1:9, KJ21).

When and if we do our part (confess our sins), God will do His part (forgive us and cleanse us from the resulting unrighteousness) because He is faithful and just. Thus, we can receive freedom from the consequences of violating the law.

Specific laws relevant to RTF ministry

As we minister, a number of God's laws are relevant. We will focus on four central ones for use in the integrated approach to biblical healing ministry:

- Sowing and reaping
- Multiplication
- Time to harvest
- Believing in your heart

The concepts and principles expressed in these laws will be used in each of the four problem areas as we bring the healing and freedom of Jesus Christ into our ministry receiver's life.

3. Hearing God's voice

Our deep desire is to hear God's voice and to follow His leading throughout each ministry session. We want the best for each person to whom we minister. We know that significant healing only occurs when the Holy Spirit leads and the Lord Jesus Christ touches. We want to hear everything that God is saying in the areas of needed forgiveness, ancestral sins and curses (SOFCs), core beliefs that are ungodly (UGBs), hurts God wants to heal (SSHs) and demonic strongholds and their legal ground (DO).

As we minister, we want to be led very specifically in each arena. Before the ministry starts, we listen to the Holy Spirit to obtain the real roots behind the ministry receiver's presenting problem(s). During ministry, we listen as the Holy Spirit guides our questions and ministry. Afterward, we listen to prepare for the next session.

Ways we hear

Our spiritual "hearing" senses can be placed into three broad
gories: hearing, seeing and feeling. We may "hear" God's voice as did
Samuel the prophet when he thought Eli was calling him[7] and as
Elijah did at Mount Horeb.[8] We may "see" God's voice as in a vision,
similar to Peter and John on the Mount of Transfiguration with Jesus.[9]
The Bible records many visions received by the prophets. We may also
"feel" God's voice with our senses. This seems to occur frequently
with intercessors as they pray for others' healing.

Most of us have one primary way that we hear God's voice most of
the time. We may hear it through any of the following (hearing,
seeing, feeling) ways: illumination of Scripture, inward vision (word of
wisdom, word of knowledge), seeing His words in our spirit, hearing
His voice in our spirit, dreams or even experiencing another person's
emotions or physical feelings. Ways of "hearing" God's voice that are
less common include seeing an outward vision and/or hearing God's
voice audibly.

Learning to hear

Many of us, like the boy Samuel,[10] do not recognize when God is
speaking. Like Samuel, we have to learn to hear Him through inten-
tional listening and hearing.[11]

The good news is that even if you are not currently confident
that you hear God's voice, you can gain confidence by practice and
receiving training to hear God's voice better. As we hear God's voice
and learn to flow in His gifts, we are much more ready to confront the
enemy of our soul and to bring His healing to others.

4. God's weapons

As ministers, we do not want to be naïve in the area of spiritual warfare. We must take our blinders off and realize there is a spiritual
battle raging. If we are blind or passive, we will sooner or later become
victims. Satan and his army are out to prevent salvation, arrest our
spiritual maturity, keep our minds full of the world's garbage and
promote disease in our bodies. Satan does not play fair! He is willing
to use every possible means and every legal access to defeat us.[12]
The good news is that we do not have to be wimpy soldiers with
wimpy weapons. We have all the "firepower" that we need. However, we have to get the weapons out of the armory and put them to
work! "For the weapons of our warfare are not of the flesh, but

divinely powerful for the destruction of fortresses" (2 Corinthians 10:4, NASB).

We have our protective, defensive weapons. They are designed to deflect and stop Satan's fiery darts. They are the helmet of salvation, the shield of faith, the breastplate of righteousness, the girdle of truth, and the boots of the preparation of the gospel of peace.[13]

In addition, we have our offensive weapons. The military teaches its leaders that "the best defense is an offense." The same is true for spiritual warfare. We want to take our "divinely powerful" offensive weapons and use them against the enemy for our own sake and for the sake of the ministry receiver. Our offensive weapons include prayer, the Word of God, the name of Jesus, the cross, the blood, praise, our spiritual prayer language and the laying on of hands. We can also ask God to dispatch angels to minister to the "heirs of salvation."[14] What an arsenal we have at our disposal!

We expect to have many victories in the Restoring the Foundations integrated approach to biblical healing ministry sessions as we use God's offensive weapons. We expect to see lives changed in significant ways so that the captives will be set free. Our mission is to use God's offensive weapons to defuse, confuse and scatter the enemy's strongholds and remove the oppression from the ministry receiver.

A final note about weapons, particularly prayer. Prayer might be better thought of as our communication link with our Commander-in-Chief and the spiritual realm in general. In the broadest term, prayer includes "commanding," "declaring," "decreeing," "breaking," "interceding" and "releasing." *In a very real sense, all of the weapons, both defensive and offensive, are put into action through prayer.*

We want to conclude this section with a portion of Psalm 18, a psalm of David.[15] We encourage you to make verses 30–50 of this psalm your own, as if God were speaking these promises directly to you as *His* spiritual warrior. May you be empowered to defeat the demonic hosts (enemies, strangers, violent men) that come against you and your ministry receiver.

> As for God, His way is perfect; the word of the LORD is proved; He is a
>   buckler to all those that trust in Him.
> For who is God, except the LORD? Or who is a rock, except our God?
> It is God that girdeth me with strength, and maketh my way perfect.
> He maketh my feet like hinds' feet, and setteth me upon my high
>   places.
> *He teacheth my hands to war,* so that the bow of steel is broken
>   by mine arms.

*Thou hast also given me the shield of Thy salvation; Thy right hand hath
   held me up*, and Thy gentleness hath made me great.
Thou hast enlarged my path under me, that my feet did not slip.
I have pursued mine enemies and overtaken them; neither did
   I turn back until they were consumed.
I have wounded them, that they were not able to rise; they have
   fallen under my feet.
For Thou hast girded me with strength for the battle; Thou hast subdued
   under me those that rose up against me.
Thou hast also given me the necks of mine enemies, that I might
   destroy them that hate me.
They cried, but there was none to save them, even unto the LORD,
   but He answered them not.
Then did I beat them small as the dust before the wind; I did cast
   them out as the dirt in the streets.
Thou hast delivered me from the strivings of the people; and Thou
   hast made me the head of the heathen; a people whom I have
   not known shall serve me.
As soon as they hear of me, *they shall obey me*; the strangers
   shall submit themselves unto me.
The strangers shall fade away, and be afraid out of their close places.
The LORD liveth, and blessed be my Rock! And let the God of my
   salvation be exalted!
It is God that avengeth me, and subdueth the people under me;
He delivereth me from mine enemies. Yea, Thou liftest me up
   above those that rise up against me; Thou hast delivered
   me from violent men.
Therefore will I give thanks unto Thee, O LORD, among the heathen,
   and sing praises unto Thy name.
Great deliverance giveth He to His king and showeth mercy to
   His anointed, to David and to his seed for evermore.

   Psalm 18:30–50, KJ21, emphasis mine

C. Sandy's Story: Who Is This Lady? What Has She Done?[16]

We want to present a marvelous account of how God used the truths
that form the basis of the Restoring the Foundations integrated
approach to biblical healing ministry to rescue a very wounded lady
from her path of destruction. We will call her Sandy,[17] this lady at the
center of the storm. Our first contact with Sandy and her husband
occurred at the church where we were meeting some of the church

elders and prospective couples to be trained and equipped to conduct Restoring the Foundations (RTF) ministry.[18] Middle-aged, well dressed and distinguished, she and her husband appeared "normal" in every sense of the word. Over the years, they had served the congregation well with much honor and respect as elders. A strong teacher of the Word, Sandy had also been the head counselor at the church—until all of "this" had come out.

They were understandably cautious and reserved as we were introduced. Why shouldn't they be? We were to be their "restorers," the ones through whom God would bring their healing (at least the initial part of it). They questioned whether or not they could really trust us; whether or not we could really help them through and out of their devastation. We learned later that Sandy wasn't at all sure she could be helped. She lived with the fear and the torment that maybe she had gone "too far." Had she committed the "unpardonable" sin? Could God really "be there" for her in spite of all she had done? Or even worse, maybe she was inherently "too defective, too evil" and beyond God's ability to restore.

We were also wondering, *Have we gotten ourselves in over our heads (again)? Could God really use us in this situation? Could we really discover the root(s) of the sin and expose the open doors through which the enemy had come? Could we clear out the "legal" rights Satan had and get the doors closed? Could we help make a way for God's restoration and healing to come?* We didn't know for sure, but we did know our God and His mercies that "are new every morning." Numerous times He had come through when we were beyond our experience and skill level. We knew that His desire to heal His people is far greater than ours. We had strong reason to believe that Sandy could and would be restored. As we visited, Sandy visibly began to relax. We soon felt that she had accepted us and would submit to the RTF ministry process.

1. The first ministry session

When we met with Sandy that first morning, it was clear that this case was not going to fall into the normal pattern of Restoring the Foundations ministry. As we had grown to expect (and desire), we would need to trust the Holy Spirit to weave the elements of the integrated approach to biblical healing ministry together in a way that would cause Sandy's healing to come. (Actually, we wouldn't have it any other way. The only worthwhile healing has to come from the Lord and under His direction.)

After the "start-up" events,[19] we launched into gathering information about Sandy. We wanted to know about her current life, the "sin" that had prompted the church to bring us to minister to her (and others); her ancestors, her family, her growing-up years, her successes and failures. We wanted to know all about her, particularly those things that would give us understanding about how she had arrived at her current situation. We wanted to listen to her *and* to the Holy Spirit's comments and illumination about what she was saying.

In order to spare you the many hours of ministry during which we obtained information about Sandy, we are going to present several main threads that ran through the fabric of her life. Then later, in the chapters on the four problem areas and in the last chapter, we will show how the Holy Spirit led us as we ministered to these "threads." It was fascinating and tremendously exciting to see how the Holy Spirit unraveled the complexity of her situation and then gave us the strategy that confounded and defeated the enemy, bringing the victory.

2. One additional note of importance

Sandy's depth of wounding and bondage was much greater than what we usually find in the Body of Christ. She was not the "typical" church leader or member ministered to by RTF lay ministers. As you will see, the severity of the demonic strongholds and the intensity of the lies she believed, along with the soul/spirit hurts, required much more ministry than the normal five sessions of the thorough ministry format.[20] So, dear reader, please don't read Sandy's story thinking that this is "normal" RTF ministry. It is the "extended" format. Rather, read it to learn the lessons God wants you to learn, so you will be better equipped to minister to those God brings your way. Also, read it to rejoice with us at God's wonderful mercy, power and grace that He would bring such freedom and healing to one of His children and allow us to participate in it. He truly is doing amazing things on the earth today!

3. Her sin

What had brought Sandy's life to a halt and stopped her ministry in its tracks as a much-loved church counselor and Bible teacher? It was a shocking adulterous affair. With paramount courage she had faced her friends in the congregation and confessed her eight-year adulterous relationship with their (and her) pastor. If a Richter scale could have measured personal devastation, her reading would have been an "8" and the church's a "7.5." The revelation of her sin caused a "faith quake" that left almost nothing standing. It exposed the deception behind their pastor's resignation several months previously for reasons of "fatigue."

Filled with grief and self-hate, Sandy realized how her sin was shattering the very people she had helped shepherd for eight years.

4. The key threads

It was soon obvious that Sandy was coming out of years of *deception* and a life ruled by *fear*. We were dealing with an intertwining of complex problem areas, including strong evidence of much occult involvement in Sandy's family line. In our years of RTF ministry, we have learned that when the symptoms of control, deception, fear, sexual sin and infirmities are present, there is almost always occult background somewhere in the family line. Sandy had all five of these indicators, big time!

The foundational wound appeared to be *abandonment*. This was the primary door through which everything else had entered and become established. It was the basis for many other strongholds and oppressions.

Abandonment was given opportunity right from the start. Sandy was an unwanted child. Her young parents were struggling financially and had two children already. These stresses generated much strife in the family. While still in the womb, Sandy was essentially "abandoned" by both parents. Her mother did want a girl and eventually even came to idolize her daughter. The damage to Sandy, however, had already been done.

In her early years, Sandy's father was often away from home. He essentially became *an absentee father*.

Fear also got an early grip on the young child. The occult immediately began to use both fear and terror to bring her into submission. As a little girl, she would often experience a "presence" at the door of her bedroom in the late night hours. "I'll kill you if you move," the evil voice threatened. The sound of eerie music that seemed to come from the church across the street added to the fear. Lying in her bed and paralyzed with fear, Sandy wondered if she would survive the night.

Sandy's sense of abandonment, along with the whispered lies of the demons, caused her to conclude early in life that she must be a "bad" girl. It was "obvious" since nobody wanted to be with her, and all those terrorizing things kept happening to her. Believing herself to be "bad" helped Sandy move into a "deceptive, secret life." By age six, she felt isolated and all alone, with nobody to help her.

Often left alone at night, Sandy would lie for hours on the floor in the center of the house. She picked a spot where no one could see her if they looked through any of the windows. Feeling too abandoned and afraid to tell her parents, she blamed herself and often thought, *I'm stupid to be afraid.* As a result, she led a double life that made her appear good and happy on the outside but fearful, abandoned, isolated and bad on the inside. Between six and ten years of age, the fears became even more paralyzing.

Like many little girls, Sandy worked hard to get her father's attention when he was home. This proved successful in her early years and she enjoyed being known as "Daddy's little girl." Between the ages of eight and twelve, she performed with him on the stage numerous times. He was so proud of her. Things changed, however, as she approached the teen years. Sandy became clumsy and awkward. On one occasion, when she even forgot her lines in their play, sheer terror and panic overtook her. After this traumatic turning point, she lost her special place as Daddy's little girl.

Many of these early events dramatically reinforced her feelings that she was "just a bad person."

At age twelve, at a camp meeting, Sandy's mother abandoned her (she didn't protect her, but put her "at risk") with an evangelist (spiritual authority). At their first contact, he asked her to look into his eyes. Overtaken by his hypnotic power, which, in this case, was a form of occult control, Sandy became helpless to resist. When it was over, she was his and would do whatever he suggested. At first her mother would visit the evangelist alone but later he told her to bring Sandy, also. He would engage them in "prayers" and other activities that left Sandy feeling tremendous shame, embarrassment and humiliation. Once again, the belief that she was "bad" was reinforced. After all, if she were normal, these things wouldn't be happening to her. Adding to her confusion was the fact that, in spite of all of her negative feelings, she also liked the attention. Being needed by this man made her feel special.

After two summers of being captivated by the evangelist, Sandy was abandoned by him when he told her mother not to bring the child anymore. While relieved to be free from his control, she felt abandoned and rejected once again. This became the first of three rejections she experienced from a spiritual authority, after being used by each one.

In the sixth grade, Sandy had a special relationship with a boy who liked her. After her jealous girlfriends persuaded Sandy to reject him, they began to pursue him. This experience further enforced Sandy's feelings of abandonment and betrayal. The young man later became a brilliant doctor with a balanced personality. For years, Sandy carried regrets and "what ifs" concerning this traumatic episode. Once again she concluded that she was to blame. If her girlfriends could betray her so easily, she must just be "bad." Perhaps she deserved to miss the opportunity for a good marriage.

In her late teens, Sandy felt abandoned once again when her two older brothers went away to college. With one brother, she had experienced a special protective relationship. His departure left her feeling vulnerable and unprotected.

By the time Sandy arrived at college, she had an interesting dichotomy with respect to the issue of control. On the one hand, she was easily dominated by authority figures, boyfriends or an important friend. She would be or do almost anything to receive acceptance and approval. If occult power was being used, she was completely passive while being controlled.

When *she* was in control, however, Sandy became strong-willed and assertive. With the presence of many controlling figures in her life and family line, it was natural for Sandy to be controlling. She was a "survivor." She was determined to protect herself from exposure of her "bad" self and the resultant hurt and pain.

Sandy did smoke and do the usual "college" sins, but, interestingly, she was not sexually promiscuous. This points to the fact that sexual sin was not the main stronghold, but it was "used" by the other strongholds.

In high school and college, others saw her as popular, fun, outgoing and a good friend. Sandy, however, saw herself as not close to anyone. She had to *hide* her "true" self (which she saw as *"bad"*) from them. As she put it, "I have defilement on the inside, so I have to look good on the outside."

One year after college, Sandy married. Her husband, however, *emotionally abandoned* her and caused further separation as he "picked at" and verbally abused their oldest daughter.

Sandy felt a great *fear* of other people's *anger* and *rage*. Her father had almost hit her one time when he was in a rage. He did hit her brother.

This *fear of anger* being directed at her carried into Sandy's marriage, causing further separation from her husband.

Moving into her adult years, Sandy continued her *double life*, hiding the deep hurts and disappointments on the inside, yet acting, on the outside, as if everything was fine.

During the eight years of adultery with the spiritual leader (her pastor), her *double life* continued. This pattern of behavior was normal for her now. She actually *believed* that God wanted her to participate in the adultery in order to help this man's self-esteem and bring about his eventual healing. Like her previous seducers, this pastor had hypnotic eyes, which she felt powerless to resist. Interestingly, Sandy reported, "Every time I was with him, I fully believed that it would be the last time."

Two years before the end of their affair, God gave Sandy a revelation, including specific questions and Scriptures, which directed her to "come out." She wrote out the revelation and even showed it to her pastor. He merely laughed. The grip of her strongholds were so intense that she was unable to break free. As a result, she continued in her sin.

In the end, this pastor also *abandoned* her for another woman, leaving Sandy *feeling discarded, betrayed* and used.

Much more could be revealed about Sandy's history, but this synopsis provides a good overview of some key themes and the "stealing, killing and destroying"[21] work of Satan in her life. As we continue through this book, we will present different parts of Sandy's story to illustrate how God used the integrated approach to biblical healing ministry to bring forth her freedom and healing in each of the four problem areas. If you can't wait to read the rest of her story, you can "skip ahead" by looking in the table of contents (pages 5–7) for the page numbers of several parts of "Sandy's story."

D. What's Ahead

The next five chapters contain the "meat" of the integrated approach to biblical healing ministry. First, we will take a fresh look at forgiveness, followed by chapters covering in depth the four problem areas briefly mentioned earlier. The order in which the four problem areas are presented is also their usual order in the ministry process. The ministry builds to a climax as we recover the legal ground given over to the enemy in each of the problem areas.

First, we reclaim the ground given due to the iniquity of our ancestors being "visited" down the family line. Then we proceed to root up any ungodly thinking that agrees with the enemy. We want to replace this thinking with God's view of things, by exchanging ungodly beliefs for godly beliefs. The third area restores "broken hearts," as we use "Waiting upon the Lord" Listening Prayer for God to heal the soul/spirit hurts. Exposing and redeeming the associated sin further recovers legal ground from the devil. We are then ready for the fourth problem area, which involves casting out the demons that have used all of the above mentioned types of "legal ground" as the basis for their demonic oppression. This is usually easy to do after we have completed the first three problem areas.

Each of these chapters on the four problem areas has a detailed list of ministry steps at the end of the chapter. You can use these as you work with the Holy Spirit to bring more healing into your life.

The final chapter, "Getting Free and Staying Free!" includes two "applications" of the integrated approach to biblical healing ministry. "Soul Ties, the Ties That Bind" is a key concept and a widespread problem. "Demonic Strongholds" shows how the four problem areas can sometimes occur within one demonic structure that requires the application of the integrated approach to biblical healing ministry to bring the freedom. Sandy's story is also brought up to date as we find out how she is doing since her time of ministry. We finish the book with some final comments to help you answer the question, "Where do I go from here?"

Each of the seven chapters ends with a section entitled "Thought-Provoking Questions" to help you further understand and receive the different aspects of the integrated approach to biblical healing ministry.

We have included one appendix. It contains an "Ancestral Open Doors" form that you can use as a starting point for your own ministry.

At the end of the book, you will find information about how to contact Proclaiming His Word Ministries for other resources and training possibilities that are designed to help you in your Christian walk and in your ministry to others.

We hope you enjoy *Biblical Healing and Deliverance*. We want this book to be a blessing to you. Our prayer is that you will learn much more about God's provisions and how to receive them for yourself and for others. We also pray that the Holy Spirit will minister to you as you read and study these pages.

E. Thought-Provoking Questions

1. Does your life contain any physical and spiritual wounds or injured relationships?

    ....

    ....

2. What is God's purpose for your life?

    ....

    ....

3. What do you think about the idea that all Christians struggle with the same four problem areas?

    ....

    ....

4. What are three ways in which your relationship with others can be improved?

    ....

    ....

5. Have you ever seen or experienced a temporary or brief healing or spiritual victory? If so, please describe it. Have you held on to that spiritual victory?

    ....

    ....

6. Can you see why Satan would try to block Christians from seeking help and joining God's army? What would Satan want you to do about Restoring the Foundations Ministry?

    ....

    ....

7. Explain the RTF integrated approach to biblical healing ministry. Explain how it is different from other ministry approaches that you have learned.

    ....

    ....

8. Do you desire a closer walk with God? What have you done recently to cause this to happen?

    . . . .

    . . . .

2

Forgiveness: The Key to Freedom

"Forgive, and ye shall be forgiven."
Luke 6:37, KJ21

Recently, Betsy heard a story about two old-maid sisters, Mary and Mabel, who lived together. Because of their extreme differences, they had irritated each other for years. Now in their eighties, each one had developed a bundle of resentments toward the other. One January, Mabel became seriously ill and was hospitalized. The sisters' well-meaning Christian friends, knowing well the bitterness between them, encouraged Mary to ask for Mabel's forgiveness while there was still time to set things right. Obligingly, Mary made her way to the hospital and said to her frail sister, "Mabel, you've been so hard to live with all these years, but I just want you to know that I forgive you for all the horrible things you've done, and you need to forgive me, too." Then, after a pause, she added, "But Mabel, if you should happen to get well, just forget everything I just said."

In this chapter, that is *not* the kind of forgiveness that we are going to be writing about! In God's economy, *forgiveness is the principal activity and heart attitude needed to pave the way for freedom.* It is the *key to freedom.* As long as unforgiveness is present, God's hand of protection, mercy and restoration is hindered at best and stopped at worst. Although often the hardest part of the ministry process for the ministry receiver, forgiveness is the prerequisite for lasting healing.

Directions of Forgiveness

We want to discuss forgiveness from the three essential directions: the ministry receiver forgiving *others*, the receiver asking *God's* forgiveness, then the receiver forgiving *self*, which allows the fullness of God's forgiveness to be received. The Scriptures underlying these different directions of forgiveness are given in Table A on page 38.

A. Forgiving Others

Forgiving others. The words are easy to say, aren't they? Forgiving others may be the greatest challenge the ministry receiver faces. In this section, we want to look at what is involved in forgiving others, the scriptural principles and some common misconceptions and hindrances to forgiveness. We will also study ways the minister, working with much grace, can help the receiver to overcome the hindrances. Table A on page 38 contains some relevant Scriptures.

In the ministry process, forgiveness sets the stage for unhindered healing in the four major problem areas: sins of the fathers and resulting curses, ungodly beliefs, soul/spirit hurts and demonic oppression. As soon as the initial interview is completed, we want to begin the process of forgiveness, unless we hear the Holy Spirit say otherwise.

1. Illustrations

Most Christians know the power of forgiveness to change lives and to bring healing to bodies. Forgiveness breaks the powerful spiritual bond that locks people into a negative way of relating to each other. To our amazement, we have even seen the person who has been forgiven begin to act differently, even when he does not know that forgiveness has taken place.

Several years ago, we worked with a young Bible college student whose father was a pastor. It was one of those situations where the ministry had come first. As a result, her father had not been present at those meaningful moments and events. The daughter's bitterness had created a deep estrangement between them. As we worked through the process of forgiveness with her, she was able to forgive her father. Then we said to her, "You can expect your relationship with your father to change." We said that in faith because we had seen it work so many times.

A month later, over Thanksgiving, she attended the traditional service at her father's church. After giving a Thanksgiving message, her father became uncharacteristically personal and began to share his heart with the people. He said, "You know, there are a lot of ways that I've failed, and one of them is in my relationship with my daughter. And yet I am thankful that we have a God of new beginnings, and I am very thankful for my daughter." With that, he walked out of the pulpit and into the congregation. He put his arms around her, asked for her forgiveness and expressed his love for her. Shocked but also thrilled, she immediately realized why this had happened. By forgiving her father, she had helped set in motion the restoration of their relationship. The families in the congregation, touched by this reconciliation, began to follow suit by sharing their love for each other and giving thanks for that which is most precious in life. When we forgive, we break a negative bond or bondage that exists with those people against whom we are holding something. This young woman's forgiveness set her father free to express the love in his heart.

Several years ago, Betsy was ministering with a young woman who had been an incest victim. Abused by her brother over a period of four or five years, she had allowed hatred to dominate her life. Over the months, as she expressed her anger and pain, Betsy often mentioned, "God wants to bring you to a place where you can begin to forgive your brother." At the time, the young woman was so hurt that she didn't want to hear anything about forgiveness. At this point, Betsy prayed and interceded for God to somehow break through and touch her life.

One day she called Betsy saying, "I'm home from work. I have ulcers that are bleeding; I'm in such incredible pain that I cannot go to work. The doctor says that I may need surgery. I don't see how I can come to my ministry session this afternoon." Encouraging her to try to come anyway, Betsy began asking the Lord how to minister to her. What the Lord revealed really shook Betsy. He said, "Her bitterness has already caused the stomach ulcers. If it goes on, it will destroy her colon, and eventually affect a third area of her body. It will then progress into a life-threatening condition." After Betsy conferred with the pastor who had referred the young woman to her, they both felt Betsy should share what God had shown her. Betsy was not thrilled at the prospect.

As they met that afternoon, Betsy said, "I have to tell you something. I just have to. I don't feel as if I have a choice. God loves you too much to want you to go on like this." While sharing with the young woman, Betsy began to weep. She was feeling the grief of God over the destruction taking place in the woman's life: the destruction from the sexual sin and now the consequence of this woman's own bitterness. In answer to prayer, the message found its way into the young woman's heart, and God's amazing grace helped these tentative words come out of her mouth: "God, please bring me to a place where I can forgive my brother." It was a horrendous thing. Betsy could see the physical and emotional struggle taking place as the woman gave up her bitterness. Afterward, she looked wilted. Suddenly, she stood up, looked at Betsy and cried out, "The pain is gone, the pain is gone, the pain is gone!" They danced around the living room glorying in God's instant healing miracle. The pain never returned. As she forgave and released that bitterness, her body was healed right there and right then.

A story once told by a Methodist pastor sums up the importance of forgiveness.

Once upon a time two men went into the forest to cut wood. As they labored together, one of the men was bitten on the ankle by a poisonous snake. As his foot and leg began to swell to threatening proportions, the man became frightened and angry. Grabbing an ax, he started beating the brush into which the snake had disappeared. His friend attempted to dissuade him from his search, telling him how important it was that they get immediately to the hospital. He knew time was limited to stop certain death from creeping into his friend's bloodstream. But the wounded man refused to listen. He flailed angrily at the tall grass and bushes as he shouted, "I'm not leaving here until I've killed that snake."

In all of life's attacks upon us, Jesus is our Doctor, and Jesus is our Healer. We must make the choice to rush ever so quickly into His loving mercy and provision of grace, or . . . we can choose to kill snakes until the venom of unforgiveness and bitterness claims our spiritual lives.

2. A definition of forgiveness

Forgiveness is the setting of one's will, the making of a decision (a decree, a decision at the spiritual level) *that a release is granted to the offending person or situation* (sometimes it's an organization or a body of people more than just an individual). When we forgive, we choose to set them free. We don't hold the resentment; we don't hold the bitterness; we let go of our plans for retaliation. We let go of the feeling, "They owe me something." We set them free. It's important for the receiver to forgive all who have contributed to his hurts and bondages.

Webster's definition of *forgive* is helpful, as is the definition of *pardon*, which really comes closest to the biblical meaning of forgiveness.

Definition

Forgive: "to give before or ahead of"
1. To cease to feel resentment against (an offender)
2. To grant relief from payment

Definition

Pardon: "to grant freely"
1. The excusing of an offense without exacting a penalty
2. Divine forgiveness

---

3. Scriptural principles

Have you, like us, ever wanted God to make a special exception in your case, as you attempted to avoid reexperiencing a painful memory? As painful as forgiveness can be, it ultimately brings about our healing in God's providential plan. His principles are very clear. As we discuss them, please refer to Table A on page 38.

a. God requires us to forgive each other.

God's Word clearly spells out His requirement for Christians: We are to relate to one another without bitterness, grudges or anything that puts up a barrier between us and our brother or sister. When it comes to forgiveness, the scriptural principles are uncompromising and non-negotiable. Forgiveness does not depend on fairness, on whether a person feels like it or not, or who was in the wrong. God simply tells us repeatedly that we *must* forgive.

God, our loving heavenly Father, not only cares about how we relate to Him, but He also cares about how we relate to our brothers and sisters in Christ, how we relate to everyone in His creation. He doesn't want us to have coldness toward each other, or to mentally "X" people out. Chester used to think it was all right to avoid people. God made it clear that His way was different. He said, "Your avoidance of people is unacceptable. It is not My nature." God wants us to forgive one another, so that we have "cleaned-out," right relationships. That's His expectation. He permits no "ifs," "ands," "buts" or "special situations." No matter what the offense, He simply says, *"Forgive."*

b. God covers all of the angles.

We must forgive if we have anything against anyone, or if we know that someone is having a problem with us.

Table A: Scriptures Concerning Forgiveness

▶ *God's minimum requirement is that we forgive.*

Luke 17:3–10
We are unworthy servants; we have only done our duty (when we forgive).

▶ *Forgive those offending you.*

Mark 11:25–26
Forgive if you have anything against anyone, or else God won't forgive you.

Matthew 6:14–15
If you forgive men when they sin against you, God will also forgive you.

Matthew 18:15–17
These verses provide the procedure for reconciliation with an offending brother.

▶ *If you have offended someone, offer reconciliation.*

Matthew 5:23–24
For God to accept your gift, you are required to go and be reconciled to your brother.

▶ *God wants forgiveness from the heart.*

Matthew 18:35
You will be turned over to the tormentors if you do not forgive from your heart.

▶ *God wants as much forgiveness as necessary.*

Matthew 18:21–22
Forgive up to seventy times seven.

▶ *After we have given and received forgiveness, God's heart is to forgive.*

Isaiah 43:25
"I, even I, am he who blots out your transgressions, *for my own sake*, and remembers your sins no more" (NIV, emphasis mine).

Isaiah 1:18
"Come now, let us reason together.... Though your sins are like scarlet, they shall be white as snow" (NIV).

Jeremiah 31:33–34
"I will put My law within them ... for they will all know Me ... for I will forgive their iniquity, and their sin I will remember no more" (NASB).

▶ *God's forgiveness and cleansing.*

1 John 1:7–2:2
If we confess our sins, He is faithful and just to forgive us our sins, and to cleanse us from all unrighteousness (verse 9, KJ21).

The gospel of Mark describes how we should respond when someone has offended us:

> "If you have anything against anyone, forgive him and let it drop (leave it, let it go) in order that your Father Who is in heaven may also forgive you your [own] failings and shortcomings and let them drop. But if you do not forgive, neither will your Father in heaven forgive your failings and shortcomings."
>
> Mark 11:25–26, AMP

How could anything so plain take so much grace? The gospel of Matthew covers it from the other direction, when we know someone is offended with us:

> "Therefore if you are presenting your offering at the altar, and there remember that your brother has something against you, leave your offering there before the altar and go; first be reconciled to your brother, and then come and present your offering."
>
> Matthew 5:23–24, NASB

God asks us not only to forgive but also to be willing to take the initiative for reconciliation when needed.

Scripture offers no loopholes. God covers forgiveness from both directions. In the first case He says, "If you have aught against anyone, then you must forgive." Then He comes at it from the other direction and says, "If you think anyone is holding something against you, then go and get it worked out." In both cases, we are to initiate the forgiveness.

c. God wants forgiveness from the heart.

God wants us to forgive from the heart. Jesus says:

> "My heavenly Father will also do the same to you [send tormentors], if each of you does not forgive his brother from your heart."
>
> Matthew 18:35, NASB

That takes God's grace. We can't always start by forgiving from our heart, but we can begin by making the decision to forgive. Then we can enter into a healing process that, if we persevere, can bring us to the place of wholehearted forgiveness.

d. God's consequences of unforgiveness are sure

If we do not forgive others, God will not forgive us.[1] God may also remove his protection from us, causing us to be turned over to the tormentors.[2] It appears that the tormentors can come in many forms: from bodily illness to tormenting demons.

That is enough for me, knowing that if I don't forgive, He's not going to forgive me. I'm not willing to pay the price of having Him not forgive me, of being out from under His protection or of being turned over to the tormentors. I'm willing to do whatever it takes.

e. God wants as much forgiveness as necessary.

How much forgiveness is enough? Forgiveness needs to take place as long as there is remaining hate, bitterness, resentment, blame or a desire for vengeance or punishment toward another person. In Matthew 18:21–22, Jesus told the disciples that we need to forgive in an unlimited way. We need to live in an attitude of forgiveness. Author Larry Lea, in his teaching on the Lord's Prayer, said that he would begin the day by setting his will to forgive whatever happened to him that day. He prepared himself to hold no offense.

4. Two common misconceptions concerning forgiveness

Two common misconceptions frequently hinder a person's ability to forgive. It is important for the minister to be sensitive to the Holy Spirit and to the ministry receiver to discern if these misconceptions are in operation.

a. Forgiveness equals healing?

A common misunderstanding is that once the offender is released, all the pain will automatically leave one's heart. No! That is not true. Frequently, because a person still feels pain, he thinks, *Well, there must be something wrong with my forgiver,* so he "cranks up" and forgives again. When the offense is forgiven, the healing has only just begun. The person then *needs God to come and heal his heart and take away the pain.*[3] That is the way the pain will leave.

If the person experienced the kind of hurt/offense that follows a generational pattern, he also needs *generational sins and curses* to be broken in his life. If these are not broken, the same type of hurt may be repeated. It is likely that he needs his *mind renewed* from any lies he has come to believe about himself, others and God. If not, he will continue to attract the same types of hurtful situations to himself. Also, please note that he still frequently needs *deliverance* from the demons that otherwise will keep reminding him of the painful incidents.

b. Forgiveness is only a decision?

Another misconception is that forgiveness is limited to being a *decision only*—over and done with, period. Although forgiveness is a decision, it is more than the simple act of deciding. In most situations (and this is certainly true for the more seriously wounded person), forgiveness is a process that takes time. The wounded person must also do his part by acknowledging unforgiveness, looking at the full impact of his hurt, working through painful memories and then reaching a place of forgiveness. There are no shortcuts. Pretending would only sabotage true healing. Forgiveness can be both a gut-wrenching matter and the initial start for the healing process. Much patience, prayer and leading of God's Spirit are needed for both receiver and minister during this time. The minister should be true to what the Scripture says about forgiveness while at the same time not threatening, shaming or pressuring the receiver into a form of meaningless forgiveness that is only lip service. At the same time, he must be willing to confront a ministry receiver's endless excuses for not forgiving, if that should be the case.

5. Blocks to forgiving others

In this section, we want to address some of the major issues or blocks with which people wrestle during the forgiveness process.

a. Some are ignorant of the Scriptures.

Some people are simply ignorant of what Scripture says. They may be new believers or simply come from churches that don't teach much on forgiveness or emphasize reading the Bible. We need to explain the Scriptures so that they can understand what the Bible says. Once they hear the Word, they will have to decide whether or not to be obedient concerning forgiveness.

b. Some think: *I have to feel forgiving.*

Do we have to *feel forgiving* in order to forgive? No! Forgiveness starts with a decision. First it is an act of the will. We have discovered that if a person will ask God to bring him to a place where he can choose to forgive, God will honor that. When forgiveness has been chosen and acted upon, eventually the feelings of forgiveness will follow.

c. Some think: *It's too big to forgive.*

Sometimes an offense has been so overwhelming and devastating in the receiver's life that he or she feels, *I know that I should forgive, but I just can't.* The wrong done seems insurmountable. Forgiveness takes time, and it takes God's grace.

d. Some fear forgiveness.

The ministry receiver may *fear* forgiving. This often happens if he *mistakenly* equates forgiveness with *excusing or ignoring* the offense. He must realize that it is possible to release the offender from blame while, at the same time, acknowledging the full impact of the hurt and/or abuse in his life. He needs to be reassured that by forgiving, he is *not* saying the offense is "okay." It is *not* tacit acceptance that he should accept more hurt or abuse of the same kind.

The ministry receiver may *fear* that if the offender is released from blame, he gets off "scot-free." Forgiving, however, does not negate holding the offender responsible for his actions.

Some receivers *fear* that if they forgive, then the minister will expect them to be healed, and they know that they won't be. As a result, they do not want to risk having expectations put on them that they know they can't fulfill.

Some receivers *fear* that if they forgive, they will be in a more vulnerable position to the one who has offended them. "Maybe I was unable to protect myself from hurt, but at least I don't have to forgive." A ministry receiver sometimes *fears* that if he forgives, the situation will get worse. He feels a kind of protective power in not forgiving. Because thoughts of vengeance generate power, some people may resist forgiving because it means laying down a cherished defense at a time when he is still feeling helpless.

e. Some may think they have already forgiven.

Occasionally, we think we have forgiven everything when we haven't. That happened to Betsy once in a prayer group setting. She asked the leader to pray about a concern she had. He replied, "I would be glad to, but the Lord is saying that you are holding unforgiveness. We need to deal with that first." Surprised, she responded, "No, I don't think so. I know I've forgiven everybody." Betsy thought that she was squeaky clean. "Well," he gently added, "would you be willing to ask the Holy Spirit one more time if there is any unforgiveness in any part of your life?" Feeling foolish, but wanting her concern prayed for, she agreed. Led by the Holy Spirit, Betsy spent the next 45 minutes forgiving many people in her past that the Holy Spirit revealed to her while the prayer group interceded. We don't always remember what needs to be forgiven.

f. Some may want to retain power.

This one is interesting. Somehow, the ministry receiver feels that as long as he holds unforgiveness (and probably anger as well), he has power over the other person. It appears that this is a way to counter being a victim. Unfortunately, this strategy for survival is not in agreement with God's Word. God says to be empowered by His Holy Spirit, not by carrying unforgiveness.

g. We must recognize a spirit of unforgiveness.

The demonic *spirit of unforgiveness*, which tends to be passed down family lines, will do everything it can to prevent forgiveness. An entire family can be bitter and unforgiving. It's like the Hatfields and McCoys without the shootout. Instead, they "shoot it out" in hostile words or with cold, undermining behaviors accompanied by unforgiveness. It is wise for the minister to do deliverance if he discerns this spirit in operation. Then the receiver is much more able to forgive.

Demons of control also promote confusion and strife within a family through continual defensive reactions. They hinder the forgiveness process by promoting the above-mentioned fears and feelings of inadequacy and shame. Frequently the control spirits are actually religious spirits, manifesting as control. Again, do whatever deliverance is necessary in order to free the ministry receiver enough so that forgiveness can be accomplished.

6. Aids to forgiving others

The minister can be a significant resource in helping the ministry receiver to forgive. His intercession, his love and patience and his ability to confront or encourage as the Spirit leads him make a big difference. The following are ways we have encouraged and confronted during the forgiveness process.

a. The enabling power of the Holy Spirit

When a person is wrestling with forgiveness, don't merely pray a simple prayer. Call on the enabling power of the Holy Spirit to help that person do what he couldn't do on his own. He also needs to seek the Holy Spirit's help. We remind the receiver that he has full access to the same Holy Spirit who enabled Jesus to say, "Father, forgive them, for they know not what they do."[4]

b. The cross as the model of God's forgiveness

Although we always pray for wisdom to present the great realities of our faith with anointing, the Holy Spirit will never lead us to manipulate or force people. In this regard, breakthroughs have come by asking the receiver to ponder the price Jesus paid for him personally to receive forgiveness. When led, we ask him to focus on his specific sins. This helps him gain a more personal appreciation of the cross. Then a thought-provoking question may be posed: "Is forgiving others truly asking you to do more than Jesus has done for you?" Forgiving others acquires a different perspective when we see ourselves in the light of the cross.

c. Consideration of the offender

"Hurt people hurt people," Sandra Wilson is fond of saying.[5] That simple statement spells out a tremendous truth. It can soften the receiver's heart toward his offender to consider the pain in the other person's life. Did he get the love he needed? What hurts and traumas did he experience? Was he emotionally abandoned, abused or caught in some web of deception? Again, the purpose is not to coerce through pity, but to help look at the facts and provide the Holy Spirit an opportunity to work compassion through this information.

A note of caution is due here. In ministering with people who are survivors of physical, sexual or severe verbal abuse, forgiveness is usually a long process. It takes time for the receiver to go through numerous painful events and let go of his blame, hate and desire for vengeance. It takes time for God's healing to come into his heart. No deeply hurt person is ready to begin the forgiveness process by looking at the hurts of his offender. This compassion usually comes later as the forgiveness and healing process works deeper into the ministry receiver's life.

d. Knowing Satan's schemes

In 2 Corinthians, Paul made a direct connection between not forgiving others and Satan's ability to outwit us. He wrote:

> If you forgive anyone, I also forgive him. And what I have forgiven—if there was anything to forgive—I have forgiven in the sight of Christ for your sake, in order that Satan might not outwit us. For we are not unaware of his schemes.
>
> 2 Corinthians 2:10–11, NIV

Sometimes it helps us to decide to forgive others when we realize that, by holding unforgiveness, we have fallen into one of Satan's traps and allowed him to outwit us. As a result we have left wide-open doors for demonic oppression.

Prayer

Father, You have made it clear that You require me to forgive. You desire the healing and freedom for me that forgiveness brings. So today, I choose to forgive all who have set me up to enter into sin and all who have hurt me. I choose to release them, each and every one. I let go of all judgments against them, and I let go of all punishments for them I have harbored in my heart. I turn all of this, and all of them, over to You.

Holy Spirit, I thank You for working forgiveness into my life, for giving me the grace I need to forgive and for continuing to enable me to forgive. In Jesus' name. Amen!

B. Asking God's Forgiveness: Repentance

Once we have completed the process of forgiving others, then we can come before God's throne and, with faith, ask for and receive the forgiveness He promises us, *if* we meet His conditions.

Let's look at this part of forgiveness called repentance. After we have forgiven others, we are in a position to confess our sins to God and to ask for His forgiveness. If we ask God's forgiveness with a repentant heart—a heart that is sorry and ready to change direction—God promises that He will grant forgiveness and cleansing to us. We read in Psalm 51:

> A broken and a contrite heart, O God, Thou wilt not despise.
>
> Psalm 51:17, KJ21

1. An illustration

An Englishman had lived a racy life filled with gambling, women and drugs. As a result, he became powerfully addicted. God drew him out of his gutter life, miraculously saved him and set him free. The man became an evangelist. Some years later, as he was preaching in one of London's famous old cathedrals, he faced an unexpected challenge. As he mounted the pulpit of the packed-out service, he noticed a letter lying open on top of the Bible. Immediately, he saw that it was from one of his former gambling buddies, one who knew the most sordid details of his life. The letter said, "How dare you bring God's message! I know what you're really like. I am here in the audience, and if you dare to preach, I'm going to get up and expose you. I'm going to tell everyone what you have done." The letter went on to list a number of the evangelist's specific sins. It ended by saying, "If you've got any sense in this world, you will walk away from that pulpit right now and never try to do this again."

By the time the evangelist finished reading the letter, he had already made his decision. In hushed tones, he began to read this letter to the audience. Concluding, he said, "I want you to know that everything this man has said about me is true, and there's a whole lot more that he didn't even list. But more important than that, I want you to know that I have taken all of this to the Lord. I have repented, and I have received so costly a forgiveness, paid for me at the cross. Tonight I want to talk to you about the power of true repentance and God's great forgiveness."

As he was speaking, the people began silently to weep. In their faces, there was no judgment, and there was no condemnation. They saw in front of them a repentant, healed man who clearly knew the grace of God. It was as if the light of God shone out of him that night. Some of the people made their way to the altar while others stood and began to publicly confess their sins and desire to repent. As God's Spirit of repentance filled the people, revival broke out in the meeting and spread to neighboring villages until it had touched much of England. It all started with the simple sharing of what God can do when we come in a true spirit of repentance.[6]

2. The meaning of repentance

The act of repentance is simple. It is coming to God to confess our sin with a heart of regret about what we have done and a heart commitment to turn and go God's way. Repentance means *to turn around and go in a different direction*, purposed intentionally to change. It translates into, "God, I am sorry and I am willing to take action. I am willing to work, to change and to let You help me stand against temptation. I set my face against sin. I am willing to pay the price to remove myself from all 'setups' that could draw me back into it." The consequences of true repentance are radical. They can include changing patterns, confronting, getting rid of things and letting go of "friends" and avoiding places where we like to hang out. We become careful about what we let come into our ear gates and our eye gates, what we let come out of our mouths and what we let dominate our minds. Repentance is radical. The arrow that represents one's life points in a new direction.

3. Scriptural basis: God's heart concerning our repentance

The apostle John lovingly assures us that:

> If we confess our sins, He is faithful and just to forgive us our sins, and to cleanse us from all unrighteousness.
>
> 1 John 1:9, KJ21

God promises two things: forgiveness and cleansing. His response to our confession is restoration: restoration of our lives and of our relationship with Him as we are freed from guilt, shame and defilement. He not only pours Holy Ghost "Clorox" on us; He also reaches out and takes us by the hand.

It is important for the ministry receiver to be assured, to have it settled in his heart that he is truly forgiven. Often, we speak God's promise directly to him, affirming that he is now forgiven. Two wonderful Scriptures allow us, as elders in the Body of Christ, to be God's representative when this confirmation is needed.

> *"If you forgive anyone his sins, they are forgiven;* if you do not forgive them, they are not forgiven."
>
> John 20:23, NIV, emphasis mine

> Is any one of you sick? He should call the *elders of the church to pray over him* and anoint him with oil in the name of the Lord. And the prayer offered in faith will make the sick person well; the Lord will raise him up. *If he has sinned, he will be forgiven.* Therefore confess your sins to each other and pray for each other so that you may be healed. The prayer of a righteous man is powerful and effective.
>
> James 5:14–16, NIV, emphasis mine

4. Hindrances to repentance

In some instances, ministry receivers have trouble asking for God's forgiveness. Others have no difficulty in asking but have trouble receiving. We need to discuss these possible trouble spots.

a. Besetting sin

Failure, shame and hopelessness encompass the person who has a *besetting sin*.[7] He has known the joy of temporary victory, only to fall again to the hated thoughts or behavior. He feels guilty and hypocritical for "asking again." The *unqualified nature of God's promise* needs to be emphasized. Just as God has required of us unconditional forgiveness of others, so, too, He has required Himself to forgive us unconditionally if we confess our sins with a right heart.[8]

b. Sin too great

A similar problem occurs when the receiver believes that *his sin is too great*. He considers his sin "humongous" because it is so heinous and of such long duration. He continually "whips" himself, because he knew better but chose sin anyway. In all cases, he feels totally unworthy to ask God to forgive him. As RTF ministers, we try to help him realize that God's Word is true and valid for him, regardless of his feelings. A person struggling with unworthiness needs a *revelation of God's heart toward him* before he can face God, asking for forgiveness.

c. No realization of sin

An opposite problem occurs when a person has *no realization that he has sinned* and, thus, no awareness that repentance is needed. People have to come to a place of repentance by being first brought to a knowledge of the truth. This was the case in our own lives regarding some experimental activities we later came to realize were in the occult arena. Conviction and repentance came as our eyes were opened to the passages of Scripture defining how abhorrent these things are to God. Actually, many people are blind to the need to repent from "dabbling in the occult," especially when it was entered into with innocence or as a game.

d. Disappointment with God

Trauma, tragedy, difficult life circumstances and "unanswered prayer" all can *cause our faces and hearts to be turned away from God*. Trust is broken and alienation takes over. Searching seems to produce no satisfactory answers. When there is *disappointment with God*, it is hard for a person to deal with God at all, but particularly to repent, because he is in the habit of blaming God for the pain in his life.

Our approach is to acknowledge the distress and not gloss over the pain of unanswered questions, while at the same time helping the person to see that it was never God's desire for him to be hurt. So many times we are putting the blame in the wrong place. We're shaking our fist at God when we need to be shaking our fist at the enemy or acknowledging the weakness of our own flesh. Sin is operating in the world, and Satan is out to destroy whom he may.[9] Sometimes there are no satisfactory answers, and we have to reach a place of choosing to trust God's goodness even when we do not understand. In Chapter 5, "Soul/Spirit Hurts," we discuss in depth various aspects of ministering to this hindrance in the "Anger/Disappointment toward God" section.

5. Receiving God's forgiveness

What about the person who is repentant and can eat plenty of "humble pie," but who can't accept that God truly forgives him? His "forgiven" receiver isn't working. Have you known anyone like that? Betsy had a dear friend who spent hours on her face repenting, only to come away saying, "God hates me, God hates me." She had trouble receiving His forgiveness.

Wouldn't it be great if there were a shop for broken "forgiven" receivers? You, dear friend, may be that shop! Broken "forgiven" receivers are repaired as people come to have an understanding, *a revelation*, if you please, *of the Father's heart*.

How well Betsy remembers the day that she came upon this verse in Isaiah:

> "I, even I, am he who blots out
>   your transgressions, *for my own sake*,
>   and remembers your sins no more."
>
> Isaiah 43:25, NIV, emphasis mine

For "Your own sake," God? Yes, that is Your heart. That's the Gospel message. For Your own sake because, above all, You want to be in fellowship and in loving relationship with us. The light began to break in on Betsy's heart. The God of the universe wanted to forgive *her sin* for *His own sake*.

Yes, forgiveness was always His plan. Yes, the Lamb was slain from the foundation of the world.[10] God has always made a way for restored relationship, from the institution of the sacrificial system to the cross, where He forgave sin and it became a settled issue. Relationship is the Gospel message. Why? Because God wants a relationship with us. God forgave Moses the murderer and David the adulterer. Jesus forgave the woman taken in adultery and the thief on the cross next to Him. To illustrate God's heart toward the repentant sinner, Jesus told the story of the watching, waiting Father opening His arms to his repentant son. That is the Father's heart. It was while we were yet sinners, while we were still in the pig pen, that Jesus died for us. Our heavenly Father provides forgiveness for the sake of relationship because *He* wants it. God says in Jeremiah:

> "I will put My law within them and on their heart ... *for they will all know Me*, from the least of them to the greatest of them," declares the LORD, "for I will forgive their iniquity, and their sin I will remember no more."
>
> Jeremiah 31:33–34, NASB, emphasis mine

Prayer

Father, now that I have forgiven all others, I thank You that I can come to receive Your forgiveness. So I come to You, through the shed blood of Jesus and the power of His cross, asking You to forgive me of all of my sins. I acknowledge and take responsibility for each and every time I have violated Your commandments, as well as for the iniquity that is in my heart.

Holy Spirit, thank You for working forgiveness into my life, for healing me and for cleansing me from all unrighteousness. Thank You, Father, for restoring me to fellowship with You. In the name of Jesus Christ, I pray. Amen!

C. Forgiving Self

When the ministry receiver has received God's forgiveness, then, because he has been forgiven, he is in a position to forgive himself, if needed. Whether self-forgiveness is needed or not depends on the receiver and how he feels about himself. Has he been holding guilt, self-condemnation or self-hate because of some foolish or very painful sin of the past? Forgiving himself may be needed before God can flush away the guilt, self-condemnation and self-hate. At times, he must forgive himself to keep God's available gift of forgiveness from being blocked. Our goal is to help him *thoroughly and completely receive God's forgiveness*, which sometimes includes forgiving himself.

1. Scriptural basis for self-forgiveness

There is no Bible verse that directly instructs us to forgive ourselves. Therefore, if someone wants to avoid this step, he can justify it as "non-scriptural." We submit, however, that certain principles are expressed in the Bible that strongly encourage self-forgiveness. Also, we frequently see great freedom and release come when a person forgives himself. Why avoid a step that might bring more healing, deliverance and freedom?

We start out with the second commandment, as Jesus declared in Matthew.

> "And the second is like unto it: 'Thou shalt love thy neighbor as thyself.'"
>
> Matthew 22:39, KJ21

When a person is holding self-hate, he is not loving himself, and he is usually not loving his neighbor, either. Self-forgiveness can lead to self-acceptance, peace and the "loving" of oneself. Then the "neighbor" can benefit, as well.

Now, let's go back to the verses that direct us to forgive others. For example, in Mark, Jesus said:

> *"Forgive if ye have aught against any,* that your Father also who is in Heaven may forgive you your trespasses."
>
> Mark 11:25, KJ21, emphasis mine

The "any" that a person may have "aught against" could be himself! Let's clear out all "aught"!

2. Blocks to forgiving self

In actual fact, sometimes the hardest part of forgiveness is to forgive oneself. Pride says, *Your sin is too big to forgive,* and unworthiness says, *You don't deserve forgiveness; you deserve to keep feeling miserable.* Both try to block self-forgiveness.

In addition, the demonic spirit of unforgiveness, which works to prevent a person from forgiving others, will also work to keep him from self-forgiveness. This spirit will also team up with the demon of self-hate to stop the ministry. Deliverance may be needed, as well as helping the person choose to love himself as God loves him.

3. Procedure

We have found it effective to have the receiver say his own name and declare his forgiveness. For example, Susie would say, "Susie, because God's forgiven you, I choose to forgive you, also." It is also acceptable to say, "I choose to forgive myself for..."

It is so important to speak this release to ourselves when needed. The Holy Spirit will show you when the ministry receiver needs to do this.

Prayer

Father, because You have forgiven me, I choose to forgive myself and to release myself from all accusations, judgments, hatred, slander, mistakes, stupidity and falling short of the mark. I choose to accept myself just as I am because You accept me. I choose to love myself because You love me. I even expect to begin to like myself.

Holy Spirit, I ask You, I give You permission and I expect You to work Your work of sanctification in me. I fully embrace this truth and look forward to working with You so I can be changed into the image of Christ. In the name of Jesus Christ, I pray. Amen!

D. Procedure Used to Minister Forgiveness

At the end of each chapter on the four problem areas, we will list the ministry steps for that problem area. The first steps *always* involve *confession* and *forgiveness*. This is truly the *key to freedom*. In this chapter, we provide an overview of the procedure for ministering forgiveness, since it is used throughout the entire ministry process.

We follow the biblical prescription for forgiveness, which is to first forgive others and then ask for God's forgiveness. If self-forgiveness is needed, it should come last, since it is based on God's forgiveness of us.

While we present an order of forgiveness in the following paragraphs, the order may be varied as circumstances and the Holy Spirit directs.

1. The Forgiveness Cross

We use a memory aid that we call "The Forgiveness Cross," as shown in Figure 1. First, we consider the horizontal bar of the cross. It

Figure 1: *The Forgiveness Cross*

reminds us that we are to speak out forgiveness toward other people who have hurt us or injured us in any way. The vertical part of the cross reminds us to look upward, saying, "God, forgive me, a sinner," and we receive His forgiveness coming down. The circle reminds us to forgive ourselves, completing the forgiveness process.

We have the person receiving ministry follow the forgiveness procedure by starting with the horizontal arm of the cross (*himself to others*), then proceed to the vertical arm (*God to him*) and then, if needed, finish with the halo/circle (*himself to himself*).

2. Forgiving others: phase one

In forgiving others, we follow an order. While it has no spiritual value in itself, it does help us keep our place in the process. We work from the past to the present. We start on the father's side of the family. If there has been a father and a stepfather, we start with the father, because he is the actual bloodline. We go back to the grandfather or great-grandfather if sinful patterns are known that far back.

If the people are deceased, we follow the biblical pattern and have the ministry receiver *confess* the sin to God. It is *not* appropriate, however, to speak forgiveness to dead relatives because what they have done is settled and sealed. We no longer have the authority to release *them* from their sin. However, as part of confessing their sin, it is very appropriate, and essential, that we appropriate the power of the cross to *release ourselves* from the effect or consequences of their sin.

If the ancestors are living, we have the receiver both *confess* and *forgive*, i.e., *release* and *pardon*.[11]

Once the father's side is taken care of, we repeat the process with the mother's side. We again start from the past and work toward the present.

We take care to be thorough in the area of parents. Most of our hurts come from family. Most people have extreme loyalty to their parents—even those parents who were hurtful. For this reason, they tend to deny negative experiences. Some describe their parents as they wish they had been. In this case, the person ministering needs to ask the Holy Spirit for revelation. We need to know how hard to press the receiver to remember and forgive, and when the receiver is ready to remember and forgive. Sometimes this comes after several sessions have occurred. At other times, God says, *Save it for the future.* In other words, the person is not yet ready for ministry to the deeper memories and hurts.

Once sins have been confessed and forgiveness spoken, we ask the receiver to *repent* of any ways he has entered into his ancestors' sin. (He may need to forgive himself, as well.) We are now ready to break generational sins and curses. This problem area is discussed in depth in the next chapter.

3. Forgiving others: phase two

Phase two of forgiving others involves the rest of the ministry receiver's family. We continue moving from the past to the present, so his siblings and others who impacted his early years, such as step-parents, come next.

We continue with the growing-up years, covering possible *significant relationships* such as teachers, scout leaders, coaches, past romantic relationships, pastors, church leaders and friends. Just mentioning each category usually causes the receiver to be aware of those people needing forgiveness.

Next, we bring up people involved with the ministry receiver's adult life. We usually start with bosses and other authority figures. Then his spouse, if he is married, and/or ex-spouse, if he is divorced. Then we come to his children, when applicable.

Before leaving the "forgiving others" area of forgiveness, we ask the ministry receiver to seek the Lord, asking Him to reveal any further forgiveness that may be needed.

More forgiveness will be needed in other parts of the ministry process. As ungodly beliefs are revealed, as hurts are exposed and during deliverance, we remain alert to the possibility that more forgiveness may be necessary. We take care of these issues as they surface in each problem area.

4. Repentance: asking God's forgiveness

Frequently, as the receiver is forgiving others, he will see his part or involvement in a situation and naturally, without being prompted, ask God's forgiveness. For example, a wife who is forgiving her husband for foolish spending, might pray, "And God forgive me for not being financially accountable, either, and not helping to establish a budget." If repentance has not naturally occurred, then it is appropriate for the minister to suggest areas where it is needed.

5. Forgiving self

It is always wise to provide an opportunity for the receiver to forgive himself. You can facilitate this by saying, "Just take a moment and see if you have really received God's forgiveness. If you have, do you now need to forgive yourself?" Don't be in a hurry. Sometimes very significant healing occurs during this time as the receiver releases for the first time guilt, self-condemnation, self-hate, worthlessness, etc.

E. Thought-Provoking Questions

1. Why should you bother to forgive those who have hurt or wronged you?

    ....
    ....

2. Why won't God accept partial forgiveness?

    ....
    ....

3. What situation in your life do you feel God should overlook
    (unforgiveness toward someone else, anger, resentment, etc.)?

    ....

    ....

4. What would you be free of if you forgave?

    ....

    ....

5. In what specific areas are you changing, conforming, getting
    clean or letting go of old/sinful patterns and relationships?

    ....

    ....

6. For what do you find it difficult to forgive yourself? Is God willing
    to forgive you in this area? Why is self-forgiveness important?

    ....

    ....

7. Are you using any excuses or justifications not to forgive?

    ....

    ....

8. What can you do if you are angry and disappointed with God?

    ....

    ....

9. What are some consequences of not forgiving?

    ....

    ....

3

Sins of the Fathers and Resulting Curses (SOFCs)

You were ... redeemed ... from your futile way of life
inherited from your forefathers ...
with ... the blood of Christ.
1 Peter 1:18–19, NASB

The sins of the fathers (and mothers) and the resulting curses (SOFCs) are a major source of oppression for all mankind. Why? Because we, our father's descendants, "take on," or "enter into," these same sins. This controversial and misunderstood problem area has unfortunately been neglected and seldom addressed, even among Christians. When the sins and curses coming down a family line are alcoholism, drugs or sexual abuse, the problem is easily identified. The root cause and how to eradicate it from the family line, however, remain a mystery. With "less serious" sins, the source of the problem is usually not even identified as generational. People simply explain the behavior by concluding, "Oh, he's just like his father, and you know what he was like!"

This chapter presents Scriptures and relevant information showing how we are "set up" for problems because of the sins of the fathers. This leads into a discussion of the curses that result from these sins. Then we discuss the "good" side of this topic, examining the Scriptures that reveal God's solution to the sins and to the curses and explaining how to minister to this problem area.

A. Definition of Sins of the Fathers

One purpose of this chapter is to explain clearly the meaning of "sins of the fathers" and the "resulting curses" (SOFCs). Let's begin by considering this simple definition for sins of the fathers. Curses are defined later in this chapter.

> Sins of the fathers represents the accumulation of all sins committed by our ancestors. It is the heart tendency (iniquity) that we inherit from our forefathers to rebel against (i.e., be disobedient to) God's laws and commandments. It is the propensity to sin, particularly in ways that represent perversion and twisted character. The accumulation of sin continues until God's conditions for repentance are met.

Here is a modern-day example showing how the sins of the fathers affect an entire family line.

Illustration: sexual sin and divorce
Delores, a woman who loves and serves God, came from a family in which sexual sin was one of the sins of the fathers. It affected her life, as well as her children's lives and her grandchildren's lives. Sexual sin frequently links itself with marriage failure (as well as with shame). As we look at her family tree of descendants, note the amount of sexual sin and marriage failure.

1. Delores's first child, Samuel, was born out of wedlock and later given to a distant uncle and aunt to raise. He grew up, married, divorced and remarried. He was faithful in marriage, but both of his daughters are sexually permissive. One had been molested.

2. Her second child, Barbara, is living with her boyfriend and doesn't intend to marry.

3. Her third child, Beverly, has been married several times. She has three children. The oldest was married and is now divorced and sexually permissive.

4. Her fourth child, Paul, is separated from his former wife and sleeps with many women. He has never had any children.

5. Her fifth child, Steven, is having serious marriage problems and is temporarily separated from his wife. Their children are still young.

Some of Delores's children are Christians, but they still have not escaped the pressures of sexual sin. Not a single one is happily married to his or her original mate.

B. Understanding the Interrelationship among the Ministry Areas

God has revealed to us an integrated approach to biblical healing ministry. This means that the four major problem areas negatively affecting a person's life must *all* receive ministry in the same general time frame in order to bear lasting healing and freedom. These four areas are the "sins of the fathers and resulting curses," "ungodly beliefs," "soul/spirit hurts" and "demonic oppression." The ancestral sins and curses must be worked through and cleared out, the mind must be renewed with God's truth, the invisible hurts of the inner person must be healed and demonic forces must be removed. Each of these problem areas is unique, and yet they are very interrelated. If one or more of these areas is not ministered to, the already healed areas may be undermined, and the healing already gained might be lost.

In each of the four core chapters of this book, we present one of these four problem areas. In each core chapter we have included a section showing how that particular area is integrally related to the other three problem areas. We hope you will come to appreciate the value of this integrated approach to biblical healing ministry as it is expressed in Restoring the Foundations ministry.

1. How sins of the fathers and resulting curses are related to ungodly beliefs

Parents often repeat the sins of their fathers (and mothers). They may replicate sinful attitudes, prejudices and/or values, which their children then assimilate from them as parents. In addition, the parents' sin usually has hurtful consequences in the lives of the offspring, causing them to form wrong or ungodly beliefs based on their own hurts.

Recently, we ministered to a woman who came from a family line that, for at least two generations (as far as we knew), had physically abandoned their children and left them for others to raise. As this woman experienced the wounding of sudden abandonment, she formed many ungodly beliefs about herself and her value, about what life is like and about her parents. Later, she had a very difficult time loving or trusting God. Her beliefs were very divergent from God's truth. Now in her fifties, she is weeding out these ungodly beliefs and replacing them with God's truth, i.e., godly beliefs.

2. How sins of the fathers and resulting curses are related to soul/spirit hurts

Sins of the fathers put pressure on the next generation to enter into those same sins. Sometimes a person, through godly teaching and/or commitment, is able to withstand those pressures. Most commonly, however, the sins are continued with the usual consequence of the hurts being inflicted on others, as well as on the person who is sinning. Think of the number of hurts caused by an alcoholic, especially if he is married and has children. Usually, the immediate family, extended family, friends and business associates are all affected. The resulting curses usually involve some form of alienation, destruction or death that causes major hurt to all involved.

3. How sins of the fathers and resulting curses are related to demonic oppression

Sins of the fathers and resulting curses work hand in hand with demons to create an ugly, vicious cycle. The initial sin gives an opening through which demons can oppress. Then, once established, the demons endeavor to continue down the family line, where they exert pressure on the descendants to sin in the same way as their fathers. The sin provides license for the demons to continue their oppression, causing the cycle to continue generation after generation. In many cases, demons are the agents (or mechanisms) that carry out the curses coming from the sins of the fathers.

C. God's Point of View

As we get ready to explore this topic in detail, let's start by considering God's point of view. How does He evaluate our fathers and mothers, our grandparents and great-grandparents, in terms of their actions and thoughts?

1. God sees us as families.

The 21st-century Western mind sees man very individualistically, as if we can look at one man at a time. *It's my life, and I'm responsible for it. Period. No one else is affected*, is a typical attitude. This is *not* how God thinks. God sees man in terms of families. He thinks in terms of generations. How often do we find in Scripture, "I am the God of Abraham, Isaac and Jacob?" He sees us not just as individuals, but as integral parts of families that have existed over the generations.

At times, He speaks of several hundred years as if it were an extremely short time. Consider His promise to give Abraham the land of Canaan.[1] Over 400 years passed between the time of the promise and the realization of the promise.

From the foundation of the world, God planned every individual. In His mind, we already existed (a very real existence from His point of view) before we were born. The book of Hebrews portrays Levi as having already tithed because he existed in Abraham's loins when Abraham tithed. This verse is representative of God's view:

> And, as I may so say, Levi also, who receiveth tithes, paid tithes through Abraham, for *he was yet in the loins of his father* when Melchizedek met Abraham.
>
> Hebrews 7:9–10, KJ21, emphasis mine

Levi was part of Abraham. In this case, Levi received the blessings of Abraham's actions. They were credited to him, as well as to Abraham. God also sees us this way. We are a part of, and credited with, both the blessings and the iniquity of our fathers. We can "shed" the iniquity by following the wonderful pattern God provides for our freedom. This includes sharing His viewpoint. Are we willing to receive His view and lay down our own way of thinking?

2. The God of mercy is also a God of justice

When first considering the effects of the sins of the fathers, it is natural to cry out, "But God, this is unfair! I shouldn't be affected by what others have done. I don't even know most of them." We begin to complain from our point of view, without considering the nature or character of God. Let's attempt to shift our perspective, and see what God says about Himself.

> The LORD, the LORD God, *compassionate* and *gracious, slow to anger*, and *abounding in lovingkindness and truth*; who *keeps lovingkindness* for thousands, who *forgives iniquity, transgression* and *sin*; yet He will by no means leave the *guilty unpunished, visiting the iniquity* of fathers on the children and on the grandchildren to the third and fourth generations.
>
> Exodus 34:6–7, NASB, emphasis mine[2]

The New International Version translates this last phrase, "He *punishes* the children and their children for the sin of the fathers to the third and fourth generation" (emphasis mine). This passage is similar to the one in Exodus 20:5, the foundational Scripture for the idea of the sins of the fathers and resulting curses.

God is good, merciful and *just*. He stands ready to forgive, and will forgive, as soon as His conditions are met. Otherwise, His justice, so basic to His nature, prevails, and the iniquities of the fathers are passed down upon their children. He must *punish the guilty*.

God's justice results in the children being affected by the pressure of inherited iniquity (perverseness), as well as by the pressure of possible curses because of their father's (and mother's) sin. Someone has said, "The moral is, we need to choose our parents carefully!"

The bad news is that we are affected by our parents' sins. The good news is that God has provided the way for our freedom from all the effects of their iniquity.

3. What God requires, God provides.

Ever since God instituted with the Israelites His requirement of the sacrificial system, He has provided a way, His way, for man's sins to be forgiven and his guilt to be cleansed. God's plan culminated in Jesus, the "Lamb slain from the foundation of the world."[3] What is man's part in this plan? It is to confess his sin and turn from it.

In Leviticus 26:40–42, God gives us a pattern and a promise for freedom.[4] If we confess our sins and the sins of our fathers, and we humble ourselves, He will remember His covenant. That is, He "remembers" that we are part of His family. This is called "identification repentance" because we identify with our ancestors and repent on their behalf, as well as our own. This breaks the power of the pressure of the sins of the fathers and the resulting curses. Excellent examples of this principle are found in Daniel 9, Ezra 9 and Nehemiah 2 and 9.

Confession and repentance are God's provision for us: "If we confess our sins, He is faithful and just to forgive us our sins, and to cleanse us from all unrighteousness" (1 John 1:9, KJ21, emphasis mine).

When the father (or mother) has sinned, that sin stands in need of being confessed. If it is not confessed by him, then it passes on to his children. Like an "outstanding" debt, the father's sin hangs "out there," impacting the man's descendants (and most likely also others) until it is addressed through confession and cleared out. God's grace will eventually enable a descendant, or perhaps a spiritual leader, to confess the sin. This person is effectively "standing in the gap," identifying with the family and confessing on its behalf. This is why this procedure is called "identification repentance."

4. God is the same; He does not change.

Some people contend that God's conditions applied only to the Israelites because He entered into the covenant with them through the Ten Commandments and the Mosaic Law. Scriptural evidence clearly opposes this position and indicates that God "weighs" all nations of the earth with the same scales. If you are unsure about this, remember that the books of the Prophets contain many "oracles" against the nations surrounding Israel, as well as oracles directed toward Israel. God spoke forth judgment when sin exceeded His mercy "limit" and there was no indication of repentance.

Jesus declared the fate of the "sheep" and the "goat" nations.[5] This shows that there are many different groups of people, some godly and some ungodly, who would be judged by His standards.

We believe that God's Word, both Old and New Testaments, clearly shows forth His character and nature, as well as His mercy and justice. Since we are made in His image,[6] He expects us to have the same character and nature, regardless of our nationality. In either the Old or the New Testament, God is the same. We read in Hebrews and in James:

> *Jesus Christ is the same* yesterday, and today, and for ever.
>
> Hebrews 13:8, KJ21, emphasis mine

> ...the Father of lights, with whom is no variableness, neither shadow of turning.
>
> James 1:17, KJ21

We must conclude that all of us are subject to God's laws: both the blessings and the curses. All we have to do is to look around and we see them in operation.

5. Appropriation is important.

"But wait," someone will say. "Why do we have to go and dredge up all this stuff from the past? Didn't Jesus pay the price for the required justice?"

Praise be to God! Yes, Jesus did take the judgment and wrath of God that is due us.[7] We submit that the correct question to ask is, "Have we *appropriated, personally received and applied* what He has done for us?" We need to receive the freedom Jesus bought for us by using God's provision. How do we do that? By confessing the sins of our fathers and our own sin and then appropriating what Jesus has done at the cross to break the power of the sin to continue to affect us.

Salvation through Jesus Christ has been available for nearly 2000 years, yet none of us is automatically "born again" at our birth. We must, by faith, "receive" (i.e., appropriate) salvation for ourselves. The same is true for physical healing, deliverance, finances, direction, gifts of the Spirit, love, etc. *All* are received by faith. Faith is believing that a promise of God applies to us and receiving that promise as realized. Until we know about these promises and provisions, we cannot, by faith, *receive*[8] what Christ has provided for us. This is true for everything that we receive from God. We must receive and apply the wonderful freedoms gained for us at the cross. We receive by faith. Sometimes we receive by somebody else's faith, and sometimes it's by our own, but we must always appropriate God's provision by faith.[9]

6. The world is not fair.

As we mentioned earlier, some people want to say, "It's not fair; the world is not fair." For those who think life should be fair, all we can say is, "Sorry." Things haven't been "fair" since the Garden of Eden when sin entered into the world. Jesus has made a way for victory to be enforced in our own individual lives and those of our families, but life and the world still aren't "fair." The only "fairness" comes from God who has provided the payment for the penalty of sin if we choose to accept it.

7. We aren't forced to sin.

Understand that the passing down of iniquity is just that: *the passing down of iniquity*. The iniquity does cause a pressure to be applied to us (and our descendants), but it does not *force* us to sin. Iniquity does not mean automatic condemnation or death.

> The fathers shall not be put to death for the children, neither shall the children be put to death for the fathers: every man shall be put to death for his own sin.
>
> Deuteronomy 24:16, KJ21[10]

Inheriting iniquity is very different from being condemned to death. God makes it clear throughout His Word that each person is going to die for his own sin. For example, the entire eighteenth chapter of Ezekiel clearly spells out how each man will die for his own sin and not for his father's, even if his father was a terrible sinner.

While the above statements express the general rule, it must be pointed out that the Bible gives us some exceptions to this rule. There are situations when the children *do* die because of their parents' sin. When we offend God past His limit of righteousness, then entire family lines may be sentenced to death.

Without God's intervention into His own laws of justice, without God Himself paying the penalty for our sin, there would be no hope for us.

> For *all have sinned* and come short of the glory of God.
>
> Romans 3:23, KJ21, emphasis mine

> For the *wages of sin* is death....
>
> Romans 6:23, KJ21, emphasis mine

This very important topic is further discussed in the scriptural basis section.

8. We must take personal responsibility.

Another frequently asked question is, "Why do we have to suffer for what our fathers did?" The answer is, "We don't," if we deal with the sin God's way. We will suffer only if we "enter into" the same sins and make "their" sins "our" sins, and then do not appropriate God's provision for freedom. Why not take advantage of the godly principle of identification repentance?[11] You can apply the power of the cross to nullify all the pressure of generational sins and to break the power of the associated curses from your life.

The issue is too important to ignore. God always requires us to be responsible and accountable for our own lives! Our *response* to the pressures, curses, environment and demonic forces that we inherit determines our personal standing with God.

D. Preparing for SOFCs Ministry

As we prepare to minister to an individual, we like to pray before-hand and ready ourselves to hear God on behalf of our ministry receiver. We ask him to fill out an application form to help us as we prepare.

As we prayerfully consider the information on this form, the Holy Spirit highlights and pinpoints the major issues in the person's life. In addition, He usually identifies the root causes underneath the symptoms. This information helps reduce the ministry interview time by making us aware of the most important information and the Lord's direction for ministry.

Are you ready now to open your mind and heart to further explore the Scriptures concerning the sins of the fathers?

Prayer

Lord, I desire to be fully cleansed and restored so I can be an effective warrior in Your army and also come to know You more intimately. I ask that Your Holy Spirit reveal to me those areas where I need freedom from the sins of my fathers and the resulting curses. As I read this book, show me what applies to me, along with the underlying roots. Thank You, Lord, for Your death on the cross that provides the basis for my freedom. In the mighty name of Jesus Christ. Amen!

E. Scriptural Basis for Sins of the Fathers

The need for ministry to sins of the fathers and resulting curses is rooted in the second commandment. In the following pages, we want to share with you what God has to say in His written Word about this problem area. We will be referring to Table B on pages 67–68, which contains the references to a number of relevant Scriptures.

1. Foundational Scriptures for sins of the fathers

Two foundational Scriptures express the problem area of sins of the fathers and resulting curses. These Scriptures are Exodus 20:5–6,[12] the second commandment, and Exodus 34:6–7, a Scripture expressing the same concept. We have already examined Exodus 34:6–7 (see page 61). In the second commandment, God expresses His hatred for idols and idolatry. He gets angry with jealousy, releasing a curse that causes

Table B: Scriptures Concerning Sins of the Fathers

▶ *Sins of the fathers*

Exodus 20:1–17; Deuteronomy 5:6–21
According to the Ten Commandments, the iniquity of the fathers is visited upon the children unto the third and fourth generation.

Exodus 34:6–7; Numbers 14:18
God's description of Himself, of His goodness, is that He is **merciful** and **just**.

Exodus 21:23–25
The Law of Judgment is an "eye for an eye."

▶ *Sins of the fathers at work*

Leviticus 26:39
A warning to the Israelites that they and their children will waste away in a foreign land

1 Kings 15:26, 34; 16:25–26; 22:52–53
Descendants of Solomon were corrupted by iniquity, leading the nation into idolatry and corruption. In general, each one was worse than the previous one.

Jeremiah 16:10–12
Descendants of Solomon and of Israel just before the Exile

Lamentations 5:1–15
Children of Israel in Babylon during the Exile

Matthew 23:30–32
Scribes and Pharisees identify with their ancestors who killed the prophets (particularly clear in the NIV).

▶ *Each dies for his own sin*

Deuteronomy 24:16
Original declaration: Each dies for his own sin.

2 Chronicles 25:3–4
King Amaziah of Judah applies Deuteronomy 24:16.

Jeremiah 31:29–30
The end of a proverb about sour grapes

Ezekiel 18:1–32
A clear outline of God's judgment and repentance principles

▶ *We are all under iniquity*

Romans 3:23
"For all have sinned and come short of the glory of God" (KJ21).

Romans 3:10–18
A horrible description of the true nature of man

Romans 6:23
"For the wages of sin is death . . ." (KJ21).

Table B: Scriptures Concerning Sins of the Fathers (*cont.*)

▶ *Special exceptions in which children die for their father's sin*

Numbers 16:27–34
  The rebellion of Korah, Dathan and Abiram results in the earth
  swallowing them and their men, wives, children and all of their
  possessions.

Joshua 7:1, 18–26; 22:18–22
  The sin of Achan results in his entire family and all of his possessions
  being stoned, burned and buried.

2 Samuel 12:14–18
  David and Bathsheba's firstborn son dies at the age of seven days.

Jeremiah 11:21–23; 13:14; 16:3–4
  Death of the children as well as the fathers: Anathoth and Judah

Lamentations 5:1–16
  "Our fathers sinned and are no more, and we bear their punishment"
  (verse 7, NIV).

Isaiah 14:20–23
  Death of the children of the wicked of Babylon, no possession of their
  land and the destruction of their cities

---

the iniquities of the fathers to come onto the children to the third and
fourth generation.

> "Thou shalt not *make* unto thee any graven image, or any likeness of
> anything that is in heaven above, or that is in the earth beneath, or that
> is in the water under the earth. Thou shalt *not bow down thyself* to them,
> nor *serve* them; for I, the LORD thy God, am a jealous God, *visiting the*
> *iniquity of the fathers upon the children unto the third and fourth generation*
> *of them that hate Me,* and showing mercy unto thousands of them that
> love Me and keep My commandments."
>
> Exodus 20:4–6, KJ21, emphasis mine

This is the general curse placed on the children because of the sin
(iniquity) of the fathers. Let's analyze this passage in some detail,
looking at the words *idolatry, iniquity* and *fathers.*

a. Idolatry

God hates idolatry. He hates what it does to us. He hates the problems
we get into and the openings we give Satan to oppress us. He says
not to *"make," "bow down to"* or *"serve"* idols. In the New American
Standard Bible, the phrase "not bow down" is translated "not worship
them."

Most Americans, as well as other "civilized" people, will say, "I don't worship idols." In actuality, idolatry is as rampant in America as it was with all of our ancestors, regardless of the country from which they came.

Idolatry occurs whenever we put our *trust* in the "thing" or "situation" more than we put our trust in God. Jesus said, "For where your treasure is, there will your heart be also."[13] We can infer from this statement that our hearts and our treasure will be "at the same place." If that place is not "in" God, worshiping God, serving God, trusting God and acknowledging Jesus as Lord, then it must be some other place. To the degree that we are "other-focused" more than God-focused, we are involved in idolatry.

Idolatry includes all of the obvious forbidden areas, such as spiritualist churches, occultism, cults and all false religions (any that do not acknowledge the Lord Christ Jesus and His blood sacrifice for their atonement). This list includes psychics, witchcraft, Satanism and secret societies based on occult (or "hidden") powers and bloody oaths. This includes groups such as the Masons, Shriners and Rosicrucians, who use their lower-level members as a deceived "front."

Idolatry also includes the less obvious things: any excessive love, passion or veneration of something such as money, possessions, beauty (the body), power, fame, rock stars, ungodly causes (homosexual rights beyond normal human rights, abortion, the environment), etc. Do you agree that we live in an idolatrous nation?

God says that we shall not bow down to other things, which means we shall not worship, focus on them, admire or acknowledge them as *superior to* or as a *replacement of* God. God says He is a jealous God. He is jealous for our attention, our affection and our undivided heart.

The word for "jealous" in Hebrew is *qanna*. It is associated with the word "red." God is red in the face with anger when we ignore Him and give to other created things[14] the adoration, honor and glory due Him. Don't let your heart be drawn away from God.

The last phrase of Exodus 20:5 is also relevant. God concludes that we "hate" Him when we are involved in idolatry. This is a strong statement. If we concede that the results of hate in the one who "hates" is being separated or estranged from the one "hated," then idolatry separates us from God. He wants a relationship with us, not separation.

As our ancestors worshiped and/or served other gods, the sin of idolatry resulted in the curse, which clearly states that the iniquity in their hearts would be passed down to the next three or four generations. As these generations then "entered into" the sins of their fathers, they continued the curse unto an additional three or four generations. This cycle continues with each generation, until and unless it is broken by the power of the cross. We see this cycle in operation as God spoke to Israel through Jeremiah:

> "Then say to them, 'It is *because your fathers forsook me,*' declares the LORD, 'and followed other gods and served and worshiped them. They forsook me and did not keep my law. *But you have behaved more wickedly than your fathers. See how each of you is following the stubbornness of his evil heart instead of obeying me.*'"
>
> Jeremiah 16:11–12, NIV, emphasis mine

It is clear that God hates idolatry. He does not want anything to take His place in our lives.

b. Iniquity

The word *iniquity* is interesting. While not part of our normal, everyday English vocabulary, merely saying it creates a sense of "wrongness" or sly deceptiveness. Yuck! Who would want to be involved in "iniquity"?

The truth is: We all are! Why? Because none of us had perfect parents or ancestors. All of us have received the "visiting" of our ancestors' iniquity. Just what have we inherited, anyhow?

Iniquity is a heart condition, the inner tendency of man to *break God's heart*. God created mankind for love, companionship and fellowship. He wanted and still desires a love relation with us. But it has to be on His terms, His conditions. After all, He is God. He gave us the privilege of free will so we can freely choose, under His conditions, to love Him and acknowledge Him as Father. When Adam and Eve chose to make their own decision about God's requirement regarding eating of the tree of the knowledge of good and evil,[15] they moved into disobedience, i.e., rebellion.[16] This tendency of the heart to rebel has been with us ever since.

> The *heart is deceitful above all things*, and *desperately wicked*; who can know it? *I, the LORD, search the heart*; I try the reins, even to give every man according to his ways, and according to the fruit of his doings.
>
> Jeremiah 17:9–10, KJ21, emphasis mine

Sin has its roots in the heart condition of iniquity/rebellion. Sin is the outworking of this heart tendency. The biblical definition of "iniquity" includes the words *lawlessness, wickedness, depravity, unrighteousness, transgression* and *perversion*. When God says that we have iniquity in our hearts, He is painting an ugly picture. He is challenging us to be serious to work with Him to remove iniquity from our hearts.

c. Fathers

When the Scriptures use the word *fathers*, as in Exodus 20:5, the meaning not only includes the actual father of a person, but also the mother, the grandparents and the entire family line. All of these people have contributed to the iniquity and sin passed on to the children. We see this scripturally, and we see it experientially as the curse has its "outworking" in this world. One noteworthy example illustrating this point is in 1 Kings 16:30–31 and 22:51–53. Ahaziah is seen to multiply the evil ways of both his father, Ahab, and his mother, Jezebel.

d. Law of judgment

Now let's look at the last passage in the first group of verses in Table B (pages 67–68):

> "But if there is serious injury, you are to take *life for life, eye for eye, tooth for tooth, hand for hand, foot for foot, burn for burn, wound for wound, bruise for bruise.*"
>
> Exodus 21:23–25, NIV, emphasis mine

Here we see the law of sowing and reaping used to establish restitution for injury. This is the terrible law of judgment that expresses the "just" side of God's nature. This is God's expression of "fairness." He has arranged the universe so that every "evil" results in more evil, just as every "good" results in more good. Since He knew that we would all be helpless[17] and unable to set ourselves free from this law, His "mercy" side sent Christ to provide a way for us to be set free from this law. Jesus fulfilled this law on our behalf. Again, the key to freedom from this law is to *appropriate* by faith the truth that Jesus has already suffered (paid) the judgment for our sin.

2. Sins of the fathers at work

The second group of Scriptures in Table B (pages 67–68) allows us to observe the effects of the sins of the fathers upon the children. First, we have a summary statement from God as He lays out the consequences of Israel's potential disobedience:

And *they that are left* of you *shall pine away in their iniquity* in your enemies' lands; *and also in the iniquities of their fathers* shall they pine away with them.

Leviticus 26:39, KJ21, emphasis mine

The children will suffer and "pine away" because of *both* their iniquity and their fathers' iniquity. While God is warning them not to be disobedient, He is also stating that they are *going to be* disobedient.

Second, we can read about the various kings and how they "entered into" and, in many cases, magnified their fathers' sins. You may want to look up the following Scriptures and study them in detail. Many Scriptures could be used to show how the kings of both Judah and Israel entered into and added to the sins of their fathers. Of course, other people in Judah and Israel were also in this same fix, but their names are not recorded for us.

a. Israel's kings

"But [*Jeroboam*] *hast done evil above all who were before thee.* . . . And He [God] shall give Israel up because of the sins of Jeroboam, who sinned and who made Israel to sin."

1 Kings 14:9, 16, KJ21, emphasis mine

And Nadab the son of Jeroboam . . . *did evil in the sight of the LORD, and walked in the way of his father* and in his sin wherewith he made Israel to sin.

1 Kings 15:25–26, KJ21, emphasis mine

This sorry story continues through the lives of Israel's kings Baasha, Omri, Ahab and Ahaziah, until 1 Kings 22, when the evil became so horrendous that God could not withhold judgment any longer. God brought the Assyrian army against Israel (the northern kingdom) several different times, until every part of the nation was defeated, carried away and dispersed among the nations.[18]

b. Judah's kings

In studying Judah's kings, it is clear that although there was an occasional righteous king, the majority were very wicked. We see these stories in Jeremiah 15:1, 6 and Jeremiah 16:10–12, which culminate in God's sending the people into exile. In Lamentations, we see that the destruction that Jeremiah prophesied has taken place. The people have collectively borne their fathers' iniquities and are in a strange land as captives. The entire book is very sad. Lamentations 5:7 sums it up:

> Our fathers have sinned, and are no more; and we have borne their iniquities.
>
> Lamentations 5:7, kj21

c. Israel's descendants

In Matthew, Jesus confronted the scribes and Pharisees and used their own words to convict them that they were the descendants of murderers.

> "And you say, 'If we had lived in the days of our forefathers, we would not have taken part with them in shedding the blood of the prophets.' So you testify against yourselves that *you are* the *descendants* of those who *murdered* the prophets. Fill up, then, the *measure of the sin of your forefathers!*"
>
> Matthew 23:30–32, NIV, emphasis mine

Many more Scriptures illustrate the sins of the fathers at work and coming down the generational lines. Just as God became weary with the sin of the Israelites, we become weary reading about it! It is grievous to our spirits. To prevent overdoing it, let us move on and look at God's justice concerning our own sin.

3. Each dies for his own sin

The third group of Scriptures in Table B on pages 67–68 clearly confirms God's general law that each person dies for his own sin. Even though we are set up by our ancestors, we are all responsible for our deeds.

> Fathers shall not be put to death for their children, nor children put to death for their fathers; *each is to die for his own sin.*
>
> Deuteronomy 24:16, NIV, emphasis mine

4. We are all under iniquity

The three verses in the fourth group in Table B on pages 67–68 contain an unpleasant description of the fallen state of mankind and the "wages" that we have earned because of our sin. God leaves no room for escape.

> But *we are all as an unclean thing*, and *all our righteousnesses are* as *filthy rags*; and we all do fade as a leaf; and *our iniquities*, like the wind, *have taken us away.*
>
> Isaiah 64:6, KJ21, emphasis mine

We *all* need a savior. Praise God that He provided One for us.

5. Special exception where children die for their fathers' sins

The last group of passages in Table B on pages 67–68 shows some exceptions to the general rule of each person dying for his own sin. These exceptions occur when one's father or mother has exceeded God's limit and brought upon themselves and their children complete destruction. We see these exceptions in the examples of Korah, Achan, David and Bathsheba. As we discussed in the introduction, God looks at families, and He looks over generations. If the sins of the fathers become excessive, there is the possibility that He will remove the entire family line.

6. Mercy triumphs over justice

Let's end this section with the last three verses in Ezekiel 18, in which God shares His heart. He desires mercy rather than justice.

> "*Therefore*, O house of Israel, *I will judge you, each one according to his ways*, declares the Sovereign LORD. *Repent! Turn away from all your offenses; then sin will not be your downfall.* Rid yourselves of all the offenses you have committed, and *get a new heart and a new spirit. Why will you die*, O house of Israel? *For I take no pleasure in the death of anyone*, declares the Sovereign LORD. *Repent and live!*"
>
> Ezekiel 18:30–32, NIV, emphasis mine

Let's be sure we are operating in God's mercy for ourselves, and then help as many as possible also find God's mercy.

F. Thoughts Relevant to Sins of the Fathers

Here are a number of related and relevant topics that will help increase our understanding of sins of the fathers and how they operate.

1. Number of people involved in four generations

One of the staggering aspects of "visiting the iniquity of the fathers upon the children unto the third and fourth generations" is the number of people involved. Adding up two parents, four grandparents, eight great-grandparents and sixteen great-great-grandparents, gives a total of thirty people! Thirty human beings, with their mixture of fleshy and godly desires, actions, beliefs, stumbling, falls and besetting sins pass their iniquity on to each of us.

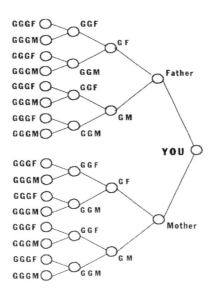

Figure 2: *The Number of People in Four Generations*

If there has been divorce and remarriage or adoption of children, even more people within four generations are involved. The greater tragedy, however, is that our parents also each had thirty people whose sin affected them, and the four grandparents each had thirty people, etc. In other words, if we really trace it back, we inherit the iniquity (and, praise God, also the blessings) of all past generations back to Noah and his sons, and they inherited from all of their generations back to Adam and Eve. This is the source of the innate, sinful nature of man. There would clearly be no escape from the consequences of so many generations of sin if God had not planned from the beginning[19] for our release, healing and freedom. Only when confession and repentance are "entered into" does the "visiting" come to a stop.

2. Inconsistencies

Some inconsistencies do exist in the way that generational sins operate and affect people. Sometimes certain sins may skip a generation or two. Other times, there seems to be a concentration or amplification of curses manifesting in a particular individual. *When one descendant seems to be a focus of the iniquity, past ancestral occult involvement is often the reason.* The results can be devastating.

We have seen occult focuses on one or more individuals in the family line, resulting in unbearable oppression. Other family members, however, will seem not to be particularly affected. The occult iniquity keeps bouncing from here to there, wreaking its havoc on individual lives. Within three or four generations, some descendant will always be affected. This person will receive the iniquity, take it for his own and pass it on down three or four more generations. However, if the person can receive Restoring the Foundations ministry, he can begin the process of freeing himself and his descendants from the occult focus.

3. Mechanisms transmitting the sins of the fathers

For those who are curious about how sins of the fathers are transmitted, we do not have a sure answer. The most likely ways, however, appear to be through the genes, through the growing-up environment, through sowing and reaping and via demons. Probably a combination of these factors are at work. Most likely they occur in different proportions and frequencies within different people.

4. Frequently occurring sins of the fathers

Table C on page 77 shows a list of sins frequently found within family lines. A minister ministering to sins of the fathers and the resulting curses should be particularly attuned to these possibilities.

Some of these are both sins and curses. The sins cause man to be disobedient, breaking God's law. Curses are the result of the sin, pressuring our descendants to enter into the same sin as their ancestors.

Fear is a good example of this "dual" role. Giving place to fears beyond normal human caution and prudence is sin because God has not given us a spirit of fear.[20] Fear is also a curse that frequently operates as a result of occult involvement. Regarding these sins, we minister to them both as sins to be freed from and curses to be broken.

Table C: Frequently Occurring Sins of the Fathers

Abandonment	Parental inversion
Abuse: emotional, physical, mental or sexual	Physical infirmities
	Pride
Addictions	Rebellion
Anger, rage, violence	Rejection, insecurity
Control, possessiveness, manipulation	Religious bondage, cults
	Sexual sin and perversion
Emotional dependency	Unbelief
Fears—of all kinds	Unworthiness, low self-esteem, inferiority
Idolatry	
Money extremes, greed, lack	Witchcraft, occult, Satanism
Not caring for children	

a. Illustration: a granddaughter of a Mason

One evening after everyone else had left the church offices, Betsy was still there ministering to Anna, a woman struggling to stay emotionally afloat. During the gathering of her generational history, it came out that Anna was the granddaughter of a thirty-third degree Mason. As Betsy was having Anna confess the sins of her fathers, she came to the Masonic grandfather. "Now Anna, just confess the sin of Masonry in your family line, and . . ."

That was as far as Betsy got. Anna rose up out of her chair a foot in the air. The demons associated with Masonry were manifesting. They were not happy that their "legal" ground was being taken away. Betsy decided that she would not go any farther until Chester could join her. She and Anna bound the demons, prayed protection over Anna and brought the session to a close. A few days later, we all gathered and proceeded through the rest of the SOFCs quite easily, including deliverance as necessary.

Anna herself was facing numerous problems in her marriage. She also had a very debilitating disease. Some months later, her precious, talented son died of a medical drug-related overdose. Anna's oldest daughter married a man after becoming pregnant. He later served a prison term for using and selling drugs. Her youngest daughter also has symptoms of a serious disease. Could these problems relate back to the sin of Masonry and its resulting curses? We also have to ask, "What occult sins of the fathers and the resulting curses were in operation in the first place that deceived and drew her grandfather into the clutches of this occult organization?"

Much that has been said about the sins of the fathers also applies to the subject of curses, since the major source of curses comes from breaking God's laws (or commandments). After looking at another portion of Sandy's story, we will shift the focus of our attention to curses. Then we will discuss the scriptural basis for freedom and ministering to sins of the fathers and resulting curses.

G. Sandy's Story: Ancestral Deception

The ancestral sin and resulting curses were so intertwined with everything else in Sandy's life that we did not minister to SOFCs in the normal way.[21] It was necessary to continue to minister to ancestral sins as a part of attacking the UGBs, SSHs and DO as new problems were uncovered.

God showed us several different ways that deception had created a powerful stronghold in Sandy's family line. During one of our sessions, we suggested to Sandy that deception could be a major part of her immoral behavior. Shocked at the possibility, Sandy was sure that deception had never been an issue. (This was deception about the deception!)

During the next session, however, she came back to this topic and admitted that God had been speaking to her. She concluded, "Maybe deception had a small role in the total scheme of things, after all."

Sandy's eyes were being opened. By the following session, she realized that deception had indeed created a major veil over her mind. She began to acknowledge that she had led a double life, a deceptive life, for essentially her entire life. We continued to "cut away" at the area of deception, but it wasn't until we dealt with other major strongholds that she truly saw the magnitude of the deception in her life.

In one of Sandy's recent letters to us, she writes:

> This new life isn't just "the old life, cleaned up and made better." Even before my birth, Satan had begun his work in my ancestors that would limit and even control me. After I became a Christian, I was a "new creature in Christ," but I was still *me*. Generational sins, sins committed against me, and my own sin had already begun their deadly work. The salvation Christ brought to me now enabled me to overcome all of the works of the enemy—past, present and future. However, I had been assaulted so early in life by his hateful plan that I can't even remember a time in my life that didn't have his fingerprints all over it.

My cooperation with Satan through sin increased his power over me. For that, I take full responsibility and have repented. The new life of freedom into which I have entered has always been in God's heart for me and now I am unhindered in walking into it.

H. Curses

As we look more extensively at curses, we will be using Table E on pages 87–88 as our reference for relevant Scriptures.

1. Just what is a curse?

The concept of a "curse" is found throughout the Old Testament and frequently in the New Testament. Generally, it involves a wish that "evil may befall another."[22] God's use of the word *curse* had the same meaning as in Israel's contemporary world. All peoples understood what the word meant. The purpose of a "curse" was to protect the terms of a covenant by expressing the penalties that would be exacted if and when the covenant was violated.[23]

A curse is the penalty to be paid for the breaking of a law. Thus the biblical meaning regarding God's law is "the consequence that will occur because of disobedience and rebellion against God's law."

In concept, it is completely analogous to our government specifying penalties for breaking the law. The fine of $95 for speeding, i.e., for breaking the law limiting our car speed to 55 mph, would be similar to a curse. The government would continue to search for us until we had paid the fine in full. Likewise, a curse will continue to search out the family line until the penalty is paid in full. Without the cross, however, the penalty can never be paid in full.

Unlike the world's governments, which accept money for their penalties, God's penalties can only be paid by the shedding of blood. God has always required the shedding of blood as payment, even in the garden with Adam and Eve.[24] The blood that He requires now is the blood of the perfect Lamb, Jesus Christ.

Through His sacrifice on the cross, we can by faith apply His blood to cover our sins, to pay the penalty, to stop the curse.

In fact, the law requires that nearly everything be cleansed with blood, and *without the shedding of blood there is no forgiveness.*

Hebrews 9:22, NIV, emphasis mine

Another good definition of a curse comes from Kenneth Copeland.[25] His definitions of both curses and blessings are:

> A curse is being "empowered to fail."
> A blessing is being "empowered to succeed."

While this is a simplistic definition, it does get the point across.

Derek Prince, a knowledgeable Greek scholar, has a more elaborate definition of a curse.[26]

> Curses are words spoken with some form of spiritual authority (either good or evil) that set in motion something that will go on generation after generation. Behind the words is a spiritual power: God or Satan.

The Israelites did indeed experience being "empowered to fail," as they repeatedly broke their agreement with God. They have also experienced "something" set in motion that has gone on generation after generation. As a result of these curses, their history shows that they have gone through two complete exiles and scatterings. They are now being regathered for the third time, which is the final time according to Bible prophecy.[27]

2. Curses operating in several people's lives

In ministry, when we see the "unexplained," we become suspicious that a curse may be in operation in a person's life. In some cases, the reason behind the operation of the curse is evident; in other cases, we depend on the Holy Spirit to bring revelation. Consider the following examples.

- The man who had so many car accidents had been living with a woman who was heavily involved in the occult and was angry with him for refusing to participate. She had been placing curses on him, setting the stage for accidents.

- The businessman who began to experience losses had ancestors who had owned slaves. Apparently the slaves had cursed the family.

- The woman with the terrible leg pain saw a picture in her spirit of her ancestors involved in slaughtering the French Huguenot Christians. This woman had experienced a remarkable number of near-death experiences. The spirit of death and pain were part of the curse that had come through the family line since the murdering of those Christians.

- The Holy Spirit revealed that the family whose middle child was handicapped had two ancestors who had witnessed the murder of a little boy. They had been "party to the crime" by remaining silent. Being involved in this crime had opened the door for physical curses to come on their descendants. We will have to wait for another generation to see whether the ministry was effective in breaking the curse causing birth defects. In the other cases, freedom and healing either has come or is in the process of coming.

3. Where do curses come from?

Generally, the most severe curses affecting a person's life are those that result from the sins of the fathers. Curses, as penalties for sin, come from only one source: God. Curses, as a desire to bring distress and failure into a person's life, can come from other sources. Unfortunately, we can also curse ourselves. In all cases, eliminating the effect of the curse from our lives is a wise thing to do!

a. From God
The main source of curses is God. Shocking, isn't it? God, our heavenly Father, the Source of all good and perfect gifts,[28] is also the source of curses. God issued the first curses against the serpent and against the land in chapter three of Genesis. While the word *curse* is not used by God in His pronouncement against Adam and Eve, His words clearly convey a curse upon them. Other divine curses are seen in the flood[29] and in Moses' pronouncements against Egypt.[30]

Moses formalized God's curses in the Pentateuch. Statements expressing the curses are "scattered" throughout the text, but the majority are found in Leviticus 26 and Deuteronomy 27 through 32. God lays out the curses (or penalties) that will come upon the Israelites if they do not "keep the commandments, and the statutes, and the judgments, which I command thee this day, to do them."[31] God makes it very clear in Deuteronomy 11:

> "Behold, *I set before you this day a blessing and a curse*: a blessing, if ye obey the commandments of the LORD your God which I command you this day; and *a curse, if ye will not obey* the commandments of the LORD your God, but turn aside out of the way which I command you this day, to go after other gods which ye have not known."
>
> Deuteronomy 11:26–28, KJ21, emphasis mine

Table D below shows the main categories of curses (and also of blessings, for which we are grateful). These categories are from the book, *How to Read the Bible for All It's Worth*, by Fee and Stuart.[32] They show that the entire range of life can be affected by curses as a result of breaking God's law.

While these curses were specifically directed to the Israelites, as part of God's covenant with them, it is clear that all peoples are cursed for rebellion against God, as we discussed earlier. The general condition for blessings or curses from God for all of mankind is summed up in the book of Proverbs:

> The curse of the LORD is on the house of the wicked, but He blesseth the habitation of the just.
>
> Proverbs 3:33, KJ21

Because any curse set into motion from God certainly has spiritual authority behind it, Derek Prince's criteria for a curse is met.

You may be wondering: Is God just waiting for us to make a mistake so He can activate a curse against us? No, revenge is not God's nature.

Table D

Curses	Blessings
Death	Life
Disease	Health
Drought	Prosperity
Dearth	Agricultural abundance
Danger	Safety
Destruction	Respect
Defeat	
Deportation	
Destitution	
Disgrace	

Instead, it is likely that the "mechanism" for curses is in place as part of the fabric of the universe.

Judgment is brought forth as His laws are broken or violated. It is an expression of the law of sowing and reaping. "Plant" a seed of disobedience, "reap" a harvest of judgment. This mechanism was probably put in place at the time of the Fall.[33] Since there is no way for us to escape by our own efforts from this continual cycle of sin and judgment, it was necessary for Christ to come to set us free.[34]

b. From others: word curses

This is perhaps the more familiar source of a curse. We have all experienced someone "cursing" us or someone else. This type of curse usually doesn't have much power behind it, unless it comes from someone with spiritual and/or relational authority. If these people put forceful energy into cursing us and/or our ancestors, it may cause serious damage.

People whom we or our ancestors have wronged by stealing, cheating, lying, deceiving, holding them in slavery, etc., may have cursed us (or them). These people may have released spiritual "pressures" and/or demonic power against us or our ancestors. This is particularly true if the people doing the cursing were witches, and/or if they were involved in any occult organizations, and/or if they were very emotional.

A number of times, we have encountered one particularly dangerous practice. Those in satanic or occult organizations often dedicate their descendants to the god of the "organization," or to Satan. This has happened several times with ministry receivers who had grandfathers active in the higher ranks of the Masons. Great demonic oppression can result from this curse placed on the family line until the "dedication" is broken.

Closer to home, we find our loving parents "curse" us with such warnings as "If you go out in the rain, you'll catch a cold" or "Don't play in the street; you'll get run over." Even worse are the curses that come from anger or "put-downs." For example, statements such as "You'll never amount to anything" and "You are a lousy daughter" are curses. The more subtle curses result from negative comparisons between siblings. A mother may say, "Linda is so pretty." Sister Judy, however, gets the message that she must be ugly. Dad may remark that "John is the smart one in the family." If you are John's brother, you begin to realize that you will never measure up to Dad's expectations. It is clearly by God's grace that most of us survive the growing-up process and are able to function and be productive in society. Yet the number of scars and unhealed wounds of the soul and spirit, along with spiritual pressures and demonic oppression, can be astounding. This is why the integrated approach to biblical healing ministry is so essential.

We find a chilling example from the Bible of both a word curse and a self-curse when the Jews shout:

> "Let his blood be on us and on our children."
>
> Matthew 27:25, NIV

This is a self-curse for the shouting Jews and a major ancestral curse for all of their descendants. Not a pleasant thought.

James wrote a profound statement about cursing and the wrong use of the tongue. He admonished us to be careful what we say and not to bless God and curse men out of the same mouth.

> Therewith we bless God, even the Father, and therewith we curse men, who are made in the similitude of God. *Out of the same mouth proceedeth blessing and cursing.* My brethren, these things ought not so to be.
>
> James 3:9–10, KJ21, emphasis mine

The guiding directive for all of us comes from Jesus, who gave us this command:

> "But I say unto you, love your enemies, bless them that curse you, do good to them that hate you, and pray for them that despitefully use you and persecute you."
>
> Matthew 5:44, KJ21

c. From self: self-curses

Even more sad than having our parents or others curse us is our cursing of ourselves. Unfortunately, we learned to do this from our parents, from our peer group and from society, i.e., the media.

Familiar examples are:

- *I have nothing to offer anyone.*
- *I can't speak in front of people.*
- *I will probably "blow" this job (expected failure).*
- *I can't remember names.*
- *My children will always be left out.*
- *I will always be poor.*
- *I can't start the day without my first cup of coffee.*

Even the secular world realizes the power of repeated suggestions that program the "subconscious" to carry out what we instruct it to do. Again, with sufficient emotion, repetition and believing,[35] spiritual pressures and demonic forces can be loosened to help carry out the curse.

Paul, writing in 1 Corinthians,[36] shows us that we are not to be under bondage to anything (other than to the Lord Jesus Christ). He teaches us in Philippians[37] to be content in every situation, not to be dependent on our coffee, etc. Paul certainly doesn't even include "I can't" in his vocabulary:

> I can do all things through Christ who strengtheneth me.
>
> Philippians 4:13, KJ21

Paul believes in "self-blessing," not in "self-cursing."

4. Summary

There is the potential for a vast array of possible curses to come against us. Some come from God because of our ancestors' sins and our own sins. Others result from people cursing our ancestors and/or us. It is also possible to curse ourselves by speaking ungodly words from our hearts. Negative speech, of course, by itself does not produce a curse. However, when someone with spiritual and/or relational authority speaks evil against us, a resulting curse is a definite possibility.

There is some comfort in Proverbs 26:2: "As the bird by wandering, as a swallow by flying, so a *curse without cause shall not alight*" (KJ21, emphasis mine).

If we can stay pure before the Lord and appropriate what Christ did for us on the cross,[38] then there is no cause for a curse to come upon us.

I. Scriptural Basis for Curses

Table E on pages 87–88 contains a number of Scriptures relevant to curses. These Scriptures will help the minister encourage repentance and instill faith in the ministry receiver. Also, they are helpful in defending the application of the Gospel to this problem area of sins of the fathers and resulting curses, i.e., apologetics.

In the sixth group of Scriptures in Table E, Jesus commands us to "bless them that curse [us]."[39] Paul put this very succinctly: "Bless and curse not."[40] We are commanded to bless and not curse because when we curse another person the law of judgment is put into motion, resulting in the fruit of the curse coming back on us.[41]

The last statement in the Bible about "the curse" is found in Revelation 22:3. This beautiful promise makes it clear that one day, "No longer will there be any curse." We can say with John, "Even so, come, Lord Jesus."[42]

J. Self-Sins

Having discussed the sins of the fathers (and mothers) and the resulting curses, it is time to turn to the very important topic of self-sins. As the minister, you should be well versed in this information as you help lead your ministry receiver in repentance.

1. Response to the setup of sins of the fathers and curses

We respond to the various pressures and temptations coming against us—self-curses, sinful acts, ungodly beliefs, the hurts we carry inside, demonic influence, etc.—in one of two ways. We can respond in a godly way, or an ungodly way. How we respond determines whether or not we are sinning, i.e., whether or not we are creating more ancestral sins and curses.

a. What is sin?

Where do we draw the line between sin and non-sin? Let's take a brief look at what Scripture defines as sin.

In Romans 14:23, Paul declared, "For whatsoever is not of faith is sin" (KJ21). Ouch! This doesn't leave us much room at all. Can we walk in faith 100 percent of the time?

We see sin from another angle in 1 John 3:4: "For sin is the transgression of the law" (KJ21). This view is also very general, but it clearly equates breaking God's law with sin.

We can turn to 1 John 2:16 for a very practical definition of sin.

> For all that is in the world—the *lust of the flesh*, and the *lust of the eyes*, and the *pride of life*—is not of the Father, but is of the world.
>
> 1 John 2:16, KJ21, emphasis mine

These three highlighted phrases seem to comprise the main categories and motivations of sin. We have the *pride of life* inherited from our father, Adam. It has come all the way down the family line to us. This

Table E: Scriptures Concerning Curses

► *Reason for curses from God*

Daniel 9:11
Transgression and disobedience of God's law lead to curses and sworn judgments.

Deuteronomy 11:26–28
God sets before us a choice. We decide whether we will obey or disobey His commandments.

Deuteronomy 28
Many curses listed for disobedience

► *First curses in the Bible*

Genesis 3:14
To the serpent: cursed above all animals, will crawl on belly and eat dust, head will be crushed

Genesis 3:16
To the woman: greatly increased pains in childbearing, desire for husband, will be ruled over

Genesis 3:17–18
To the ground: cursed because of Adam, hard to produce good food, easy to produce thorns

Genesis 3:17–19
To the man: painful toil and sweaty work to produce food

► *First curse spoken by a man*

Genesis 9:25
"And [Noah] said, 'Cursed be Canaan! A servant of servants shall he be unto his brethren'" (KJ21).

► *Jews cursing themselves and their children*

Matthew 27:25
"Let his [Jesus'] blood be on us and on our children" (NIV).

► *General statements about curses*

Proverbs 3:33
"The LORD's curse is on the house of the wicked" (NIV).

James 3:9–10
"[With the tongue] *we curse men....* Out of the same mouth proceedeth blessing and cursing" (KJ21, emphasis mine).

Proverbs 26:2
"Like a fluttering sparrow or a darting swallow, an undeserved curse does not come to rest" (NIV).

Table E: Scriptures Concerning Curses (*cont.*)

▶ *Jesus has the last word about curses*

Matthew 5:43–44; Luke 6:27–28
> "But I say unto you, love your enemies, bless them that curse you, do good to them that hate you, and pray for them that despitefully use you and persecute you. . . ." (Matthew 5:44, KJ21).

▶ *Jesus provides freedom from the curse*

Galatians 3:13
> "Christ redeemed us from the curse of the law by becoming a curse for us" (NIV).

▶ *Last statement about curses in the Bible*

Revelation 22:3
> "No longer will there be any curse" (NIV).

---

is the basic iniquity of the human heart: a tendency to rebel, to go our own way. Every person is born with this natural tendency. We have to receive God's salvation before we have an opportunity to stop being rebellious.

The other two areas, *lust of the eyes* and *lust of the flesh*, are inherited from our ancestors, from our environment and from our peer groups. We "absorb" the standards of those around us. We are told that life is not complete and that we won't be happy unless we have whatever we want. So, until we get what we want, we are not happy.

Remember, you and I are each responsible for our own sin. Even though we enter this world "set up" and have all these influences working against us, we enter into the sins of our fathers and the resulting curses in only one way: by our own choice. God holds us accountable for the exercise of our free will. It is by His mercy and grace that He also gives us a choice to enter into His family through the sacrifice of Jesus Christ on the cross.

K. A Biblical Example of Sins of the Fathers and Curses

A number of biblical examples portray the sins of the fathers and resulting curses in action. One example, however, stands out above all the rest. The nation of Israel provides information about more generations than any other example. Technically speaking, this nation started with Abraham and continues until this day. For our illustration, however, we will use King David as the starting point.

1. King David and his descendants

King David sits as a premier example of king, priest and prophet. He is the foreshadowing of the One who was yet to come, the Lord Jesus. As we read about his life in 1 and 2 Samuel and in 1 Kings, David's many accomplishments are described, including his numerous victories in battle, his favor with the people and his favor with God. He had everything going for him.

Then came his encounter with Bathsheba—an encounter that both caused and marked the pinnacle of his career. From that point on, events in his life began to deteriorate.

Now, you may be thinking, *Wait a minute, wasn't David forgiven?* The answer is, "Yes, he was forgiven," but the sins of the fathers and the resulting curses operating on his family line did not stop simply because he was forgiven. Forgiveness does not normally stop the "outworking" of curses. The cross stops curses when we *appropriate* its freedom into our lives. If we don't appropriate the cross, even if we don't know we need to do so, the consequences/ curses continue.

Some consequences continue, no matter what. Why? Because a seed was planted that produced a harvest. The child conceived and born out of wedlock provides a simple example. The child is still with us even after the parents have repented and received God's forgiveness. At the other extreme, a person murdered does not come back to life after the murderer repents. Forgiveness is a wonderful gift from God, but it is only part of what needs to be done in order to stop curses.

David entered into the sins of *adultery*,[43] *deception*,[44] *conspiracy*[45] and *murder*.[46] After David's (and Bathsheba's) sin, he was confronted by Nathan the prophet. Besides the humiliation of being exposed by Nathan, David received a multipart curse[47] from God. The curses are penalties of like nature. Because of the sins he had committed, David and his descendants would reap what he had sown. As we discussed earlier, this curse included the death of the child from the affair,[48] but this was only the beginning.

David repented. We can read his confessional prayer in Psalm 51.

This is a wonderful psalm, one with which we all can identify. However, this didn't stop the curses.

Later, one of David's sons, Amnon, *raped* Tamar,[49] which led to Amnon's being *murdered* by Absalom.[50] *Deception, lying* and *conspiracy* were all involved. Then Absalom himself *rebelled* against his father, the king, and *conspired* to take over the kingdom.[51] The story ends with Absalom's *death*[52] and with much *destruction* in Israel, just as the prophet had spoken.

If we continue to follow the history of Israel and the line of David, we find the same sins of the fathers and the outworking of the resulting curses occurring time after time after time.

Solomon, the second son of David and Bathsheba, became king. While he was one of the wisest men to ever live, he was not wise in his later years. He married many foreign women and fell into the *traps of women, gold, horses and idolatry.*[53]

While David's descendants (in Judah) included both good and bad kings, the overall pattern reveals definite flaws. God finally stopped the royal succession from coming through Solomon. He did this even though He had promised David:

> "And thine house and *thy kingdom shall be established for ever* before thee; thy throne shall be established for ever."
>
> 2 Samuel 7:16, KJ21, emphasis mine

God cut off Solomon's line with Jehoiachin,[54] the son of Jehoiakim,[55] and let Israel go into captivity.

> Thus saith the LORD, "Write ye this man as childless, a man that shall not prosper in his days; for no man of his seed shall prosper, sitting upon the throne of David and ruling any more in Judah."
>
> Jeremiah 22:30, KJ21, emphasis mine

Since we have the benefit of knowing the historical accounts, we can see that God did fulfill his promise to David through David's son Nathan (the third son born to David and Bathsheba).[56] This family line eventually led to the birth of Jesus, the "supposed" son of Joseph.[57] Jesus *is now sitting* upon the throne of David *forever*.

Thus we have the fascinating situation of God keeping *all* of his promises to King David and Israel/Judah, both the curses and the blessings. Yet the outworking of the curses caused an ever-deepening spiral of wickedness and destruction. David's sin put in motion much trouble and heartache for his descendants.

2. King David and his ancestors

It seems fair to ask, "What about David's ancestors? Did David fall into sin just 'out of the blue,' or did family pressures 'set him up?' Where did all of this sin begin?"

We know that David's grandmother was Ruth, a Moabite,[58] and that his great-grandmother was Rahab,[59] a Canaanite, the "keeper of the inn" in Jericho. So there were two heathen nations known for their *idolatry* and *sexual sins* grafted into the Israelite line preceding David, *within four generations.*

Going back farther, we do not know much about David's ancestors until we get back to Judah, a distance of ten generations.

In Genesis 38, we read about Judah, who had sexual relations with his daughter-in-law, Tamar, thinking she was a temple prostitute. We do not know Tamar's nationality, but Jewish tradition indicates that she was an Israelite. *Deception, fornication* and *lying* were all involved in this sin, and perhaps *occult/idol worship.*

Judah's father, Jacob (Israel), revealed his tendency for *deceit, lying, cursing, cheating,* etc. All of these sins were evident in his life, at least before his encounter with the angel of the Lord at the brook Jabbok.[60] His mother, Rebekah, entered into *deception* with Jacob, even *calling for the resulting curse* to be upon herself.[61] His wife, Rachel, *stole* her father's *household gods* and *lied* about them. This resulted in Jacob's *unintentional cursing* of her[62] and her early death.[63]

Both Abraham and Isaac were guilty of *lying,*[64] saying that their wives were their sisters. This, for Abraham, was a half-truth, since his wife was his half-sister.

While the blessings of the fathers far outweighed the cursing, it is clear that David did not have a "pure" family line. Even though we don't know about his ten nearest ancestors (except for Boaz, who was a righteous man who followed the Mosaic Law), we know enough about David's family line to state with confidence that David was "set up" by his ancestors. Although he did indeed have a heart after God, David chose to enter into the sins of his fathers in his sin with Bathsheba.

David is a reminder to us all to be on guard. We must be careful not to assume that we cannot fall. God's favor may be on us, He may be using us mightily to further His kingdom, but that is no guarantee that we cannot be tempted and fall. Satan lies in wait like a roaring lion ready to pounce and bring us down in that one weak or unguarded moment. It is wise to be on the alert for the enemy's attack, particularly at the time of a great victory. Scripture shows that a counterattack often follows such a time. Our best defense is to be on guard and to stop the counterattack before it begins.

L. Scriptural Basis for Freedom from Sins of the Fathers and Resulting Curses

Once Christians discover that sins of the fathers and the resulting curses may be providing an opening for failure and oppression, most of them want to appropriate freedom. The Scriptures in Table F on page 93 provide us with the basis for freedom.

1. Confession of fathers' and own sins

God first states His condition(s) for restoration in Leviticus, surrounded by His warnings and the dire consequences of Israel's anticipated rebellion.

> "*If they* shall *confess their iniquity and the iniquity of their fathers*, with their *trespass* which they *trespassed* against Me, and that also they have walked contrary unto Me . . . if then *their uncircumcised hearts be humbled* and they then *accept the punishment of their iniquity, then will I remember My covenant* with Jacob, and also My covenant with Isaac, and also My covenant with Abraham will I remember; and I will remember the land."
> Leviticus 26:40–42, KJ21, emphasis mine

As we prepare to apply the principles of this Scripture to ourselves and our families, it would be helpful for you to reread the section "What God Requires, God Provides" (pages 62–63). In the above Scripture, God has provided us a tremendous pattern to follow. One significant aspect of this pattern is that we are *not required to take responsibility* for our fathers' iniquity. Rather the passage models our *acknowledging and confessing* their iniquity. But God *does* expect us to accept responsibility for our own iniquity, to repent and to be humbled. When we do this, God states that He will remember His covenant(s). In other words, He will fulfill His promises of forgiveness and cleansing—to us and to the land. Of course, the "land" represents us also, since we are God's promised land.

This Scripture is the basis for *identification repentance*, a modern term meaning that we "stand in for" and represent our ancestors in confessing their sin.[65] This is a form of intercession. This concept,

Table F: Scriptures Concerning Freedom

► *Confession of father's (and own) sins*

Leviticus 26:40–42
"If they shall *confess their iniquity and the iniquity of their fathers*, with their *trespass* which they *trespassed* against Me, and that also they have walked contrary unto Me ... if then *their uncircumcised hearts be humbled* and they then *accept the punishment of their iniquity, then will I remember My covenant* with Jacob, and also My covenant with Isaac, and also My covenant with Abraham will I remember; and I will remember the land" (KJ21, emphasis mine).

Daniel 9:4–20
"And I *prayed* unto the LORD my God, and *made my confession* ... 'We *have sinned and have committed iniquity*, and have *done wickedly* and have *rebelled*, even *by departing from Thy precepts* and *from Thy judgments* ... all Israel have transgressed Thy law, even by *departing*, that they might *not obey Thy voice; therefore the curse is poured upon us*, and *the oath that is written in the Law....' I was speaking and praying, and confessing my sin and the sin of my people Israel*, and *presenting* my supplication before the LORD my God for the holy mountain of my God" (KJ21, emphasis mine).

► *Appropriating the cross*

Galatians 3:10–14
"All who rely on observing the law are under a curse, for it is written: *'Cursed is everyone who does not continue to do everything written in the Book of the Law.'* Clearly no one is justified before God by the law, because, 'The righteous will live by faith.' The law is not based on faith; on the contrary, 'The man who does these things will live by them.' *Christ redeemed us from the curse of the law by becoming a curse for us*, for it is written: 'Cursed is everyone who is hung on a tree.' *He redeemed us in order that the blessing* given to Abraham *might come* to the Gentiles through Christ Jesus, *so that by faith we might receive the promise of the Spirit"* (NIV, emphasis mine).

Colossians 2:13–14
"And when *you were dead* in your transgressions and the uncircumcision of your flesh, *He made you alive* together with Him, having *forgiven us* all our transgressions, having *canceled out* the *certificate of debt* consisting of decrees against us ... and He has taken it out of the way, *having nailed it to the cross"* (NASB, emphasis mine).

1 Peter 1:18–19
"You were not *redeemed* with perishable things like silver and gold *from your futile way of life inherited from your forefathers*, but *with precious blood*, as of a lamb unblemished and spotless, *the blood of Christ"* (NASB, emphasis mine).

when applied at the larger level, allows spiritual and civic leaders to "stand in for" the former leaders and inhabitants of the land, confessing their sin. Applying this principle to an organization or a geographical area—a church or business, or a city or region—can yield great results in weakening and eventually clearing out demonic principalities and paving the way for awakening and spiritual revival.

Scripture provides several very important examples of identification repentance. Daniel, Nehemiah and Ezra[66] all prayed and confessed the sins of their fathers. Again, note that they did not ask forgiveness for their forefathers, but only for themselves and their people. They confessed their forefathers' sin.

In Daniel 9:4–20, we see that Daniel prayed a tremendous confessional prayer of identification repentance during his and Israel's exile in Babylon. While reading in the book of Jeremiah, Daniel realized that the seventy years of captivity prophesied by the prophet[67] was nearly completed and so he interceded for God's prophecy to come to pass.

In this awesome prayer, Daniel identified himself and the nation of Israel with their forefathers. He *confessed* his and their sins. He *agreed* with God that they were wrong and that God was right. He agreed with God that He had every right to bring the curses upon them "because we have sinned against [God]." Then he called on God's righteousness and mercy, and asked Him to restore the situation "for thy own sake." This prayer is a great model for us.

In Nehemiah, we find two similar prayers.[68] These prayers have essentially the same ingredients as Daniel's prayer and serve as additional example prayers for us. Nehemiah 9:3 shows the Israelites following the Leviticus 26:40 pattern as they confessed their sins and the iniquities of their fathers before beginning their corporate prayer. Ezra 9 follows a similar pattern.

As we choose to follow this biblical pattern to humble ourselves and repent of the sins of our fathers, we and others are experiencing newfound freedom. Tremendous testimonies are also being reported from around the world that identification repentance is breaking the power of demonic strongholds over geographic areas, and revival is coming forth.[69]

2. Appropriating the cross

On this side of the cross, Jesus has completely satisfied the requirements of God's judgment. He has provided freedom for us from the curses originating from the sins of the fathers and resulting curses, as well as from our own sin. Even better, whereas God also required the Israelites to accept the appropriate punishment for their sin (see Leviticus 26:40–42 on page 92), Jesus has already taken the punishment for us. All we have to do is to appropriate His work on the cross by faith!

In Galatians, Paul wrote:

> *All who rely on observing the law are under a curse,* for it is written: *"Cursed is everyone who does not continue to do everything written in the Book of the Law."* Clearly no one is justified before God by the law, because, "The righteous will live by faith." The law is not based on faith; on the contrary, "The man who does these things will live by them." *Christ redeemed us from the curse of the law by becoming a curse for us,* for it is written: "Cursed is everyone who is hung on a tree." *He redeemed us in order that the blessing* given to Abraham *might come* to the Gentiles through Christ Jesus, *so that by faith we might receive the promise of the Spirit.*
>
> Galatians 3:10–14, NIV, emphasis mine

This promise is further amplified in Colossians:

> When *you were dead* in your transgressions and the uncircumcision of your flesh, *He made you alive* together with Him, having *forgiven us* all our transgressions, having *canceled out* the *certificate of debt* consisting of decrees against us . . . and He has taken it out of the way, *having nailed it to the cross.*
>
> Colossians 2:13–14, NASB, emphasis mine

Peter also showed us the way out and explicitly tied redemption through the blood of Christ to the "futile" lifestyle inherited from our fathers:

> *You were* not *redeemed* with perishable things like silver and gold *from your futile way of life inherited from your forefathers,* but *with precious blood,* as of a lamb unblemished and spotless, *the blood of Christ.*
>
> 1 Peter 1:18–19, NASB, emphasis mine

We cannot keep God's law, and the Israelites could not and cannot today keep God's law. Our disobedience in breaking the law results in curses coming upon us. God Himself, in the likeness of man, "redeemed us from the curse of the law." Jesus is our substitute if we will receive Him as such by faith. He provides a legal answer to the outworking of God's judgments and to the curses that Satan wants to impose upon us. Jesus "canceled out the certificate of debt, consisting of decrees against us and which was hostile to us." Jesus is the answer. He alone sets us free.

3. Bringing freedom to our children

We have been asked many times, "What effect will my ministry have on my children?" and "What can I do to also help my children get free?"

One of the awesome things about breaking sins of the fathers and the resulting curses is that the person receiving this ministry brings the "passing down" to a halt at his generation. His descendants can have a fresh start. Babies born after the time of ministry are the first generation of a new family line, one rooted in the family of God. This is a tremendous blessing that one can give his descendants— perhaps, the most significant inheritance possible, next to helping them know the Lord Jesus personally.

For children who are already born, the effect of the parent's SOFCs ministry on them depends on their age, particularly their age relative to the age of accountability.

a. Young children

Young children, from infants to four to five years, can be ministered to while they are asleep. Then, through prayer, you can move into a position of authority as both parent and intercessor. Using the same strategy you used to obtain your own freedom, continually apply the SOFCs ministry steps, moving from grouping to grouping. At the same time, you may want to cast out related demons.

b. Older children

Older children, over four to five years old, are less likely to receive significant freedom from their parent's ministry. We usually suggest that they be prayed for in person. For approximately nine- to twelve-year-olds, explain the basics of SOFCs to them and enlist their cooperation. Lead them through the ministry steps, following the same "family" strategy order of going through the SOFCs groups that you used in your ministry. If they are not yet born again, this ministry may give them the freedom needed to make a godly choice. It would also be wise to continue to bind all demons oppressing them.

c. Adult "children"

For mature children, the suggested approach is really the same as for "older" children. Help them become informed so they desire to receive the ministry for themselves. Perhaps you might share your testimony with them. Consider asking their forgiveness for the ways your sins and hurts have caused them to be hurt. Let them know your heart, how much you desire their freedom. Depending on the age and personality of the child, you might share a copy of this book and encourage them to read it.

Obviously, wisdom is needed if the children are unsaved. How you actually approach them will depend on a number of factors. As always, seek the Holy Spirit for God's wisdom in all things, including whether or not to pray with them in this area—and if so, when, where and how.

M. Ministering Freedom to SOFCs: Specific Steps

Ministering to the area of sins of the fathers and the resulting curses is very important. This is analogous to clearing away the faulty foundation upon which the ministry receiver's life has been built. At times, this ministry to an individual may seem very straightforward and "cut and dried," while at other times it can be extremely dynamic and powerful.

Regardless of the appearance, let us assure you that significant things are happening in the spiritual realm. Powerful forces are being released like rubber bands flying across the room. Demons are losing their place and heading for the unemployment line. The unseen universe is shaking as the profound reverberations of broken curses echo out from the cross. A great cheer goes up in heaven. Another saint is being set free!

1. Strategy for ministry

We have found that the most effective ministry to the sins of the fathers and resulting curses problem area takes place when we have a strategy. Our strategy involves grouping the core areas of sins that have most affected our ministry receiver's life and beginning with these. We start with the most significant and end with the least significant. Most often, these important sin areas are closely related, as with abandonment and sexual sin. (People who miss out on being loved look for love through sexual relationships.) Next, we include other closely related areas, such as the shame, fear and control areas, associated both with abandonment and with sexual sin. Frequently there seems to be a cluster of about six to eight interrelated, core sin areas. After ministering to these, we move to the groups of lesser impact. We use a list of groups of "ancestral open doors" as a ministry sheet to plan and organize the SOFCs. A copy of this ministry sheet is included in the appendix.

2. Receiving God's blessings

In the ministry steps used for sins of the fathers and resulting curses, the last step can have deep, personal significance for the receiver. This is a time when God can bring the blessings that He has always wanted for him. The cross has been applied. The pressure of the sins and the power of curses have been broken. The slate of his life has been wiped clean. Now he is in a fresh position to receive from the Lord.

We ask the ministry receiver to listen to the Lord in the last step. We either tape record or write the personal, life-giving blessings he receives as the Lord speaks.

If our receiver is unable to hear the Lord, then we share what the Lord is speaking to us or showing us. Don't let your ministry receiver miss the joy of this blessing!

3. Final thoughts before ministry

The minister needs to be particularly sensitive to the Holy Spirit during this time of ministry. He needs to be able to identify sins of the fathers and resulting curses operating in his receiver's life, including those known by the person himself and those unknown. The unknown ones, particularly those from more distant ancestors, may be discernible only by the gifts of the Holy Spirit.

Exercise
As you pray the Submission Prayer on page 100 (or one similar to it in your own words), and work through the following ministry steps, you can use your completed Ancestral Open Doors form to help you and the Holy Spirit minister to those sins and curses that He has selected for this time.

4. Submission prayer

The prayer on page 100 can be used as a model as you help your receiver prepare to appropriate the freedom God desires for him. Please, however, avoid becoming "religious" and using this prayer by rote. We want our prayers to be of the Spirit and not of the letter.[70]

5. Steps to freedom in ministering to sins of the fathers and resulting curses

The progression of ministry is outlined in the following list of detailed steps. Generally, the minister will pray/declare ministry steps 8 and 9. Sometimes, however, the ministry receiver will include these as he is moving through the other steps. If so, that is great. It means that he is "grabbing hold" of the Gospel and applying it. Obviously, there is no need for the minister to repeat the same steps.

Ministry Steps

1. **Confess**: Have the ministry receiver confess the sins of his fathers and his own sins.
2. **Forgive**: Have the receiver forgive his ancestors and parents who are still alive for any and all sins that they have committed that have affected his life. Have him forgive them for specific sins as appropriate.
3. **Forgive**: Have the receiver forgive every living person who has spoken word curses against him and/or his ancestors.
4. **Repent**: Have the receiver ask God's forgiveness for entering into the sins of his fathers and for yielding to the curses affecting him. Have him choose to turn away from any and all sins of the fathers, as well as from his own personal sins.
5. **Forgive**: Have the receiver forgive himself for his own personal sins, for self-curses and for carrying guilt, shame and self-hatred.
6. **Receive**: Speak forgiveness[71] and pray for cleansing.[72]
7. **Renounce**: Have the receiver renounce any more involvement or "putting up with" the sins and curses.
8. **Appropriate**: Appropriate and apply the power of the cross and the shed blood of Christ to stop all judgments and curses.

SOFCs Submission Prayer

As a child of God, purchased by the blood of the Lord Jesus Christ, I choose to confess and acknowledge the sins of my ancestors. While I don't like the results of their sins on my life, I choose to forgive and release them and not to hold them accountable for each and every way that their sins have affected me.

I now renounce all of the sins of my ancestors and release myself from their effects, based on the finished work of Christ on the cross.

Lord, I am sorry for all of the ways that I have entered into these same sins and allowed the curses to affect me. I ask You to forgive me for this and to wash me clean. I choose to receive Your forgiveness.

I affirm that I have been crucified with Jesus Christ and raised to walk in newness of life. On this basis, I announce to Satan and all his forces that Christ took upon Himself the curses and judgments due me. Thus I break every curse that has come upon me because of my ancestors. I also break all curses that have been released onto me by others. I also break all curses that I have spoken or thought about myself. I receive my freedom from every one of these curses.

Because of the above and because I have been delivered from the power of darkness and translated into the Kingdom of God's dear Son, I cancel the legal rights of every demon sent to oppress me.

Because I have been raised up with Christ and now sit with Him in heavenly places, where I have a place as a member of God's family, I renounce and cancel each and every way that Satan and his demons may claim ownership of me. I cancel all dedications made by my ancestors of their descendants, including me and my descendants, in the name of Jesus. I declare myself to be completely and eternally signed over to, owned by and committed to the Lord Jesus Christ.

All this I do on the basis of the truth revealed in the Word of God, and in the name and with the authority of my Lord and Savior, Jesus Christ. Amen!

9. **Break**: Break the power of any and all curses in the authority of the name of Jesus and in His finished work on the cross.[73] Refuse Satan any right to carry out any curses.

10. **Affirm**: Have the receiver affirm that he has a new Father. Not only is he in a new kingdom,[74] but he is in a new family, where there are no sins of the fathers.[75]

11. **Receive**: Have the receiver listen to the Holy Spirit, to reveal the blessing that God has for him in place of the sins and curses.

N. Thought-Provoking Questions

1. Please describe three problems and three blessings in your own family that are generational.

   . . . .

   . . . .

2. What is good about actually confessing ancestral sin?

   . . . .

   . . . .

3. Describe the greatest inheritance you can pass on to your children.

   . . . .

   . . . .

4. When does God know that you hate Him?

   . . . .

   . . . .

5. Why are Masonic/secret society memberships and oaths a curse to a family?

   . . . .

   . . . .

6. What does a curse empower you to do? What does a blessing help you to do?

   . . . .

   . . . .

7. Where do curses come from? (Name three sources.)

    . . . .

    . . . .

8. How can the cross stop curses?

    . . . .

    . . . .

9. How can your family be changed by the confessing, forgiving and breaking of ancestral sins and curses?

    . . . .

    . . . .

4

Ungodly Beliefs (UGBs)

Be ye transformed by the renewing of your mind,
that ye may prove what is that good and acceptable
and perfect will of God.
Romans 12:2, KJ21, emphasis mine

Everyone, to some extent, contains, in their belief system, beliefs that are not true. When these beliefs are contrary to God's truth, we call these beliefs "ungodly beliefs" (UGBs). They are "lies" about ourselves, about others and about God. These beliefs are dangerous. Why are they so dangerous? Because they affect our perceptions, our decisions and our actions. They even affect our destiny. These lines of poetry illustrate this powerful progression.

Belief System
If you accept a Belief
You reap a Thought.
If you sow a Thought
You reap an Attitude.
If you sow an Attitude
You reap an Action.
If you sow an Action
You reap a Habit.
If you sow a Habit
You reap a Character.
If you sow a Character
You reap a Destiny.

Author unknown

Have you ever thought about the fact that what you believe will shape your destiny? You can see why God wants our minds renewed!

As we start this chapter, we will share Tim's testimony and how the discovery of his ungodly beliefs resulted in the renewal of his mind. In other words, his ungodly beliefs were changed into godly beliefs (GBs).

Also in this chapter, you will learn the difference between ungodly beliefs and godly beliefs. As we discuss how and why ungodly beliefs are formed, you will learn to identify the most common ones. Since we Christians are also "infected" with ungodly beliefs (sorry!), we will explain the damaging results of living our lives based on them. We will then explore the Scriptures that provide a basis and a methodology for identifying and changing ungodly beliefs into godly beliefs. You will learn how to "reprogram" your mind so that it is filled with godly beliefs. Lastly, we present ministry steps that allow you to break the power that ungodly beliefs have over your mind and appropriate God's power through godly beliefs. It will change your life!

Tim's exposure to ungodly beliefs

Our hearts trembled as our new friend and recent ministry receiver, Tim, approached the podium to give his testimony. Waves of compassion mixed with tension swept over the congregation. A few short months before, Tim's pain-wracked existence had wavered between life and death when he overdosed twice in one week on cocaine and alcohol. But as Tim began to speak, a clarity and a steadiness came forth, confirming that God had truly done a deep, personal work in our friend's life. Tim shared about the recommitment to Christ that had taken place in his first ministry session, how his old belief system had been leading him to destruction and how his new godly beliefs were bringing him into stability and new life.

> I want to touch on one core ungodly belief. This one came right out of my experience and combined with others for my destruction. *I believed that I had to fend for myself because God could not be trusted.* During my childhood, my father neglected me and failed to provide for my needs. As a result, I wandered through life feeling scared, insecure and wondering how I was going to make it. I did all kinds of crazy things to provide for myself. The worst was allowing my body to be bought sexually. My looks and my body were the only things that I had any confidence in.
>
> The Kylstras helped me to see that I was believing a lie about God. We did some deliverance, prayed and asked God to help me to begin believing the truth about Him. Then they told me to begin to pray/ meditate every day on the godly belief that God loves me, and He is my provider. Over time, I began to change on the inside. At first I doubted that anything in my life would change since I was in deep financial

debt at that time with no obvious way out. Although it was hard to keep believing, I started repeating these new phrases every day. After all, I didn't have anything to lose. As a result of this new belief about God, I started acting differently. I began by obeying God about tithing and learned how to manage my money better. Little by little, I began to believe that God *did* care and that He would provide.

Before long, the miracles started happening. My salary increased by four times in four months, and I've taken home over half of it. At times I still fret a little bit. This past week I needed nearly $200 to fix my car. To make matters worse, I lost a few hours from work because I was sick. While I was sitting at home, I asked myself, *Why aren't you worried? Why aren't you upset?* To my amazement, I began to see that my belief system really *was* changing. I was saying, *Well, I know in my heart God is going to provide*, and I really believed it. That was a major turning point for me.

Changing my beliefs about God's provision has had other implications. I no longer have to do those old, awful, sinful things to get someone else to take care of me.

As Tim finished, the congregation rose to their feet with a cheer. They clapped and shouted as they gave thanks to the Lord and rejoiced for the obvious changes God had worked in this young man they all had known.

A. Understanding the Interrelationship among the Ministry Areas

Ungodly beliefs are interrelated with the other three problem areas. This is why they must be ministered to in concert with each of the other problem areas if the ministry is to be permanently effective. Although some measure of healing would come by ministering solely to UGBs, it will become apparent to you how *interrelated* UGBs are with each of the other problem areas.

1. How ungodly beliefs are related to sins of the fathers and resulting curses

After finishing a ministry session in which much generational sin had been exposed, Betsy commented to Chester, "Tell me the sins of the fathers affecting a person's life, and I will tell you most of his ungodly beliefs." Think about it. The two are integrally related. The same sins that have plagued families for generations cause deception, clouded minds, rationalization and unbelief in these same sin areas. For example, sexual sin causes many wrong, twisted beliefs about sex. Violence results in rationalization and "normalizing" of violence and wrong beliefs about it, as well as affecting the victim's beliefs about self-worth. The specific sin of the fathers is like the hub of a wheel and the UGBs are like the spokes going out from it. They become an extension of the sin. To deal with the spokes but not the hub would produce incomplete results, as the roots would be left in place.

2. How ungodly beliefs are related to soul/spirit hurts

When a child becomes the victim of his father's drunken rage, his young heart is broken. Think for a moment about some of the UGBs that he could have. Eventually ideas might develop such as *I must not be a lovable person* or *It is my fault that Dad is so angry.* Many of the negative beliefs that we have about ourselves, others and God result from the ungodly, hurtful ways we have been treated. Hurts and wrong beliefs are like two hands that are placed together with the fingers intertwined and locked. The hurts must be healed, as well as the mind renewed. If not, the hurts will cry out messages of denial to override the attempted process of renewing the mind. Hurts are like an infected wound and the UGBs are like the pus coming from it. We can wipe away the pus, but more will develop unless the wound is healed. The wound affects the heart; the pus affects the mind. Both need to be healed.

Because sins are generational and sin causes hurts, the same types of hurts tend to be repeated generation after generation. As a result, the same kinds of UGBs continue to be generated and passed down. Sins of the fathers, soul/spirit hurts and the resulting ungodly beliefs form a threefold, negative cord that is only broken by our understanding, our faith and the appropriation of God's freedom.

3. How ungodly beliefs are related to demonic oppression

Our understanding of the importance of the integrated approach to biblical healing ministry was greatly strengthened the day we supervised a ministry team that was trying to deliver a man named Clyde from a spirit of lust. The demon would not budge. The Holy Spirit revealed to the team that the demon's legal ground involved two UGBs based on this man's childhood experiences. Clyde's father had kept *Playboy* magazines under his bed and the boy often sneaked a look at them. Without realizing it, Clyde formed the beliefs that *it is normal and manly for a man to have pornography in his house* and that *pornography is a normal part of the husband/wife relationship*. When the ministry team identified and exposed these two beliefs as revealed by the Holy Spirit, Clyde repented and renounced them. The demon of lust was then easily and immediately cast out.

Ungodly beliefs provide legal permission for demons to stay. Why? Because we are in agreement with the devil—rather than God—when we have an UGB. This connection between UGBs and the demonic has been validated in deliverance sessions many times. It is best to minister to UGBs *before* doing deliverance since this removes "legal" ground for the demonic. Sometimes, however, the deliverance must be done first before we can begin to minister effectively. When this is the case, we still come back later—after finishing the ministry to sins of the fathers and resulting curses, ungodly beliefs and soul/spirit hurts—to do some "clean-up" deliverance. We want to insure that any demons that were able to enter in the interim are removed.

4. Summary

Thus we see how UGBs are clearly tied to the other three problem areas. To minister only to UGBs—or to deal with the other problem areas without including UGBs—would leave the ministry process incomplete and the ministry receiver vulnerable to losing his healing. We hope that you see the connections between the different areas and that you will not return to dealing with only one or two problem areas such as deliverance or praying for hurts.

B. Definitions/Descriptions

What is a belief system? It includes our *beliefs, decisions, attitudes, agreements, judgments, expectations, vows* and *oaths*. It includes everything that involves our mind and our thinking, particularly our decision-making power. Look at the complete definitions in the box on page 108.

Unfortunately, the major areas of our belief system are usually made up of UGBs. For example, what we believe about our right to exist, our purpose, our value and the very source of our security—as well as what we believe about our relationships with other people and with

---

Ungodly Beliefs

All *beliefs, decisions, attitudes, agreements, judgments, expectations, vows* and *oaths* that *do not* agree with God (His Word, His nature and His character).

Godly Beliefs

All *beliefs, decisions, attitudes, agreements, judgments, expectations, vows* and *oaths* that *do* agree with God (His Word, His nature and His character).

God—may generally be ungodly. As the Holy Spirit begins to sanctify our mind,[1] our belief system begins to change from a mixture of mostly UGBs to more and more GBs.

We can make some statements about "real" godly beliefs, that is, beliefs that do indeed "agree with God" rather than beliefs that we "think" agree with God.

- A real godly belief is reflected in our actions.
- A real godly belief is rooted in our heart.
- A real godly belief stands firm in the face of challenge.

On the other hand, a godly belief is not something that we say that sounds spiritual and yet something by which we do not live.

The goal is to be transformed into the image of Christ,[2] having only GBs. While this goal may seem impossible to attain, we can decide to work with the Holy Spirit so that He can change us as rapidly as we can handle.[3] Perhaps the day will come when we can say with David:

> How precious to me are your thoughts, O God!
> How vast is the sum of them!
>
> Psalm 139:17, NIV

When we are tuned in to His mind, we realize that God has much to say to us. Paul wrote of this possibility in 1 Corinthians, as he discussed Christians who were spiritual: "But we have the mind of Christ" (1 Corinthians 2:16, KJ21). If God has promised us His mind, let us not draw back, but instead pursue a renewed mind with faith.

C. God's Plan and Purpose for Our Beliefs

The verses in Table G on page 111 show God's plan and heart for our beliefs. While our spirits were redeemed when we were born again, the redemption of our soul is "in process."[4] Renewing of the mind is a key element of the sanctification process. Our responsibility is to give ourselves to the process, cooperating with God rather than resisting Him.

1. Renewing the mind

Romans 12:2 is a key verse illuminating the sanctification process. In Romans 12:1, Paul had just finished writing about presenting our bodies as a "living sacrifice," stating that it's only reasonable for us to do so. Then he penned, "Do not be conformed to this world . . . but be transformed (changed) by the [entire] renewal of your mind" (AMP). The translators of the Amplified Bible qualify what this phrase means by adding the phrase, "by its new ideals and its new attitude." Then comes the purpose statement, the reason for the renewing of our minds: "so that you may prove [for yourselves] what is the good and acceptable and perfect will of God, even the thing which is good and acceptable and perfect [in His sight for you]" (AMP).

2. Knowing God's perfect will

How many of us would like to know the perfect will of God in our lives? Of course, we all want this. In every situation, we would like to know God's good, acceptable and perfect will in our lives. How do we obtain this? The answer is this: We must have our minds renewed. As our minds become renewed, we think more like God, we become aware of how He looks at things, and we begin to look at things as He does instead of out of our own selfish, self-centered ways. We learn to know what is on His heart, how He wants us to pray, where He wants us to go, what He wants us to do. And so, we can begin to move in His good, acceptable and perfect will.

As we receive His healing, we are not so fearful about what He might be wanting us to do. We grow in trust and confidence, working toward complete and absolute confidence in God. This enables us to hear His voice and to know His will better and better. Thus, there is a one-to-one correspondence between having our minds renewed (which means getting rid of our UGBs and replacing them with GBs) and being able to know the good and acceptable and perfect will of God.

We expect that most of us want our minds renewed so we can know

God's good and acceptable and perfect will. Then we can choose His perfect will.

3. Renewing the spirit of your minds

In Ephesians 4:23, Paul again stressed the same theme. Here the phrase is, "Be renewed in the *spirit* of your *mind*" (NASB, emphasis mine). Isn't this an interesting phrase? "The spirit of your minds." We have been taught to think of the mind as being in the soul region, but here, the spirit of our mind is to be transformed, to be renewed.

In 1 Peter 4:1, Peter wrote, "Arm yourselves likewise with the same *mind*" (KJ21, emphasis mine), or we could say "with the attitude of Christ." As our mind is renewed, it should function more and more like the mind of Christ.

Colossians 3:10 is another wonderful verse, expressing being "renewed in *knowledge* after the *image of Him*" (KJ21, emphasis mine). Knowledge has to do with the mind (and spirit), with "knowing." This passage could be paraphrased: "Be renewed in (your) mind with knowing Him as He is."

4. New Age and Christianity

The Colossians passage above shows us the difference between humanism, or New Age philosophy, and Christianity. New Agers promote self-improvement, a better self-image, etc., all of which are *self-centered*. Christianity, on the other hand, offers a *"Christ-centered"* life. It offers a "new self" that is being conformed to the image of Christ, taking on *His* nature, character, attitudes, beliefs, likeness and mind. It doesn't try to "improve" the "old self."

5. Taking thoughts captive

The well-known passage in 2 Corinthians 10:3–5 instructs us to pull down strongholds, cast down *imaginations* and use our spiritual weapons to come against "every high thing that exalteth itself against the *knowledge* of God, and [to bring] into captivity every *thought*...." (verse 5, KJ21, emphasis mine). *The battleground is in the mind.* We need to apply God's weapons against everything that would try to keep our thought patterns and habits in the old way. Strongholds of fear, worry, bitterness, anger, shame and control need to come down and be replaced by Christ's thoughts.

All of these points lead to one conclusion. We can only believe the truth by having our minds renewed. Otherwise, we are in danger because Satan has access to our minds through our UGBs.

Table G: Scriptures Concerning Ungodly Beliefs (Set 1)

▶ *God's plan and purpose for our beliefs*

Romans 12:2
"Do not be conformed to this world (this age), [fashioned after and adapted to its external, superficial customs], but be transformed (changed) by the [entire] *renewal of your mind* [by its *new ideals* and its new attitude], so that you may prove [for yourselves] what is the good and acceptable and perfect will of God, even the thing which is good and acceptable and perfect [in His sight for you]" (AMP, emphasis mine).

Ephesians 4:22–23
"In reference to your former manner of life, you *lay aside the old self*, which is being corrupted in accordance with the lusts of deceit, and . . . be *renewed in the spirit of your mind*" (NASB, emphasis mine).

1 Peter 4:1
"*Arm yourselves* likewise with the *same mind [attitude] . . .*" (KJ21, emphasis mine).

Colossians 3:9–10
" . . . seeing that ye have *put off the old man* with his deeds, and have *put on the new man*, which is *renewed in knowledge after the image* of Him that created him" (KJ21, emphasis mine).

2 Corinthians 10:3–5
"For though we walk in the flesh, we do not war according to the flesh. For the weapons of our warfare are not carnal, but mighty through God for the *pulling down of strongholds, casting down imaginations* and *every high thing* that *exalteth itself against the knowledge of God*, and *bringing into captivity every thought* to the obedience of Christ" (KJ21, emphasis mine).

D. How Ungodly Beliefs Are Formed

Ungodly beliefs originate primarily from two sources: experiences of hurt, and the natural, or unredeemed, mind of mankind. Let's look at these. We also want to explain how beliefs, once formed, are strengthened through a process we call the Belief-Expectation Cycle.

1. Ungodly beliefs from experiences of hurt

The possibility of being hurt exists at every stage of life. These hurtful experiences add to the strength and intensity of our negative beliefs about ourselves and others.

a. Childhood years

Most of our UGBs result from childhood hurts, traumas and negative experiences. These make a very strong impression on us. For example, the child whose father misses all of his ball games, all of his birthday parties, and is never there when he needs guidance, may form such beliefs as the following:

- *I am not important because my dad does not have time for me.*
- *Significant people in my life will not be there for me when I need them.*

These UGBs will become incorporated into the very core of the hurt from which this child begins to live his life. These lies of abandonment embedded within his hurt will powerfully affect his life until he *learns how to get his hurt healed.* Even if he comes to recognize the lies, mental awareness is not enough. These UGBs will not be totally rooted out without heart-level, Jesus-level healing. This is also true for most of the UGBs we have.

Even more serious UGBs are formed by the child who tries to intervene as his parents are fighting and is told, "Shut up, you pipsqueak. We didn't have all these problems before you came along." From this devastating experience, the child concludes:

- *Things would be better if I had not been born. My life is a mistake.*
- *It is better to keep my mouth shut and my feelings to myself. If I express them, I will just get in trouble. I will just "stuff" or "hide" my feelings.*

In the same way a potter molds and shapes the clay, our hurtful experiences mold and shape our beliefs. If the foundation of our belief system laid during childhood is misshapen and distorted, the life that we built upon that foundation will also be misshapen and distorted.

b. Repetition of hurts reinforce the ungodly beliefs

We are particularly influenced by our families' often repeated statements, especially ones about ourselves. Some families continually reinforce with such statements as "You will never amount to anything" or "You are no good." In a friend's family it was "Don't be a weenie," meaning "Don't be a coward."

Our peers and schoolteachers also can play an important role repeating and reinforcing lies about ourselves. Have you ever heard your friends jeer, "Joey is a sissy, Joey is a sissy" or "Teacher's pet, teacher's pet"? Such statements are often part of the child's daily diet.

As a result, they become the bone and marrow of his UGBs system, a belief system that undermines his self-worth and ability to succeed.

c. Adult years

In addition, negative experiences occurring during our adult years can cause further UGBs to be formed. The impact of problems in business, marriage and church, or the experience of accidents, natural disasters or tragedies can cause us to believe lies about ourselves, others and God.

2. Ungodly beliefs from the natural mind

The other large, tainted source of UGBs comes from the *natural*, unredeemed mind of mankind. While these beliefs often seem logical and appealing, they reek with the worldly standards of man. In today's world they permeate and infuse our society. Concepts of worldly success, popularity and the *self-made* man are held up as the ultimate goal. These ungodly beliefs encourage us to "be in charge," to "do our own thing" or, in the words of various cult organizations, "to create our own reality." If God is mentioned, He is limited to the "God within" and considered more a "tool" than Lord. These beliefs are like poison gas—unseen but lethal. Surrounded by the beliefs that pervade our culture, we as Christians fail to detect how tightly they are woven into the fabric of our own partly sanctified minds.

It is the natural, unsanctified mind, attempting to handle and make sense out of life's hurts and traumas, that is chiefly responsible for the negative belief system that we have. As we attempt to protect ourselves from hurt, our mind wrestles with the "what if?" As we allow our imagination to run wild, we worry about terrible things happening to us and convince ourselves that we are no good and even shameful. Because of our unredeemed belief system, God "insists" that our minds be renewed.[5]

a. Family heritage

Just as our families pass on to us a special fishing rod, a set of old china or the corner cupboard, our families also pass on their beliefs, for better or for worse. Without realizing it, we "inherit" their beliefs about almost everything: life, politics, religion, education and relationships. We receive their prejudices about other people, other races, other cultures and even their pet peeve about the neighbor's dog. Our inheritance is very complete. Think of those times you've said, "I sound just like my mother (or father)." As one relay runner smoothly passes the baton to another, so parents pass on to their children their beliefs. Families are belief-shapers without even realizing this truth!

b. Unintentional teaching by our parents

Ungodly beliefs can be formed even when a parent has good motives, like comforting and protecting his child. Jackie Clifton, a friend and colaborer in ministry, shares the example of what a mother might say when her "precious" child comes home crying because the neighbor's "awful" child hit him. The comfort sounds something like this: "There, there, don't cry. It doesn't hurt. You are just fine." Sound familiar? What UGBs might the child form if this kind of comfort were repeated? Perhaps the following:

- *It must not be "okay" for something to really hurt.*
- *People who love me don't accept my real feelings.*
- *It is not all right to cry.*

Most parents would not want their children to adopt such beliefs.

3. Test your understanding

Ungodly beliefs are so much a part or our everyday way of thinking that we do not even recognize them most of the time. See if you can identify the ungodly beliefs in the following situations.

a. Situation 1

A young woman is engaged and has already sent out invitations to her wedding, when her fiancé breaks off their engagement. She says to herself, *I am so embarrassed. I do not know what people will think. I do know that I will never let myself get close to a man again.*
UGB: . . . .
. . . .

b. Situation 2

A man is looking at himself in the mirror as he is shaving. He says to himself, *My nose is too big, and my ears are funny looking. My chin is too pointed. When it comes to good looks, God really short-changed me. I wish I looked more like my handsome brother.*
UGB: . . . .
. . . .

c. Situation 3

An overweight woman is going to the ocean for a vacation and has begun a diet to lose weight. She says to herself, *I have been on this horrible diet for three days now and haven't lost a single pound. It is impossible for me to lose weight.*
UGB: . . . .
. . . .

How did you do recognizing the above ungodly beliefs? Now think about what ungodly beliefs you have said to yourself today. Are there any that you tell yourself every day?

▶ *Begin today to think about what you think!*

E. Belief-Expectation Cycle

The dynamics of how ungodly beliefs are formed and continue to gain strength can be diagrammed as the Belief-Expectation Cycle as shown in Figure 3.
    In this cycle, we see this process at work:

1. Our ungodly beliefs formed out of hurtful experiences, leading to...
2. Expectations arising from these beliefs. These expectations affect our...
3. Behavior, causing us also to influence the behavior of others, leading to...
4. Experiences in line with these behaviors that confirm the ungodly beliefs.

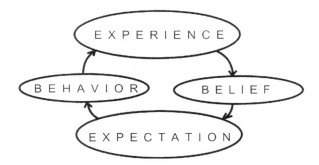

Figure 3: *The Belief-Expectation Cycle*

This cycle traps a person into a steadily worsening spiral of death.

The only way to stop this cycle is to intervene between the experience and the belief stages. *We must choose to make God's truth our new belief.* As we receive the truth and let it begin to change our beliefs, we begin to expect positive events in our lives. This leads to constructive behavior and good experiences.

The same cycle that was "killing" us now begins to reinforce the new GB, further strengthening it. The law of sowing and reaping is now working for us rather than against us. Our trust in God's faithfulness builds, as the truth of His Word[6] works in our lives.

F. The Importance of What We Believe in Shaping Situations

We can further understand the Belief-Expectation Cycle by examining the verses in Table H on page 117. These verses relate the importance of what we believe to the shaping of situations and events surrounding us.

This concept of shaping situations is frequently taught by various occult, psychic and secret societies. It is summed up in the phrase "creating your own reality." These people work hard at shaping/creating their own reality, usually for selfish reasons. Some people involved probably think their motives are not selfish, but they deceive themselves. Unless a person is born again, it is nearly impossible for his motives to be anything but self-centered. Believers, on the other hand, should be shaping situations and their responses to them under the direction of the Holy Spirit. That is the best way to plant godly seeds and reap godly harvests.

1. Sowing and reaping

When discussing the laws of God, we often refer to Mark 11:22–24. Please read it as expressed in the Amplified Version of the Bible in Table H on page 117. This important passage reveals the universality of the principle of sowing and reaping. As we plant "thought" seeds (in our heart), they do (eventually) affect our reality.

Verse 23 contains the general principle that if we *believe* in our heart—down in the soil of our heart where (thought) seeds are planted—and if we *don't doubt*, we shall *have* what we *say*. We usually

---

Table H: Scriptures Concerning Ungodly Beliefs (Set 2)

▶ *The importance of what we believe in shaping situations*

Mark 11:22–24
"And Jesus, replying, said to them, Have faith in God [constantly]. Truly I tell you, whoever *says* to this mountain, Be lifted up and thrown into the sea! and *does not doubt at all in his heart* but *believes that what he says will take place, it will be done for him.* For this reason I am telling you, whatever *you ask* for in prayer, *believe (trust* and *be confident) that it is granted to you,* and *you will [get it]*" (AMP, emphasis mine).

Proverbs 23:7
"For as he *thinks in his heart, so is he*" (AMP, emphasis mine).

Galatians 6:7–9
"Do not be deceived: God cannot be mocked. *A man reaps what he sows.* The one who *sows* to please his sinful nature, from that nature will *reap* destruction; the one who *sows* to please the Spirit, from the Spirit will *reap* eternal life. Let us not become weary in doing good, for *at the proper time* we will *reap a harvest if* we do not give up" (NIV, emphasis mine).

Hebrews 12:14–15
"Make every effort to live in peace with all men and to be holy; without holiness no one will see the Lord. See to it that no one misses the grace of God and that no *bitter root* grows up to cause trouble and *defile many*" (NIV, emphasis mine).

Matthew 7:1–2
"Do not judge, or you too will be judged. For in the same way you judge others, you will be judged, and with the measure you use, it will be measured to you" (NIV).

Luke 6:37–38
"Judge not, and ye shall not be judged. Condemn not, and ye shall not be condemned. Forgive, and ye shall be forgiven. Give, and it shall be given unto you: good measure, pressed down and shaken together and running over, shall men give into your bosom. For with the same measure that ye mete therewith it shall be measured to you again" (KJ21).

---

read this verse from the prayer point of view, since that is how Jesus applied the general principle of sowing and reaping. The power behind the law of sowing and reaping, however, is at work all of the time, not just when we are praying. Whatever we plant with faith, expectancy and absolute confidence that we shall have it, *we will have it.* Good or bad, *we will have it.*

2. When to plant

It is a fact that we can plant a seed at any time of the year. In certain seasons there is a greater chance that the seed will sprout and come to harvest, but we *can* plant all year round: winter, spring, summer or fall. Depending on where we live in the world, the seed may come up at any time of year or it may not come up at all. Likewise, we can plant thought seeds, good or bad, at any time.

3. Will there be a harvest?

Whether or not we receive a harvest, as well as its magnitude, depends on many factors. One important factor is whether we think the thought repeatedly. Continued sowing is more likely to produce a harvest. Another factor is faith. When prayer thoughts (whether out of faith or fear) go down into our heart and are received as the *truth*, the planted seed has a greater likelihood of sooner or later producing a harvest.

4. Core beliefs

The most "absolute" type of beliefs are those we grew up with, received and made our own without even realizing it. Since they were planted in the very core of our being, we don't even question whether they are true. We know that we know them without knowing that we know them. They are as *sure* as the truth that "the sun is going to come up in the morning" and "the sky is blue." These deeply planted belief/ thought seeds produce a continuous harvest, as the same thoughts go through our mind and into our hearts again and again. Usually we don't even notice them because they are such "givens." Planted again and again, they produce harvest after harvest, confirming and verifying the core beliefs. Of course, the core beliefs that are lies produce a harvest that is ungodly. These can trap us into devastating Belief-Expectation Cycles.

5. Shaping our reality

As each harvest comes to maturity, the seeds are replanted in our heart. The expectations associated with the harvest also come to pass, further validating the belief. *We have shaped our reality.* God's universe has responded to our seed planting and produced a harvest according to our expectations, good or bad. Since we all have a mixture of godly and ungodly beliefs, we experience a mixture of good and bad happenings. Demonic influences may also be at work with ungodly expectations by amplifying, accelerating or stirring up the response. They attempt to make the situations appear worse than they might otherwise.

To summarize: What we *believe* (in our heart), *say* (think) and *expect* (to have), we will *receive*. God's Word promises this. As a result, our beliefs get reinforced by our experience; what we experience reinforces our beliefs, and around we go. "See the facts, here they are. I was rejected again. It proves that my belief, my expectation that I will be rejected, is valid." Our beliefs cause our expectations, the expectations shape our reality, and our reality influences our beliefs. Eventually, we find ourselves on a downward spiral that seems out of control.

6. Breaking free of the "bad" harvest

To break out of the downward spiral takes some effort. God has provided a way if we will appropriate it and allow the law of the time to harvest to work. It takes time to change the momentum of our experiences.

7. Becoming what we believe

Continuing with the Scriptures in Table H on page 117, Proverbs 23:7 is essentially another way to state the law of sowing and reaping. We become what we believe we are. *If we don't like who we are, we need to change what we believe about ourselves.*

In Galatians 6:7–9, God states that whatever we sow—whether we sow to the flesh or we sow to the spirit—the law of sowing and reaping will bring forth a harvest. Universal in nature, this law applies in all realms and to all people. This law operates no matter who plants the seed—a saved or an unsaved person. Sowing "thought" seeds (beliefs) produces a harvest in the soulish realm and/or possibly in the spiritual realm. Then, as others respond to the spiritual pressure of our expectations, they tend to "do" in the physical realm what it takes to conform to our expectations.

While we are on the subject of sowing and reaping, please note that the Beatitudes reflect this same principle, particularly Matthew 5:7: "Blessed are the merciful, for they shall obtain mercy" (KJ21).

8. Planting "bitterness" seeds

Hebrews 12:14–15 in Table H refers to a "root of bitterness." The context of the passage is "living at peace with all men." If we are not living at peace, then we are likely to be planting seeds of unforgiveness, anger, resentment, envy and bitterness. Bitterness is a particularly hardy plant that usually underlies criticism, gossip, murmuring, complaining, etc. God is strongly admonishing us not to plant seeds of bitterness because the root will follow and the harvest will affect (defile) many others. The law of sowing and reaping is at work again. God says to follow peace and not bitterness.

9. The size of the harvest

Look next at Matthew 7:1–2. It also is an expression of the law of sowing and reaping. It confirms that the amount of seed reaped relative to the number planted will be in proportion. If we plant with teaspoons, we will reap in proportion to teaspoons. If we plant with bushel baskets, our harvest will be relative to bushels. So it is with planting expectations, i.e., UGBs. The stronger and more intense our belief is, the more we "think" it and plant it in our hearts, the larger the harvest.

10. Judging and condemning

Luke 6:37, a companion verse to Matthew 7:1–2, says, "Judge not, and ye shall not be judged" (KJ21). The verse continues, "Condemn not, and ye shall not be condemned" (KJ21). Can you recognize the sowing and reaping process in these verses? If we don't plant seeds of condemnation, then we won't reap a harvest of condemnation. The verse then reads, "Forgive, and ye shall be forgiven" (KJ21). This is the type of harvest we want to receive. This truth provides a powerful impetus for us to forgive other people—so that we will be forgiven.

11. Giving and multiplying

Everyone who wants to be rich likes to read Luke 6:38, "Give, and it shall be given unto you" (KJ21). This is God's Word. It says if we plant seeds by giving, "it" shall be given unto us. We can't avoid it. When applied in a godly way, this principle has very positive results. If, however, we apply it negatively, giving to others seeds of bitterness or hatred or anger or violence or rage or abuse, watch out! If we give away these types of "seeds," then that's what we can expect in return. And the amount will be "good measure, pressed down and shaken together and running over" (KJ21). We don't want to reap this kind of harvest, do we?

G. Results of Ungodly Beliefs: Unnecessary Limitations

Our beliefs affect our identity, how we perceive ourselves and how we relate to others, to the world around us and to God. They determine how Christlike we become and even the quality of our Christian lives. Ungodly beliefs are like a vise grip putting tight constraints on our lives, choking out the abundant life that Jesus promises.[7]

Ungodly beliefs are like spiritual termites that quietly work behind the scenes, undermining and eating away at the faith established within us. They constantly "gobble, gobble, gobble," reducing our foundations.

What are you believing today about yourself, other people or God? Are you experiencing any of the following results of ungodly beliefs?

- Erosion of your faith—weakening your relationship with God
- A divided mind (one part believes the facts of your life; another part believes God's truth)
- Demonic oppression (every UGB is an agreement/covenant with the enemy)
- Hindrance of Christ's intercession (How can the fullness of Christ's prayers be answered when we are not in agreement with Him or His Word?)
- Thinking "small," holding back, limited growth (the crippling of our God-given destiny)

For example, think for a moment about the dilemma of a pastor who is leading a growing church and is trying to determine whether or not to build a new church building. On the one hand he wants to proceed. On the other hand, he is immobilized by the following core ungodly beliefs:

- *God speaks to me about other people but not about the decisions that are important in my own life.*
- *God will not finance the things that He calls me to do.*
- *God will abandon me in my time of need, so I will fail.*

Is there any doubt left in your mind that ungodly beliefs about yourself, other people or God, can limit, cramp or short-circuit your destiny?

H. Sandy's Story: "Evil Core" Stronghold

We want to share with you two of Sandy's vicious ungodly beliefs that were key foundations holding in place a major stronghold that we named the "evil core" stronghold. Sandy's initial expression of these UGBs was:

> "No matter how much ministry I receive, no matter how much prayer goes up for me, no matter how many people pray, I am 'evil' beyond God's ability to restore me. I am so bad that even God can't help me."

Can you recognize the two lies? The first is, *I am inherently evil to the core.* The second is, *God can't help me.* In her deception, Sandy was nullifying the power of the cross![8]
Even with her desire and expectation of healing, Sandy was again leading the double life. On the one hand, she was hoping for freedom and healing. On the other hand, way down deep inside where she really lived, she believed her case was hopeless. She thought that we were wasting our time.

Once we recognized the "evil core" stronghold, we realized that it must be rooted out before we could make significant progress in Sandy's healing. The series of ministry steps we went through is not necessarily the only sequence that would have brought freedom. It is, however, the sequence that we used as the Holy Spirit guided us. Because it is atypical, it is not a model for others to use.

The Holy Spirit will likely have an entirely different approach for each ministry receiver oppressed by an "evil core" stronghold. The ministry pattern we used, however, is a good example of the need for an integrated approach to biblical healing ministry.

1. SOFCs

We started by leading Sandy through confession and forgiveness of her ancestors for their involvement in the occult, witchcraft, deception, sexual sin, hopelessness and gossip. We covered everything that might give legal ground to the "evil core." Then we had Sandy declare:

> I choose to be separated from the sins and curses of my ancestors. Your Word, Lord, says I have been brought out of darkness into Your kingdom of light. I receive that fully today. For every part of me not yet in the kingdom of light, I ask Your forgiveness, and I receive Your forgiveness.

Sandy then forgave, individually, several people who had spoken curses over her. She said, "I forgive each one who contributed to my believing that I am basically evil."

She then prayed for freedom.

> Father, I ask You to free me from deception. Let Your truth flood every aspect of my being. Free me from the power these lies have had over my life and over my very identity. Free me from falling victim to another's control. Lord, set me free from my double life and all it involves: confusion, fear and false responsibility. I renounce all demons promoting these sins and deception.

2. UGBs

Next came the UGBs related to the "evil core." Sandy confessed the sins of her ancestors and her own sins. These had set into motion the curses (coming down the family line) that promoted her UGBs. Gathering courage and determination, Sandy asked for forgiveness and then spoke boldly through her tears.

> I renounce the following lies:
> 1. *I am basically evil, rotten at the core.*
> 2. *God, You can't save me out of this mess. I am so evil that Your cross can't save me. This is too big for You, and I will never be free.*

Head still bowed, she forgave herself for the pride and arrogance associated with her former lies.

We continued to remove legal ground she had given to the stronghold. We had her break all "word curses" and "self-curses." These were negative words others had spoken to her or about her. She had agreed with them, taken the negative words and internalized them, repeating them to herself. We could see the life beginning to come back into Sandy. The horrible oppression was beginning to lift. For the first time, she spoke as a person who truly had hope.

> I break all agreements with anyone who ever told me that I am bad. I break my agreement with myself that I am bad and will never be free.

(The saga of removing the "evil core" stronghold is continued in the chapter on demonic oppression [see chapter 6].)

I. Typical Ungodly Beliefs

As we minister, we encounter a large number of UGBs that are similar from person to person. We expect that this is due to the culture-wide disintegration of the American family over the last fifty years, and thus the common hurts we all have experienced. Reviewing our ministry notes, we have extracted those UGBs shared by a majority of the people. These are tabulated on the following pages in two groups: those about ourselves and those about others.

We have divided the table of "Typical Ungodly Beliefs about Ourselves" (Table I on pages 126–127) into a number of "theme" categories. It is likely that you will have other themes that are also significant for you (or for your ministry receiver).

The table of "Typical Ungodly Beliefs about Others" (Table J on pages 128–129) is a distillation of many possible inclusions. There are a large number of other possible themes and a huge number of possible UGBs. But the listed ones are a beginning as you develop an increased sensitivity to ungodly thinking!

We have also extracted some common complementary/reinforcing UGBs that men and women have about each other. These are presented in Table K on page 130. It seems that part of God's plan to conform us into the image of Christ usually includes a helpmeet who is ideally suited to draw out and expose our UGBs, as well as the other deficiencies of our flesh. This process can be particularly vicious when we have UGBs that feed into and confirm our spouse's UGBs. Once exposed, we have to choose whether to take these UGBs and our flesh to the cross, or defend our weaknesses and UGBs by resisting and fighting with our spouse and with God. God wants us to choose to humble ourselves and work with the Holy Spirit for further sanctification.

Exercise

We suggest that you use the Typical UGBs tables as a springboard for you and the Holy Spirit to identify some of your UGBs. Prayerfully consider the listed UGBs. Mark those that you relate to, that seem to apply to you. If you realize other UGBs that you have, you can write them in the space provided or on an additional sheet of paper. Later on, we will give you an opportunity to write GBs to replace the ungodly beliefs. When we present the ministry steps, you can go through each UGB to remove it and replace it with a new godly belief.

J. A Higher Level of Truth than the Facts

In order for us to be transformed into the image of God, our thinking has to be changed so it lines up with *God's truth* and not the *facts* of our experience. Here we are truly challenged.

First, there are the facts. Facts are what actually happened. For example:

- The accident happened.
- The person had a disease.
- The business closed.
- The person confessed sin.

Facts are true, based on our experience in the here and now.

But:

There is a higher level of truth than the facts.
That is God's truth.
The real truth is what He says about the situation.

God's truth is not seen by the natural man, who is looking at the facts, but by the spiritual man, who knows God's transforming power. It is seen and embraced through faith.

> But a natural man does not accept the things of the Spirit of God, for they are foolishness to him; and he cannot understand them, because they are spiritually appraised. But he who is spiritual appraises all things, yet he himself is appraised by no one.
>
> 1 Corinthians 2:14–15, NASB

Table I: Typical Ungodly Beliefs about Ourselves

▶ *Theme: Rejection, not belonging*

- ☐ 1. *I don't belong. I will always be on the outside (left out).*
- ☐ 2. *My feelings don't count. No one cares what I feel.*
- ☐ 3. *No one will love me or care about me just for myself.*
- ☐ 4. *I will always be lonely. The special man (woman) in my life will not be there for me.*
- ☐ 5. *The best way to avoid more hurt or rejection is to isolate myself.*
- ☐ 6. Any additional UGBs concerning this theme:
  . . . .

▶ *Theme: Unworthiness, guilt, shame*

- ☐ 1. *I am not worthy to receive anything from God.*
- ☐ 2. *I am the problem. When something is wrong, it is my fault.*
- ☐ 3. *I am a bad person. If you knew the real me, you would reject me.*
- ☐ 4. *If I wear a mask, people won't find out how horrible I am and reject me.*
- ☐ 5. *I have messed up so badly that I have missed God's best for me.*
- ☐ 6. Any additional UGBs concerning this theme:
  . . . .

▶ *Theme: Doing to achieve self-worth, value, recognition*

- ☐ 1. *I will never get credit for what I do.*
- ☐ 2. *My value is in what I do. I am valuable because I do good for others, because I am "successful."*
- ☐ 3. *Even when I do or give my best, it is not good enough. I can never meet the standard.*
- ☐ 4. *I can avoid conflict that would risk losing others' approval by being passive and not doing anything.*
- ☐ 5. *God doesn't care if I have a "secret life" as long as I appear to be good.*
- ☐ 6. Any additional UGBs concerning this theme:
  . . . .

▶ *Theme: Control (to avoid hurt)*

- ☐ 1. *I have to plan every day of my life. I have to continually plan/strategize. I can't relax.*
- ☐ 2. *The perfect life is one in which no conflict is allowed, and so there is peace.*
- ☐ 3. Any additional UGBs concerning this theme:
  . . . .

Table I: Typical Ungodly Beliefs about Ourselves (*cont.*)

► *Theme: Physical attractiveness*

☐ 1. *I am unattractive. God shortchanged me.*

☐ 2. *I am doomed to have certain physical disabilities. They are just part of what I have inherited.*

☐ 3. *It is impossible for me to lose weight (or gain weight). I am just stuck.*

☐ 4. *I am not competent/complete as a man (woman).*

☐ 5. Any additional UGBs concerning this theme:

. . . .

► *Theme: Personality traits*

☐ 1. *I will always be (angry, shy, jealous, insecure, fearful, etc.).*

☐ 2. Any additional UGBs concerning this theme:

. . . .

► *Theme: Identity*

☐ 1. *I should have been a boy (girl). Then my parents would have valued me or loved me more.*

☐ 2. *Men (women) have it better.*

☐ 3. *I will never be known or appreciated for my real self.*

☐ 4. *I will never really change and be as God wants me to be.*

☐ 5. Any additional UGBs concerning this theme:

. . . .

► *Theme: Miscellaneous*

☐ 1. *I have wasted a lot of time and energy, some of my best years.*

☐ 2. *Turmoil is normal for me.*

☐ 3. *I will always have financial problems.*

☐ 4. Any additional UGBs concerning this theme.

. . . .

Table J: Typical Ungodly Beliefs about Others

▶ *Theme: Safety/protection*

☐ 1. *I must be very guarded about what I say, because anything I say may be used against me.*

☐ 2. *I must guard and hide my emotions and feelings. I cannot give anyone the satisfaction of knowing that they have wounded or hurt me. I'll not be vulnerable, humiliated or shamed.*

☐ 3. Any additional UGBs concerning this theme:

   ....

   ....

▶ *Theme: Retaliation*

☐ 1. *The correct way to respond if someone offends me is to punish them by withdrawing from them or cutting them off.*

☐ 2. *I will make sure that* [insert a person's name] *hurts as much as I do!*

☐ 3. Any additional UGBs concerning this theme:

   ....

   ....

▶ *Theme: Victim*

☐ 1. *Authority figures will humiliate me and violate me.*

☐ 2. *Authority figures will just use and abuse me.*

☐ 3. *My value is based totally on others' judgment/perception of me.*

☐ 4. *I am completely under other people's authority. I have no will or choice of my own.*

☐ 5. *I will not be known, understood, loved or appreciated for who I am by those close to me.*

☐ 6. Any additional UGBs concerning this theme:

   ....

   ....

▶ *Theme: Hopelessness/helplessness*

☐ 1. *I am out here all alone. If I get into trouble or need help, there is no one to rescue me.*

☐ 2. Any additional UGBs concerning this theme:

   ....

   ....

Table J: Typical Ungodly Beliefs about Others (*cont.*)

▶ *Theme: Defectiveness in relationships*

☐ 1. *I will never be able to fully give or receive love. I don't know what love is.*

☐ 2. *If I let anyone get close to me, I may get my heart broken again. I can't let myself risk it.*

☐ 3. *If I fail to please you, I won't receive your pleasure and acceptance of me. Therefore, I must strive even more* (perfectionism). *I must do whatever is necessary to try to please you.*

☐ 4. Any additional UGBs concerning this theme:

. . . .

. . . .

▶ *Theme: God*

☐ 1. *God loves other people more than He loves me.*

☐ 2. *God only values me for what I do. My life is just a means to an end.*

☐ 3. *No matter how much I try, I'll never be able to do enough or perform well enough to please God.*

☐ 4. *God is judging me when I relax. I have to stay busy about His work or He will punish me.*

☐ 5. *God has let me down before. He may do it again. I can't trust Him or feel secure with Him.*

☐ 6. Any additional UGBs concerning this theme:

. . . .

. . . .

Table K: Husband/Wife Complementary/Reinforcing Ungodly Beliefs

Men believe:	Women believe:
Women control the household; men control at work.	*Men don't know what to do around the house. It is easier to just do things myself.*
Women are domineering and controlling.	*Men are passive.*
Women make too big of a deal about special occasions.	*Special occasions are not important to men.*
Women are loose spenders. They can't be trusted with money. They don't have any restraint. They are always buying clothes and other things.	*Men are tight with their money. They don't appreciate how hard it is to keep the house supplied with food, clothes, etc.*
Women want to talk about their feelings all of the time.	*Men don't want an intimate, close relationship, in which a woman can share her innermost self.*
Women aren't interested in making love.	*The only thing men are interested in is sex.*
Women make having children too important. They get consumed with the children's lives.	*Men see children as a bother. They would rather not have them.*
My wife and children have ganged up against me. I can't even talk to my children.	*My husband ignores me and our children. He doesn't want to be close to us.*
Women are naturally more spiritual than men.	*Men are not concerned about the spiritual life of their families.*
My wife is lazy and doesn't keep the house in order.	*My husband finds fault with my housekeeping and doesn't see all that I do.*

We are not "just" natural men. We are men and women whose spirits are alive and who have been born again. As a result, we can discern (appraise) the spiritual truth concerning what God says about a fact or situation. By the power of His Spirit working within us, we can embrace His truth.

The following examples illustrate the difference between believing factual truth and believing God's truth.

---

1. *Apparent fact*: *I am just a nobody, going nowhere.* **God's truth**: God chose me before the foundation of the world. His plans for me are good.
2. *Apparent fact*: *This church is falling apart. The leadership of this church can't be trusted to bring unity.* **God's truth**: God says, I am building My Church.
3. *Apparent fact*: *So much is changing; I can't count on anything.* **God's truth**: God says, I am the same yesterday, today and forever. Put your trust in Me.
4. *Apparent fact*: *I am going through many trials and difficulties for no purpose.* **God's truth**: *God will bring me through the trials and mature me in the process.*

Can you see the difference between believing the "reality" of our circumstances and believing and confessing God's *eternal truth*? We don't negate the level of fact, but we can say, "God, there's something more, higher than just the facts that my natural eyes are seeing and my natural circumstances are causing to happen. There's something more, and that's *Your truth*."

Prayer
Lord, help me to be that spiritual man/woman who can discern and embrace Your *truth*.

K. Replacing Ungodly Beliefs with Godly Beliefs

Now that we have studied the dynamics of beliefs, let's learn how to replace UGBs with GBs. A very important part of this process is to legally break our agreement with the ungodly belief and to legally join in agreement with God. Doing this step makes all of the difference in the ease of acquiring a belief system in alignment with God's Word, nature and character.

As ministers, using this procedure with your ministry receivers will help them gain considerable freedom from the tyranny of their UGBs. As they talk, listen to them and to the Holy Spirit to hear the UGBs underlying their conversation.

Why write out the UGBs and GBs? We want a written statement in our own words that clearly declares God's truth to replace any lie(s) we have believed. Then we want to align our beliefs with God's. Written GBs help the process of removing the wrong beliefs (UGBs) that do not agree with God's Word. They help in releasing ourselves—and our releasing others—from the beliefs, judgments (labels) and expectations that keep us locked into *less* than God's best for us. We want to line ourselves up with His plans and purposes without putting limits on His abilities or His grace.

Exercise

Continue the earlier exercise on page 125, by writing the GBs to go with your UGBs.

---

1. Procedure for replacing ungodly beliefs with godly beliefs

You may follow this procedure to help a ministry receiver change an ungodly belief into a godly belief.

1. *Identify* the ungodly belief.

   Identify a thought, belief, expectation, etc.—a "given"—that the ministry receiver has that is *not* in agreement with God's Word, nature or character. One source of UGBs is the person's application form. Also, the Holy Spirit will expose the lies underneath the person's *fears, worries, anger, resentments, hurts, unbelief, doubts, bitterness, blaming*, etc., as you listen.

   The presence of these negative emotions can be brought out by helping him think about recent occurrences of being hurt. If you will "dig" down under the emotions, you can determine the underlying beliefs.

   We encourage you to go for the root UGBs that support and undergird the obvious hurts and emotions. Every time you identify an UGB, see if you can dig deeper. Ask the Holy Spirit if there is a "more core" UGB under the identified one, until you feel you have arrived at the deepest level.

Remember that you will also identify additional core UGBs during the soul/spirit hurts session, as the lies embedded with the hurts are identified.

2. *Write out* the ungodly belief.
Write out the UGB as a declarative statement, making it stark, blunt and clear. The bluntness helps to emphasize the reality of the unbelief. Usually a belief can be stated in one or two sentences. If the ministry receiver can be honest with himself, he may be shocked at how much *fear, resentment* and/or *unbelief* the statement contains.

Make a list of the UGBs that you feel cover the core issues in the ministry receiver's life. Limit your list to about fifteen (maximum twenty) statements so he isn't overwhelmed.

Number the UGBs and write them on a sheet of paper. Leave four or five blank lines between each one so you can later add the GBs and the ministry receiver can add supporting Scriptures.

3. *Write out* the godly belief.
A *good* GB is a statement that agrees with the *truth* of God's Word. As we did with the UGB, we like to express the GB as a declarative statement.

Sometimes we write the GB for the ministry receiver. At other times, when he is more mature in the Word, we work with him to write the GB during the session. We discuss his thoughts and give input, working until we have a solid GB that really fits. We either finish writing the GBs in the session or we let him complete the writing of his GBs as homework to bring back to the next session. Make sure he has a list of UGBs and GBs at the end of the session to take with him, even if there are some still to be completed.

Hints for writing effective godly beliefs
Use these hints to help construct an effective godly belief.
- Generally a GB is the opposite of the UGB. It expresses God's way of looking at the same concept/belief/principle that is revealed by the UGB. It must agree with the principles of Scripture.
- When the GB seems too big a step from the UGB, choose an intermediate GB that your receiver can believe—one that will help him move in the right direction.

- It may help to write a "progressive" GB that reduces the pressure to change immediately. A suggestion is, "As I am healed, I will be able to . . ."
- When needed, you may include a phrase such as "by God's grace . . ." or "with His help . . ."
- Make sure the GB addresses the main issue of the UGB. It should counteract the essence of the UGB.
- Write the GB using the ministry receiver's words whenever possible. We are not looking for a nice religious statement, but one that speaks to his heart.
- When writing GBs that include other people, be careful to not impose either your own or the receiver's will on them. Write a faith statement about what is possible with God's grace and with the cooperation of the people involved.
- Of course, the new GB must agree with Scripture. Make sure you are satisfied that the GB is truly godly before giving it your "stamp of approval."

4. *Use Scripture* to support and verify that the new belief is godly.
   Assign the ministry receiver the homework task of finding Scriptures that support the GB. Pray that the Holy Spirit will lead him to the right Scriptures. Instruct him to add the Scriptures to the GB and to incorporate meditating on the GB and accompanying Scriptures as a part of his prayer time. We want his faith to be solidly attached to the Word and not onto an opinion.

5. *Minister* to the belief system.
   Use the ministry steps at the end of this chapter to remove and break the power of the UGBs and to set the stage for the GBs to be established. Go through the steps of forgiveness, repentance and renouncing. Declare and receive the new GBs.

6. *Fine tune* what has been written.
   Instruct the ministry receiver to improve the GBs using words that truly express what he knows God wants him to believe. Have him fine tune and adjust the statement until it "fits" him. Have him give you a copy of the final list so you can check it and verify that the godly beliefs truly are godly.

7. *Follow* the *most essential* steps for freedom.
   Stress to the ministry receiver that if he desires to gain real freedom, it is important to pray, meditate and think about his new godly beliefs for at least thirty days. This is the typical time that it takes to change any habit we learn and for the newly

"planted" beliefs to be well rooted and begin to manifest in his life. Have him continue to pray that the Holy Spirit will plant the new beliefs deep into his heart. Have him continue to meditate on their truth and meaning. The point is not merely positive confession but rather to have his heart/mind changed so he can begin to think, make decisions and have expectations corresponding to a GB's system.

2. Examples of ungodly and godly beliefs

We will look at several examples, starting with UGBs/GBs about ourselves, then others and then God.

a. Ungodly/godly beliefs concerning self

The following example illustrates that there are several different ways to express a godly belief. We want the one that best "fits" the ministry receiver.

Example
This is a UGB in the area of "not belonging" and "abandonment." The person for whom it was written had been left and ignored by his father. He had never bonded with either parent.

Ungodly Belief
I am alone in the world and have no one who cares.

Possible Godly Beliefs (We would choose one.)

- *I am not alone in the world because God has given me Himself, my wife and my family of God, i.e., the Church. I choose to reach out to them.*

- *God cares, my wife cares, and my brothers and sisters in Christ care for me and about me. I choose to be in relationship with them.*

- *I belong completely to God, my Father; Jesus, my brother; and the Holy Spirit, my comforter. I belong to my wife, as God has and is causing us to become one. I belong to the Body of Christ, and they belong to me. I choose to let them be part of my life.*

Observe that we have included statements such as "with God's help" or "by His grace He will enable me to . . ." so that we don't have to face the entire transition from old to new in one step. Otherwise, our new GB could sound like a *lie* to us. For example, if we try to help someone change from "I can never remember names" to "I always remember names," it would be difficult to have faith for such a dramatic transition. Sometimes in beliefs concerning self, a GB amounts to a declaration (what I will decide to do), regardless of other people or situations.

Example 1
Ungodly Belief
I will always be lonely.

Godly Belief
With God's help, I will begin to reach out to others and also to receive from them. He has designed me to fit into His Body, the Church.

Example 2
Ungodly Belief
I always drift from job to job. I will never find my real direction.

Godly Belief
I choose to submit myself to God and to go the way He leads me. He will direct me in the plan and purpose He has for me.

---

b. Ungodly/godly beliefs concerning others

In a situation in which the UGB involves another person, we need to look at what God says is *possible for that person,* and not how he is behaving now. Note that we no longer identify the problem with the person, but we separate him from the problem ("the anger," not "his anger"). We focus on what God says and on what God can do. The GB is a *statement of faith.*

Example 1
Ungodly Belief
My husband always gets angry at me.

Godly Belief
God can enable my husband not only to control the anger but to become completely free of this bondage.

---

c. Ungodly/godly beliefs concerning God Himself or His Word

Ungodly beliefs about God and/or His Word are very common. We must choose to believe what He says about Himself rather than our fears or resentments toward Him. It helps to remember that our beliefs about God are strongly influenced by our experiences and relationship with our earthly fathers.

Example 1
Ungodly Belief
God heals others, but He doesn't desire to heal me.

Godly Belief
God loves His children equally and desires His best for each one. He desires to heal me. I choose to receive His healing.

---

3. Practice

We have included Table L on page 138 as a practice page to help you become more acquainted with writing ungodly and godly beliefs. This is your opportunity to put to work the teachings in this section. The first four pairs of UGBs/GBs are completed to give you additional examples. You can use the remaining space to practice on UGBs important to you.

If you are not sure where or how to start, refer back to the lists of examples of ungodly beliefs on pages 126–130. Also, reread the instructions in this section on the procedure for replacing ungodly and godly beliefs. Then take a deep breath and make the plunge!

Our Prayer for You
May the Holy Spirit illuminate your mind with revelation in hearing, discerning, writing and ministering to UGBs. May this practice bring understanding and clarity as you work with the Holy Spirit to renew your mind. Amen!

Table L: Practice Writing Ungodly and Godly Beliefs

UGB: *Those important to me will abandon me at critical times when I need help.*

GB: *God has promised to be with me always. He has also given me others in the Body of Christ who will be faithful friends, even in my times of need.*

Scripture: Matthew 18:20; Proverbs 18:24

UGB: *My spouse will never treat me the way I want to be treated.*

GB: *As I forgive and repent of my judgments about my spouse and the way that I have treated her/him, God is free to work in her/his life to bring about loving change.*

Scripture: Ephesians 5:21–33

UGB: *I will never fully be able to give or receive love, to have intimate, satisfying relationships with people.*

GB: *God, who is love, can and will teach me how to enter into 1 Corinthians 13 love. I choose to begin to let down my defenses and to enter into His kind of love.*

Scripture: 1 Corinthians 13:1–8; 1 John 4:8

UGB: *God will not be pleased with me if I take time for myself to rest and play.*

GB: *God is holding the universe together. It will not fall apart if I rest or play. He desires for me to have a balanced life, to enjoy Him and His creation and to do satisfying and fulfilling work.*

Scripture: Ephesians 2:11; Hebrews 4:1–11

UGB: . . . .

GB: . . . .

Scripture: . . . .

UGB: . . . .

GB: . . . .

Scripture: . . . .

L. Ministering Freedom to UGBs: Specific Steps

As we have stated throughout this chapter, ministry to UGBs is among the most important of the four problem areas. It is also a very rewarding ministry in which we see God transform lives as minds are renewed.

1. Final preparation before ministry

The majority of the work in preparing to minister to UGBs takes place outside of the ministry session, when we go back over the notes taken during the interview and time of ministry to the sins of the fathers and curses sessions. At that time, we note the obvious UGBs spoken directly by the ministry receiver, as well as listen to the Holy Spirit as He shows us the UGBs "underneath" what the ministry receiver was saying. Prayerfully rereading the notes and the noted UGBs usually leads to a synthesis of the material, allowing us to see patterns of thought and expectations that group into themes of unbelief in the ministry receiver's life. Then we apply the steps in the earlier section on procedure for replacing ungodly and godly beliefs to finish preparing for the ministry.

Usually, we will try to have ten to fifteen, with a maximum of twenty, pairs of UGBs and GBs for the ministry receiver. Giving more than this at one time tends to be overwhelming. The ministry receiver may give up and not even try, particularly if one of his UGBs is that he fails at everything he tries!

The other extreme is typified by a friend who attended one of our classes. After the session on ungodly beliefs, he said to his wife, "I just can't relate to any of these people in here. They all seem so excited as they realize what ungodly beliefs their ancestors have passed down to them, but I don't identify with a single one of them. I just don't have any ungodly beliefs!" His wife looked at him and said, "Well, I know at least one ungodly belief that you have." With some surprise, he said, "You do?" "Yes," she said, laughing. "Your ungodly belief is that you don't have any ungodly beliefs!" She proved to be correct when they later went through the RTF ministry.

Exercise
You should now be ready with your written ungodly and godly belief pairs to move through the following ministry steps, allowing the Holy Spirit to help you free yourself from the UGBs and plant the GBs. Our prayers are with you as you set your will (2 Corinthians 7:1) to change the way your mind "works," so that you can grow to be more like Jesus every day.

---

2. Submission Prayer

We again have a "model prayer" that you can use as you help your receiver prepare to renew his mind.

UGBs Submission Prayer
Lord, according to Your Word in Romans 12:1–2, I choose to submit to the process of being transformed by the renewing of my mind. I ask You to search my heart today, invade my thought life and make me aware of any wrong thinking or blind spots. I thank You that You have created me in Your image and that You desire to set me free from all negative ways in which I view myself, others and You, God. I commit my way to You, Lord, knowing that You will establish my thoughts.

As You continue to renew my mind, I ask You to give me grace to cooperate with You fully in the process of changing my ungodly beliefs into godly beliefs. I receive Your mind, Lord Jesus. I declare that I have been redeemed, forgiven and sanctified. I belong to Christ, my body is the temple of the Holy Spirit, and I shall have victory today as I submit myself to this renewing and transforming process on the authority of and in the name of Jesus Christ. Amen!

---

3. Steps in ministering to ungodly beliefs

Some of the following steps take place before the actual time of ministry to UGBs. Steps 1 and 2 are accomplished by the minister during the early sessions and as he prepares to minister. Then steps 3 through 11 are accomplished by the ministry receiver for each UGB. The minister has the privilege of praying for the power of the cross to intervene into the ministry receiver's life in step 12.

Ministry Steps

1. **Listen**: Identify possible UGBs by listening to the ministry receiver and to the Holy Spirit during the interview and SOFCs sessions.

2. **Write**: Accumulate a written list of the possible UGBs. You may also write new GBs to use as initial suggestions. (Either write new GBs before coming to the UGBs session or write them during the ministry time [procedure step 3 on page 133], as the ministry receiver declares what he will believe to replace the UGBs [ministry step 12].)

3. **Offer**: Present one UGB at a time to the receiver during the UGBs session. Help him agree that he does indeed have this UGB and needs to take responsibility for it affecting his life. Fine-tune the UGB until it "fits" him. (The receiver may state that he does not relate to the presented UGB. If he doesn't relate to the UGB at all, you can either withdraw the UGB or suggest that you and the receiver pray and ask the Holy Spirit to show if and how the UGB applies to the receiver.)

4. **Confess**: Have the receiver confess the sin of believing the UGB (lie) rather than the truth and living his life according to this lie. (If applicable, the ministry receiver should confess the sins of his fathers [and mothers] in believing and acting on the same lies.)[9]

5. **Forgive**: If appropriate, have the receiver forgive his ancestors (fathers and mothers) that have passed down to him the UGB.

6. **Forgive**: Have the receiver forgive all others that may have influenced him to form the UGB.

7. **Repent**: Have the receiver ask God's forgiveness for living his life based on this UGB.

8. **Forgive**: Have the receiver forgive himself.

9. **Renounce**: Have the receiver renounce the UGB and break its power from his life based on the finished work of Christ on the cross. (Encourage him to be strong in setting his will and to make a spiritual "decree" to refuse to give the UGB any more importance in his life.)

10. **Construct**: Present the new GB or work with the receiver to construct a new GB. (Fine-tune the GB until you and the receiver have a good "first draft.")

11. **Receive/Affirm**: Have the receiver declare the GB and receive it into his belief system as the replacement for the previously removed UGB.

    (Repeat the above steps until you have gone through all of the UGBs list.)

12. **Restore**: Pray for the receiver's new set of GBs.
    - Pray that God bring to an end the effects of the UGBs in his life.
    - Pray for the GBs to be planted into his heart.
    - Pray that the Word already in his heart will be brought to the surface of his mind and be available for use as a weapon against future, ungodly thoughts.
    - Pray for the discipline needed for him to meditate on his new GBs for at least thirty days.
    - Pray that the Holy Spirit will make him very sensitive to falling back into old thought patterns and that he will be able to take captive any such thoughts.[10]
    - Pray for new habit patterns of thought to be established.[11]

Post-Ministry: "Walking It Out"

The post-ministry phase of ministering to UGBs is extremely important to the success of establishing the new GBs in the heart and mind of your ministry receiver. Cover the following areas to prepare him for the "walking it out" phase of healing. If at all possible, the help of a mature saint should be enlisted for prayer support, accountability and encouragement.

1. Inform the receiver that the *legal power of the UGBs is broken*, but that he has to keep the doors shut to the old ways.

2. Charge him to *take control of his thoughts*, "bringing [them] into captivity . . . to the obedience of Christ" (2 Corinthians 10:5, KJ21), rather than allowing them to follow their natural course. Take charge of any stray thought that "comes in."

3. Inform him that once the demonic deliverance is accomplished, any demonic temptation to continue in the old UGBs will be from the "outside," which will be much weaker than previous temptation. This *oppression will likely continue until the demons assigned to the ministry receiver become convinced that he will indeed stand firm in his new GBs*. Demons will soon see his resolve in allowing the Holy Spirit to help him develop a new belief system

and that he is not going to believe demonic lies, either the old ones or any new ones that they might throw at him.

4. Have him *take responsibility to pray* that the Holy Spirit will continue to show him other UGBs and to do self-ministry so that additional healing and freedom may come.

5. Encourage him to *continue to fine-tune the GBs* so that they really speak to his heart. Have him search the Scriptures and find verses that support the new GBs.

6. Have him *pray and meditate on his new GBs for at least one month* as part of his daily devotions. He should daily thank the Holy Spirit for planting the GBs deep into his heart.

7. Help him realize that the tendency of the mind is to continue in the old habit patterns. Help him commit to *persevere for at least a month* with his new GBs to insure that the new habit patterns of thought are established. When a new GB is replacing a major core UGB, he may need to periodically return to the GB and focus on it again while continuing to eradicate all traces of the original UGB.

M. Thought-Provoking Questions

1. In what areas does your mind need renewal and transformation?

   ....

   ....

2. What are two ungodly beliefs (UGBs) that cause trouble in your relationships?

   ....

   ....

3. What would you be like if you had only godly beliefs?

   ....

   ....

4. How were your ungodly beliefs formed?

   ....

   ....

5. List three ungodly beliefs that are popular and acceptable in the natural and unredeemed world.

   . . . .

   . . . .

6. Where do your UGBs hide?

   . . . .

   . . . .

7. What is the difference between the facts and God's truth in one area your life?

   . . . .

   . . . .

8. Why is it helpful to write out UGBs and GBs?

   . . . .

   . . . .

9. In what way is an UGB a covenant with the enemy?

   . . . .

   . . . .

5

Soul/Spirit Hurts (SSHs)

"The Spirit of the Lord is upon Me. . . .
He hath sent Me to heal the brokenhearted."
Luke 4:18, KJ21

The pain of past hurt rules many lives. It simmers, it stifles, and it sometimes shuts a person completely down. Understanding scriptural principles brings comfort and hope, but it does not necessarily bring healing. Forgiveness releases a person from bitterness and from the bondage of negative ties to others, but it does not necessarily heal hurts. Demonic deliverance brings great freedom, but it does not heal hurts.

God heals hurts. He is waiting and ready to touch our deepest pain if we will let Him. In a sense, His healing is another divine exchange, in which we offer to Him our hurt and He offers to us His healing. Most of us do not know how to go about *receiving* this wonderful gift He has to offer.

In this chapter, after showing how integrated soul/spirit hurts are with the other three problem areas, we present a definition of soul/spirit hurts, followed by a look at God's wonderful healing Scriptures. Then we examine hurts in more detail, including the consequences of hurts. Moving into the healing portion of the chapter, we present a number of hindrances to our receiving God's healing. As a minister, you will want to be sensitive to these hindrances so that you can help the ministry receiver deal with them. After a journey into the "insides of a memory," we then prepare to receive God's healing using a powerful approach we have named "Waiting upon the Lord" Listening Prayer. We can receive healing for ourselves and then lead others into the full healing God has provided. Several case studies complete the teaching portion of the chapter. We finish with how to minister to SSHs.

A. Understanding the Interrelationship among the Ministry Areas

The problem area of soul/spirit hurts seems so personal, so intimate. How can it be related to the other problem areas? As we shall see, it is very closely related. Inner wounds are caused by sins of the fathers and resulting curses, ungodly beliefs and demonic oppression. Then, these same three problem areas are propagated by soul/spirit hurts. It is important to realize and understand how these areas intertwine and impact each other in order to acknowledge the need for an integrated approach to biblical healing ministry.

1. How soul/spirit hurts are related to sins of the fathers and resulting curses

Because the same types of sins are passed down in a family from generation to generation, the same curses continue to operate. As a result, many members of a family tend to repeat the same kinds of behaviors, hurting each other in similar ways to their ancestors. These sinful, generational patterns and the resulting curses need to be broken in order to stop propagating the same hurts, sins and curses. In breaking them, we set the stage for healing from the hurts.

The alcoholic family provides the classic example. The codependent family, in which the children can't seem to leave home, offers another common example. We could continue citing examples of the same soul/spirit hurts continuing generation after generation.

2. How soul/spirit hurts are related to ungodly beliefs

Most ungodly beliefs are actually formed in hurtful situations. They result from hurtful family patterns. The hurts underlying the ungodly beliefs must be healed before the belief system can be rebuilt, founded on the truth of God's Word, His nature and His character. Otherwise, the hurt and the ungodly belief will serve to negatively reinforce each other.

If the heart says, "I'm hurting," and the mind that is being renewed says, "I'm healed," which one will win out? That's right, the heart! The unhealed hurt causes the heart to cry out, "This 'godly belief' is a lie! I can't receive it!" Why? Because the pain is still present. The hurt *must* be healed before God's truth can fully settle into the heart.

3. How soul/spirit hurts are related to deliverance

Demons do not play fair. When someone experiences hurt or trauma, certain demons frequently invade: fear, failure, isolation, loneliness, shame, control, rejection, rebellion, depression, trauma and death. Their work does not stop with the invasion. They continue to agitate and stir up the same hurts by picking off the scabs, so to speak, and arranging events to cause more hurt. Hurts also provide a launching place for demonic lies. Demons will amplify the hurt by the messages they send to the mind, such as *There is no point in trying to make friends; nobody will like me.* When we receive healing for our hurts, the demons are no longer able to amplify those hurtful memories. If demons are blocking or distorting God's healing revelation, we sometimes do deliverance before praying for healing of hurts. Otherwise, we prefer to do the deliverance afterward—when the legal ground of the sins associated with the hurts has been dealt with and the demons have no justification for remaining.

4. God's overall purpose

Deuteronomy 6:23 reads:

> But he brought us out from there to bring us in and give us the land that he promised on oath to our forefathers.
>
> Deuteronomy 6:23, NIV

God wants to bring us out of the situation of hurt into the healing we need. He wants to set us free. His ministry is to bring us out of the sins of the fathers and resulting curses, and into His family line, where He is our Father and where no hurt or sinful heritage exists. He wants to bring us out of our ungodly beliefs and renew our minds. Why? So we can think and act like Him and agree with His Word. He wants to bring us out of the snare of the devil and into the safety of His protection. He wants to bring us out of the world and into His godly Kingdom. Our job is to make ourselves available to the Holy Spirit so that our heavenly Father can accomplish His work in us.

B. The Definition of Soul/Spirit Hurts

Soul/spirit hurts (SSHs) surface when a person appears or a situation occurs that is similar to the person or situation involved with the original hurt. A common example is the stage fright people experience at the thought of being in front of a large group. Often this is related to an earlier painful experience in which the person was embarrassed or humiliated in front of others.

Soul/spirit hurts are hurts on the inside of a person. They are wounds to the soul or the spirit of man that are carried and experienced within the person himself. They are not physical, and they cannot be seen. Their presence is revealed by their symptoms, by the manifested evidence of unhealed emotions, behaviors and thoughts.

C. Scriptural Basis for Soul/Spirit Healing

God is our Healer. No Spirit-filled Christian would question that God heals, and particularly that He provides physical healing. *Jehovah Rapha*, the name for God used in Exodus 15:26 (see Table M on pages 151–152), is used in the context of His bringing the Israelites out of Egypt. It also relates to His promise that if they obeyed His commandments and followed His statutes, then He would not put on them any of the diseases of the Egyptians. We could paraphrase this Scripture as: "None of the diseases of the world will be able to be on you because I am the God that healeth thee; I am *Jehovah Rapha*" (Exodus 15:26, paraphrase mine).

The basic meaning of the Hebrew word *rapha* is "to mend," as in stitching up or mending a torn cloth. *Rapha* also means "to cure or cause to be cured, to heal, to position, to repair, to make whole." When we say *"Jehovah Rapha,"* we are saying, "God, the Mender, the One who makes us whole." Isn't that wonderful? This is one of God's redemptive names. He wants each one of us to be whole.

Many Christians would agree that God wants to heal us physically, but what about emotionally or mentally? Does He heal the inner person as well as the physical body? We have listed a number of relevant Scriptures in Table M on pages 151–152 that we feel show His heart for healing us wherever we need it.

Is God interested in healing the inner person,
as well as the outer person?

1. God heals the inner person.

Let's begin by looking in Table M on pages 151–152 at David's petition to God and see if we can identify with it. In Psalm 41:4, David petitioned God to be merciful and to heal his soul. First, he acknowledged his sin before God because he knew that taking responsibility was an important requirement in obtaining God's mercy. David was asking God to heal his soul—a soul made sick from sin. David believed that his soul, his inner self, *could* be healed by God.

In Psalm 147:3, the writer penned, "He heals the *brokenhearted* and binds up their *wounds* [or *sorrows*]" (NIV, emphasis mine). *Brokenhearted* refers to the wounds in the innermost portion of ourselves.

In Jeremiah 31:25, God told Jeremiah that He "will [fully] satisfy the *weary soul*, and ... replenish every *languishing* and *sorrowful* person" (AMP, emphasis mine). In the Hebrew, both *weariness* and *sorrow* can refer to the mental or emotional condition of the inner person. God says He will *satisfy* and He will *replenish* the deepest part of man's being.

At another time Jeremiah cried out, "Heal me, O LORD, and I shall be healed; save me, and I shall be saved; for Thou art my praise" (Jeremiah 17:14, KJ21). The prophet was talking about much more than his physical condition. He was referring to his soul.

You are probably already familiar with the verse in 3 John, in which the beloved apostle prayed:

> Beloved, I pray that in all respects you may prosper and be in good health, just as your soul prospers.
>
> 3 John 2, NASB

In addition to being a prayer for the prosperity and health of our souls, it is also a prayer for teaching prosperity in all areas of life, including financial prosperity.

2. Jesus heals the brokenhearted.

Isaiah 53 presents a powerful prophecy concerning Jesus and His coming ministry to reveal the Father's heart to the people.[1] The Father desires to heal us. In the following verses, note the words we have emphasized that have to do with emotions, or inner hurts.

> He was *despised* and *forsaken* of men,
> A man of *sorrows*, and acquainted with *grief*;

And like one from whom men hide their face
He was *despised*, and we did *not esteem* Him.
Surely our *griefs [sickness]* He Himself bore,
And our *sorrows* He carried;
Yet we ourselves esteemed him *stricken*,
Smitten of God, and *afflicted*.
But He was *pierced [wounded]* through for our transgressions,
He was *crushed* for our iniquities;
The *chastening* for our well-being fell upon Him,
And by His *scourging [stripes]* we are healed."

Isaiah 53:3–5, NASB, emphasis mine

These verses offer a powerful listing of pain-related words that mostly refer to inner pain. For example, the Hebrew word for "sorrows" is used throughout the Old Testament to refer to mental or emotional pain. *Choli*, translated "griefs," indicates afflictions, casualties, weakness and pain, as well as sickness and disease. It seems clear that more than the physical body is included in the healing and deliverance ministry of Jesus.

Isaiah also prophesied about the anointing, wisdom and tenderness of Jesus' ministry in Isaiah 11:2–4. He declared that Christ would not rely merely on the five senses, but He would be able to judge with righteousness and fairness.

In Isaiah 42:3, Isaiah expressed the divine care and tenderness with which Jesus would treat the souls of men. This is of great comfort to hurting people.

The record of the gospels shows these prophetic words repeatedly fulfilled. Right from the beginning of His ministry, Jesus defined and declared His ministry to the inner man. Luke 4:18–19 records Jesus reading from Isaiah 61. He stated:

"He hath sent Me to heal the *brokenhearted*, to preach deliverance to the *captives*, and recovering of sight to the *blind*, to set at liberty them that are *bruised*, to preach the acceptable year of the Lord."

Luke 4:18–19, KJ21, emphasis mine

These powerful words were fulfilled as the anointing on Jesus Christ brought forth healing and freedom.

Portrait after portrait is recorded of God, through Jesus, meeting people at their point of pain. Ordinary people, trapped, rejected, outcast or desolate, were touched by His heart of compassion, His words of life, His transforming power. Many encounters reveal His tremendous compassion. Consider the lepers whom He reached out and

Table M: Scriptures Concerning Soul/Spirit Hurts

▶ *The ministry of Jesus Christ*

Luke 4:18–19 (Isaiah 61:1–3)
"The Spirit of the Lord is upon Me, because He hath anointed Me to preach the Gospel to the poor. He hath sent Me to *heal* the broken-hearted, to preach *deliverance* to the captives, and recovering of sight to the blind, to set at *liberty* them that are bruised, to preach the acceptable year of the Lord" (KJ21, emphasis mine).

John 21:15–19
" 'Do you truly love me more than these?' 'Yes, Lord,' he said, 'you know that I love you.' Jesus said, 'Feed my lambs' " (verse 15, NIV).

Isaiah 11:2–4
"The Spirit of the LORD will rest on Him,
The spirit of wisdom and understanding,
The spirit of counsel and strength. . . .
And He will not judge by what His eyes see,
Nor make a decision by what His ears hear;
But with righteousness He will judge the poor,
And decide with fairness for the afflicted of the earth" (NASB).

Isaiah 42:3
"A bruised reed He will not break
And a dimly burning wick He will not extinguish" (NASB).

Isaiah 53:4
"Surely he took up our *infirmities*
    and carried our *sorrows,*
yet we considered him *stricken* by God,
    smitten by him, and *afflicted*" (NIV, emphasis mine).

▶ *God's heart for soul/spirit healing*

Exodus 15:26
" . . . I will not bring on you any of the diseases I brought on the Egyptians, for I am the LORD, *who heals [rapha] you*" (NIV, emphasis mine).

Psalm 147:3
"He *heals* the brokenhearted,
And *binds up* their wounds" (NASB, emphasis mine).

Jeremiah 31:25
"For I have *satiated* the weary soul, and I have *replenished* every sorrowful soul" (KJV, emphasis mine).

▶ *David's prayer*

Psalm 41:4
"LORD, be merciful unto me; *heal my soul,* for I have sinned against Thee" (KJ21, emphasis mine).

Table M: Scriptures Concerning Soul/Spirit Hurts (*cont.*)

▶ *David's prayer* (*cont.*)

Psalm 23:2–3
"He leadeth me beside the still waters. He *restoreth my soul*" (KJ21, emphasis mine).

▶ *John's prayer*
3 John 2
"Beloved, I pray that in all respects you may prosper and be in good health, just as your soul *prospers*" (NASB, emphasis mine).

▶ *Jeremiah's prayer*
Jeremiah 17:14
"Heal me, O LORD, and I will be healed;
Save me and I will be saved,
For You are my praise" (NASB).

---

physically touched, defying all Jewish law.[2] What about the woman at the well, whom He accepted and to whom He gave life-changing truth?[3] Who can forget the woman caught in adultery whose death sentence He revoked and whose shame He remitted, saying, "Go and sin no more"?[4] Then there were the scared, frustrated parents of demonized children, who had their precious ones healed and their own hearts mended when Jesus heeded their cries for help.[5]

In John 21, we see Jesus dealing with the heartbroken Peter. Jesus knew what to do as He ministered to Peter's deep grief and remorse. Three times, Jesus asked, "Do you love me?" allowing Peter three opportunities to express his love and receive Jesus' forgiveness and acceptance. As Jesus told Peter to "feed My sheep" and "take care of My lambs," He reaffirmed His trust in Peter to minister effectively. What healing that must have brought to Peter as he was still dealing with his act of betrayal. What could be more powerful than to be "reinstated" by the very One whom he had betrayed?[6]

Consider the question put so well by Max Lucado in his book *He Still Moves Stones*:

> Why did God leave us one tale after another of wounded lives being restored? So we could be grateful for the past? So we could look back with amazement at what Jesus did?
>
>   No. No. No. A thousand times no. The purpose of these stories is not to tell us what Jesus *did*. Their purpose is to tell us what Jesus *does*.

"Everything that was written in the past was written to teach us," Paul penned. "The Scriptures give us patience and encouragement so that we can have hope" (Romans 15:4).

These are not just Sunday school stories. Not romantic fables. Not somewhere-over-the-rainbow illusions. They are historic moments in which a real God met real pain so we could answer the question, "Where is God when I hurt?"

He's not doing it just for them. He is doing it for me. He's doing it for you.[7]

Lucado helps us see that when our hearts are broken, God wants to heal. If any of us are in emotional bondage or oppression, God wants to set us at liberty. This is Jesus' proclamation.

D. Our Personal Experiences of Healing

Long before either one of us (Chester and Betsy) had received the revelation through the Scriptures of Jesus' healing the inner person, we experienced it! For each of us it was very unexpected.

Chester's experience occurred one hot summer day while we were driving our van from our home in Gainesville, Florida, to the beach. He was laying in the back praying. When Chester was only two years old, his father died. Partly as a result of growing up without a father, he became introverted and a loner. For much of his life, he had hidden behind work and achievement. On that life-changing day, God chose to reveal Himself to Chester as the Father that he had never had—as a personal Father-God who wanted a close relationship with him. As that revelation became real to Chester, tears flowed. His heart, which had been closed for so long, began to open. He says even now,

> There are no words to describe the depth and profoundness of this experience as I realized that God, the very God of the universe, wanted a Father-son relationship with me. I still cannot talk about this in public without being filled with the awesomeness of His love.

The healing that took place that day gave him a sense of belonging that has continued to increase.

Betsy's first experience of God healing her soul/spirit hurts occurred about two years later on a wintry Sunday night. Jackie Canapa, a faith-filled friend who was visiting that evening, said that there was something Jesus wanted to touch in Betsy's life. Neither of them knew

what it might be, but Jackie suggested that Betsy bow her head and ask
Jesus to come and minister to her.

As Betsy followed Jackie's suggestion, she began to see a picture in
her spirit of a tiny baby girl being born. Betsy describes her experience:

> After a while, I saw Jesus come and pick up the baby girl. He looked at
> her with great delight in His face, and said, "I am so glad that you are
> here. I planned your life a long time ago, and I have such wonderful
> plans for it." Then I realized that the baby girl was me! As I saw Jesus
> welcoming me with tenderness and enthusiasm, I knew that He had a
> special purpose for my life. I had never experienced anything like that
> before. It had a profound and lasting effect on me.
>
> For thirty-seven years, I had carried a painful doubt that maybe my
> life was a mistake. As a baby, I had been given up for adoption by a
> young, unmarried mother. She had wanted the best for me. Although
> in God's providence I was raised in a wonderful, godly family, I had
> never been able to put to rest the nagging feeling that I was the result of
> a sinful act and that I was lacking in some way. The Lord Jesus knew
> that I needed this healing. As the reality broke over me that I truly was
> planned and purposed by Him, my heart, so full of cracks and
> uncertainties, began to be healed.

E. Information about Soul/Spirit Hurts

As we prepare to pray for soul/spirit hurts, it helps to have an overall
understanding about hurt. This section reviews some basics about
soul/spirit hurts.

1. Situations that cause hurt

We do not need to look far to find the brokenhearted. Daily, the media
bombards us with reports of gang murders, rapes and robberies.
Violence and terror is apparent on all sides. More and more families
are homeless. Witchcraft and occult practices have a stranglehold on
many young people. Those who are ritually, sexually abused are being
programmed in such a way that their personalities become fragmented,
and they are unable to function in normal society. Divorce rates
continue to escalate, leaving behind untold stories of the adults and
children whose lives are devastated. We read about the ongoing
slaughterhouses of abortion. The *Christian Herald* stated that 95 percent
of the women who have had abortions regretted doing so (1994).
The November 1993 National Aids Day yielded statistics that over 14

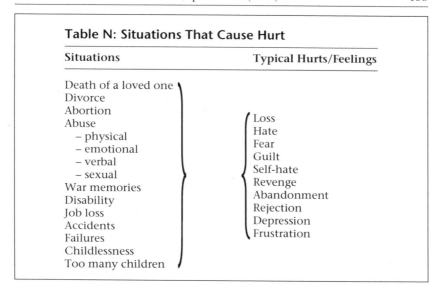

Table N: Situations That Cause Hurt

Situations	Typical Hurts/Feelings

Death of a loved one
Divorce
Abortion
Abuse
   – physical
   – emotional
   – verbal
   – sexual
War memories
Disability
Job loss
Accidents
Failures
Childlessness
Too many children
	Loss
	Hate
	Fear
	Guilt
	Self-hate
	Revenge
	Abandonment
	Rejection
	Depression
	Frustration

million people worldwide have AIDS. All of society is affected by situations and hurts, such as those listed in Table N above.

Consider the hurts experienced by each person in your family. Now think about your friends. How about yourself? No doubt you could list a great variety of hurts that have different degrees of intensity. These hurts may have resulted from generational sin, they can be caused by others, or they may even be self-imposed.

Sometimes our hurts come not from what was done to us but from what was *not* done. What about the toddler who was never cuddled or hugged? How about the child who was never made to feel special? Consider the teenager whose parents missed his graduations, did not attend his birthday parties and failed to say, "God has a plan and purpose for your life." Other hurts result from deep disappointments beyond our control: children who failed to meet our expectations, a promotion that never came or a wanted pregnancy that never happened. Some of you reading this have experienced hurts that only God knows. Isn't it good to know that He cares, and that He wants to heal?

2. Levels of Hurt

What if it were possible to measure a person's mental, emotional and spiritual "temperature" the same way we measure a physical temperature? Hurts, as we know, are hard to gauge. We can't take a traumatic experience in another person's life and calculate the depth of pain he suffered or how it affected his spirit and soul. We can't measure hurt from the outside.

The degree and the intensity of hurts cover a tremendous range from the small pain, such as being left out of a ball game, to the gut-wrenching trauma of losing a child-custody battle.

What about the long-lasting and ongoing hurt? Sometimes physical, sexual or emotional abuse goes on for years. Or the spouse is still unfaithful; the alcoholic still drinks every evening and weekend; the ridicule still continues.

Close friends of ours have a handicapped child. They say every time their son enters a new phase of development, they cry all over again, seeing what other children his age can do. *Ongoing hurt needs ongoing healing.*

At the extreme level of hurt are those deliberately and ritualistically traumatized to force disassociation. Examples of this are satanic ritual abuse and political programming. In the case of political programming, the victimizers are after a totally controlled slave that will do their every wish, yet remain undetectable.

F. Some Consequences of Hurt

It is not an exaggeration to say that the results of hurt are just as crippling to our soul and spirit as a debilitating disease is to our bodies. While the myriad of horrible consequences of hurt are far too many to discuss, we can list some of the major consequences. But before going on, take a moment to reflect on your own experience.

Exercise
Make a list of some of the major hurts that have occurred in your family of origin.

. . . .

. . . .

. . . .

Now make a second list of the ways that these hurts have affected you or your family members.

. . . .

. . . .

. . . .

Did you list any of the following consequences of hurts? Did you find consequences in addition to the ones listed here?

- Hurts can cause us to wear a "mask" to hide and protect ourselves.
- Hurts often underlie illnesses.
- Hurts can cause shame, anger, hopelessness or depression.
- Hurts can cause blocked emotions, causing us to be out of touch with our feelings.
- Hurts can result in anger and disappointment in God (even giving up on God and/or the Church.
- Hurts can provide an open door for demonic oppression.
- Hurts that are very deep can cause a fragmented personality.
- Hurts can cause restricted growth and a lack of fulfillment in life.

As we consider the area of soul/spirit hurts, it is clear that hurts begin in the family and can affect the entire family. Hurts can affect an entire person (body, soul and spirit). Hurts have multidimensional negative effects and tend to multiply. Hurting people hurt people!

Hurts block intimacy, joy and the freedom to be ourselves. Who wants to stay hurt when we can be healed? As we look at the patterns in our own lives and as we prepare to minister to others, we must be open to recognize the many different forms of hurt.

Exercise

1. Think of some of the hurts in your own life and how they have held you back from opportunities you might have had, but you were scared to take the risk.
2. Think of the dreams that you have let go.
3. Think of people to whom you would like to have talked, but you couldn't because you didn't feel comfortable.
4. Think of the intimacy you wanted to have in a relationship, but it never happened.

Prayer

If considering any of these questions causes pain in your heart, pause a moment, pray and ask the Holy Spirit to touch and heal the specific losses in your life. Then wait for Him to do so.

G. Possible Hindrances to Receiving Healing

How long have you wanted healing for your own hurts? How long have you waited for someone you love to be healed? Most of us yearn to feel more whole. As ministers, we come with great enthusiasm and anticipation to the time of healing. In about 70 percent of the people to whom we minister, the healing comes easily and without interference. It is absolutely thrilling how easily God's healing is received. In the other 30 percent, however, there are major, frustrating hindrances operating within the individual receiving healing. These hindrances can prevent him from receiving his healing. As ministers, we need to be ready to remove these hindrances. Now let's look at what we may need to confront.

The three most common hindrances are:

- unforgiveness (which can also be generational)
- unconfessed sin
- demonic blockage

There are some other important hindrances. Sometimes our ministry receiver is *unfamiliar with the process* for receiving healing. Often we may need to educate and explain to him how he can receive from the Lord. It is important to take time to answer his questions and be reassuring.

Another interference is *analytical thinking*. This can be a deeply ingrained lifestyle, as well as a method of staying in control. If our receiver remains in "analytical mode," this may prevent him from fully entering into the memory the Lord wants to heal. Ask your ministry receiver to stop "thinking" and do all that he can to listen, see or feel with his spirit.

Fear is another large hindrance to receiving healing. Often fears of being out of control, of reliving pain, of reexperiencing shame or failure inhibit a person's openness to receive healing. We may need to help him give all of his fears to the Lord. The ministry receiver also needs much reassurance that even though he will reexperience pain, there is a purpose for the pain. This time the pain will be healed.

Another hindrance to consider occurs when a ministry receiver is *unfamiliar with expressing his emotions*. There is a whole group of people who have grown up in families where emotions are totally devalued and discounted. In these families, emotions are neither talked about nor expressed. Sometimes emotions are even seen as a form of weakness and not allowed. The focus for many of these families has been survival, getting the job done or getting ahead.

A ministry receiver coming from this kind of dysfunctional background has learned to minimize his hurts and to keep his feelings to himself. He often has a very small "feeling vocabulary" and it is challenging for him to speak about feelings at all. Frequently, this ministry receiver reports feeling "fine," no matter how severe his hurts may have been. What does he need in order to receive healing? He needs godly, balanced teaching about the place of emotions in his life. He needs to see that Jesus Himself expressed a wide range of emotions, and that Jesus had much compassion on hurting people. Let him see that Jesus did not ignore hurts; He healed them.

A ministry receiver from an emotionally deprived background may need a biblical model of expressing emotions in order to legitimize his own feelings. You can use Psalm 142, which is discussed fully on page 164. Help him recognize that feelings such as anger, bitterness, grief, resentment and/or frustration may have been stuffed for years, simply because it has not been safe to express them. Encourage him that God wants him to get rid of all negative emotions. You can share with him other pertinent Scriptures such as Colossians 3:8–10 and Ephesians 4:26–32.

Two other ways people can be hindered are by *blocked emotions* and by *anger or disappointment with God*. Since these are such important hindrances, they will be discussed in greater detail in the section on "Hindrances That Need Special Attention" on page 173.

A special note about *medication* is needed, for medication also can be a hindrance. We as ministers need to recognize that medications, particularly antidepressants or anti-anxiety drugs, are designed to limit the intensity of emotions, as well as the range of emotions. It will be harder for the ministry receiver to both feel or express them. He may report, "I just feel numb." Be encouraged that the Lord can still work with root causes and bring healing even when drugs are blocking the ministry receiver's feelings. In some cases, however, it appears that he receives less healing than he could have received. From person to person, the effects of the medication on the healing can be quite variable. We never tell a ministry receiver to discontinue his medication during his ministry (or at any other time).[8] When the roots of depression are emotional and/or spiritual, however, his need for medication will diminish as the Lord's healing takes place.

H. Understanding the "Insides of a Memory"

As we minister to soul/spirit hurts, we have a primary focus on memories that the Holy Spirit brings to the ministry receiver. However, before going farther, we want to explore the "insides of a memory." Through SSHs ministry, we are providing an opportunity for people to go deep within themselves and face painful, often distressing experiences that have been stored within their memories. We are entering a private, intensely personal realm. We have no more business charging into this vulnerable area of someone's life unprepared and untrained than a medical student has performing brain surgery during his first year of medical school. We need to know what to look for in the memory and, more importantly, what to do with it. Memories needing healing contain the following ingredients:

- Hurtful situations
- Negative painful feelings
- Ungodly beliefs
- Demons (often)

1. Hurtful situations

What are we trying to do? Our goal in working with a memory is to have our receiver reexperience his memory of a *hurtful situation* in such a way that Jesus, Father God or the Holy Spirit is allowed to intervene and bring healing to all of his negative, painful feelings. (See examples later in this chapter.) Often the Holy Spirit brings revelation to the hurting person or shows him pictures that bring relief, fresh understanding and healing. In other cases, people experience the active presence of Jesus, making it possible for them to interact with Him as He directs and heals. His action and His revelation bring healing of the negative emotions and pain. With God's fresh revelation, the ministry receiver begins to see himself, as well as others, from the Lord's perspective. He will now have the healing *truth* and not just the *facts!* This usually results in the automatic replacement of the ungodly belief (lies) associated with the memory with godly beliefs.

2. Negative painful feelings

Because *negative emotions* are such a strong component of hurtful memories, we often have our ministry receiver "pour out" his *hurtful emotions* to the Lord. (See "Pouring Out His Complaint" on page 163.) This can be an important part of beginning to get unburdened of the many painful emotions in the memory. As he pours out his complaint, he begins to feel less trapped and less alone.

3. Ungodly beliefs

Ungodly beliefs, incorporated into the pain of the memory, need to be exposed and healed. Often, a core *ungodly belief* becomes very evident as the healing takes place. Jesus or the Holy Spirit may address the lie directly. For example, as Jesus tells a person, "It wasn't your fault," the lie he has carried that *everything bad is always my fault* is exposed and replaced by the truth.

We add this UGB to our receiver's list of ungodly beliefs so he can later incorporate the truth that Jesus spoke a godly belief to him. Doing this is a backup. Why? Because when Jesus brings the truth into a hurtful memory, the lie (ungodly belief), in most cases, is instantly replaced with the truth (godly belief). Sometimes, however, it is necessary to continue to meditate on the godly belief to plant God's truth permanently into the receiver's heart and spirit. We firmly believe that these ungodly beliefs (lies) and godly beliefs (truths) need to be recorded in our notes and given to the person after the session. We have been amazed at how quickly we all forget the awesome things God has done!

More of a challenge to the RTF minister are the hidden, or less obvious, ungodly beliefs that spring from the core lie(s). A person believing, *Everything bad is always my fault*, may also believe, *I am no good*, and/or, *I will never amount to anything*. Although these associated UGBs may never have been spoken, each one needs to be exposed and healed, as well.

Another group of subtle ungodly beliefs are those that can power-fully serve to block a ministry receiver in several ways. These beliefs may hinder him from being able to hear from the Lord, receive a memory or invite Jesus into his memory. A very evident example is, *I am too unworthy to receive anything from the Lord*. When we suspect the presence of such a lie, we present it as a possibility to the ministry receiver. If he is willing, we take him through the ungodly belief steps (see pages 141–142) to renounce the lie and come out of agreement with it.

If we do our job well, we will find two to five ungodly beliefs in every painful memory.

4. Demons (often)

Demons constitute the fourth component of the memory. They are often attached to both the negative painful feelings and the ungodly beliefs contained in the memory. These demons always try to block the healing. Count on it. Be prepared either to bind them or cast them out, depending on their strength and degree of interference. As usual, let the Holy Spirit direct you.

A vital part of ministry preparation is anticipating what we expect to find within a hurtful memory. Prepared and alert, we can be on the offense as we prayerfully help to guide our ministry receiver.

I. Preparing the Ministry Receiver

A key to successful ministry is the thorough preparation of the ministry receiver. This preparation will determine, at least in part, how well he will be able to enter into the soul/spirit healing experience. We discuss the following information with him to help him know what is expected: both what he is to do and what he is not to do.

1. Hearing the Lord

If needed, we review with our receiver how he usually hears the Lord. We have already shared with him the different ways God speaks. If necessary, we remind him that he may have a thought, or a "knowing," or that he may see an image of a situation where he was wounded. We assure him that God will probably communicate with him in the same way He usually does. A couple of cautions are usually needed.

a. Not "thinking it up"
First, we want the ministry receiver to be still and wait to see/hear/ sense God's voice. We emphasize that *we are not asking him to "remember" anything, or to try to "think it up," or to select one of his (known) hurts. He is to receive, to be sensitive to and to see what the Holy Spirit brings.* We also share that the hurtful memory can be connected to an event that occurred during any time period of his life, from conception until the present.

b. Sharing without censuring

Second, we tell the ministry receiver to share with us whatever the Holy Spirit may bring into his awareness. He is not to censure the memory in any way. Even if what he sees/hears/feels seems very insignificant or "fleeting"—or he doesn't understand what it means—his job is to share it. Why do we do want him to do this? Because as he shares, God usually causes his understanding to open up and become significant. In fact, we can point to numerous times when an initially foggy memory became clarified and meaningful ministry took place. We let the ministry receiver know that whatever comes into his awareness is what we are looking for. Nothing is too small, silly or embarrassing if the Holy Spirit brings it to remembrance. Also, remind him not to censure memories for which he has previously received ministry. The Holy Spirit may want to go deeper and provide a more complete healing.

2. Reviewing the ministry steps

We review the steps of the ministry process.[9] This can be helpful in surfacing any remaining questions he may have. We make it clear, however, that we will be leading him so that his focus can be on the Lord.

3. Maintaining focus on God

At this point, we prepare our receiver in terms of his focus, which is to be on the Holy Spirit and what He reveals and/or on Jesus as He comes into the memory. We remind him that, unlike the other sessions where the primary interaction has been with us, this will no longer be the case. We ask him to keep his eyes closed and focused on Jesus and the memory, even during times when we are talking to him.

4. Pouring out his complaint

Next, we share with our ministry receiver how important it is for him to be totally honest with the Lord about his pain. We teach him that there is a biblical precedent for being open and real with God. We read, or have him read, Psalm 142 out loud and share the ways he identifies with what David has written.

I cried unto the LORD with my voice; with my voice unto the LORD
    did I make my supplication.
I poured out my complaint before Him; I laid before Him my trouble.
When my spirit was overwhelmed within me, then Thou knewest my
    path. In the way wherein I walked have they privily laid a snare
    for me.
I looked on my right hand and beheld, but there was no man that
    would know me. Refuge failed me; no man cared for my soul.
I cried unto Thee, O LORD; I said, "Thou art my refuge and my
    portion in the land of the living.
Attend unto my cry, for I am brought very low; deliver me from my
    persecutors, for they are stronger than I.
Bring my soul out of prison, that I may praise Thy name; the
    righteous shall compass me about, for Thou shalt deal
    bountifully with me.

Psalm 142, KJ21

If other examples are needed to further illustrate this point, we have
him consider Moses[10] or Jesus in the Garden of Gethsemane.[11] Jesus
cried, "My soul is exceedingly sorrowful, even unto death." And then
He said to the Father, "If it be possible, let this cup pass from Me,
nevertheless, not as I will, but as Thy will." We see in Scripture
that those who are most *real* with God are those with the *closest*
relationships to Him.

5. Removing possible hindrances

It is important to alert our receiver that he may possibly experience
some hindrances, particularly demonic opposition. We reassure him
that we are accustomed to interference and are prepared to work
together to overcome all obstacles.

6. Giving reassurance

The importance of giving reassurance cannot be overemphasized. We
must assure our ministry receiver that even though he may have
intensely painful feelings when the memory returns, the pain won't
last long. This time a redemptive purpose is at work: God's complete
healing and eradication of his hurt. We assure him of the strong
likelihood that in the midst of the hurt, he will have an awareness of
the presence of Jesus. Remind him that the Lord has been present

during every part of his life, and that He promises never to leave us nor forsake us.[12] The Lord will be with him in this special time of healing.

7. Praying a prayer of submission

We let our ministry receiver know that as we start the healing ministry we want him to pray a prayer of submission, both submitting to the healing process and turning over his control to the Lord.

J. "Waiting upon the Lord" Listening Prayer

This powerful ministry approach to bring healing for soul/spirit hurts is very safe for the ministry receiver in terms of possible demonic interference or deception. It gives the Holy Spirit great latitude to control the ministry in "exactly the right way." As ministers, we merely follow along, being faithful stagehands.

In this section, we want to present an overview of this approach. Then we will describe the ministry ingredients in detail. An additional section includes how to remove hindrances based on blocked emotions and/or anger or disappointment with God. We conclude by sharing several case histories of how these ingredients were used in actual ministry sessions.

1. Overview of the ministry ingredients

Note that we are using the term *ingredients* rather than *steps*. We usually do not need to complete all of the following items with each person. We work with the Holy Spirit to move through only the *needed* ingredients. The ingredients are:

1. Thoroughly prepare the ministry receiver.
2. Have the ministry receiver pray the prayer of submission.
3. Determine the scope and starting point: general versus specific.
4. Wait on the Lord: Listen for the Holy Spirit to reveal a memory or impression.
    - Clarify memory.*
    - Deal with any hindrances to receiving a memory.*
5. Help the ministry receiver "enter" the memory.
    - Work within the memory to "specify" and "feel" the feelings.

6. Guide the process of "Pouring Out My Complaint" to the Lord.

7. Invite Jesus into the memory.
   - Keep the focus on what Jesus says and does.
   - Deal with any hindrances blocking the awareness of Jesus.*
   - Broaden what is acceptable.*
   - Conduct a three-way conversation (direct guidance from the Holy Spirit).*
   - Have the ministry receiver release any remaining pain.*

8. Take notes (1) on what Jesus says and does, and (2) on any revealed UGBs. (These will be shared later with the ministry receiver.)

9. Test the healing by "checking the results."
   - Deal with every negative feeling.
   - Follow a theme.

10. Do "clean up/follow up" of remaining healing issues.

(*These bullet points are ingredients to be used as needed.)

2. Ministry ingredients

Having presented the overview, let us now examine in detail the ingredients.

1. Thoroughly prepare the ministry receiver.
We prepare the ministry receiver by following the instructions given on pages 162–165.

2. Have the ministry receiver pray the prayer of submission.
As we prepare to start the actual soul/spirit hurts ministry, we have the ministry receiver read/pray the prayer of submission (on page 190). We ask him to read it first to himself to see if he is in agreement with the prayer. We give him permission to put the prayer into his own words if he prefers.

3. Determine the scope and starting point: general versus specific.
Where do we start? Once we have prepared the ministry receiver, we can start in a very broad and general way, or in a narrow and focused way. When a life has been so dominated by one destructive issue or theme, we often feel led to begin with that focus rather than beginning in a broad and general way. Always ask the Lord where to start. It is a matter of revelation and discernment.

We explain to the ministry receiver our plan so he knows what to expect. If we want to start "broad," we ask the Holy Spirit to reveal *any hurt* He wants to heal. "Holy Spirit, please take Sam back to the memory You want to heal." Note that there is no focus, no limitation. If we choose to start "narrow," then we focus on one area that has been a key problem/issue in the ministry receiver's life. For example, we might say, "Holy Spirit, please take Sam back to a memory that contains the roots of his lust problem." Or, "Holy Spirit, please reveal to Laura a memory of when her fear first began."

4. Wait on the Lord: Listen for the Holy Spirit to reveal a memory or impression.

We pray quietly and allow plenty of time for the ministry receiver to listen for a memory. Once he lets us know he has received a memory, we ask him to describe it in detail.

▶ *Clarify the Memory.* *

If the ministry receiver is not clear about the memory or doesn't understand it, we have him ask the Holy Spirit to clarify the memory and make it plain.

▶ *Deal with any hindrances to receiving a memory.* *

If he still cannot receive the memory clearly, we ask the Holy Spirit to show us what is hindering or blocking. We then take care of this obstacle. At this point in the ministry, the obstacle is usually either blocking demons or unfamiliarity with the process.

5. Help the ministry receiver "enter" the memory.

We want to help the minister receiver enter into the memory as much as possible, reexperiencing the event, as well as his feelings. This will enable him to embrace a deeper level of healing.

▶ *Work within the memory to "specify" and "feel" the feelings.*

Many times specific questions help the ministry receiver reenter the memory. As he begins to report the memory, we ask him questions such as "How old are you?" "Where are you?" "Is anyone else there?" "Describe what is happening and how you are feeling." "What is your fear like?" "Why are you afraid to tell anyone?" These questions will not only help the ministry receiver become more focused, but they will also assist him to specify and reexperience his feelings.

6. Guide the process of "Pouring Out My Complaint" to the Lord.

Once the ministry receiver is in touch with his pain, we ask him to begin to share his pain and feelings with the Lord. Some ministry receivers are immediately able to do this. Others may need some help getting started. If the receiver is struggling with this process, we "prime the pump" by giving him some "lines" that help him begin to describe the hurt. For example, we might suggest, "Lord, I am just so hurt and angry about how my mother treated me. I still have nightmares about it." Or we might suggest, "Just tell the Lord what it was like for you to be locked in your bedroom all those afternoons when your mother was punishing you." After the priming, he may naturally continue, or more "feeling" lines may be needed.

The Holy Spirit will guide us in how to lead the receiver. We must not get discouraged here. We may be working to reverse a pattern of many years. If the receiver says a few things and then stops, we give him another "priming" line. Also, if he reports feeling "weird" by doing this, we are understanding, but encourage him to continue. Once he has shared his pain with the Lord, we are ready to have him ask Jesus to come into the memory.

7. Invite Jesus into the memory.

In some cases, the ministry receiver will already be experiencing Jesus with him as he pours out his complaint. More often, however, at this point we ask the receiver to invite Jesus into the memory with him. We say, for example, "Ask Jesus to show you where He is." We ask him to report what Jesus is saying or doing.

▶ *Keep the focus on what Jesus says and does.*
We encourage the ministry receiver to continue to keep his focus on Jesus. It is what Jesus says or does that brings the healing. All our efforts are directed toward helping this happen.

In our role, we *never tell* the ministry receiver what Jesus is doing or saying. For example, we *do not* say, "Now Jesus is coming over to hug you." No no no! Also, we *never command* or direct Jesus to do something. We never say, "Jesus, go take the baby out of his crib and hold him." This is another no-no. We may *ask Jesus* if He will do something. For example, "Jesus, would You show this hurting child Your love?" *Asking is totally different from directing or demanding!* Sometimes Jesus responds to what we ask Him to do, and sometimes He doesn't! Our task is to stay tuned to the Holy Spirit, so that we are asking Jesus to do what He, through the Holy Spirit, is already telling us He wants to do. This is essentially the same as intercessory prayer, where the Holy Spirit has the intercessor praying God's will into a situation so that God is released to do here on this earth what He wants to do.

Attempting to direct Jesus, or the Holy Spirit, and telling Him what to do or say is manipulating, controlling and occultic. It will not result in true healing. It opens the door to illegitimate control by the minister and possible entry of spirit guides and other familiar spirits that would like to get involved.

We must leave the Lord in control. He can appear to the ministry receiver however He wishes. We *always* let Him *take the initiative!*

▶ *Deal with any hindrances blocking awareness of Jesus.* *
At this point, the main hindrances that prevent a ministry receiver from being aware of Jesus are unconfessed sin, unforgiveness, demonic interference and/or shame. If there is a problem, we ask the Holy Spirit which of these areas needs to be addressed.

▶ *Broaden what is acceptable.* *
Most often, people are able to see Jesus with them in their hurtful memory. In other instances, they sense Him. Others do not see or sense Jesus, but rather have an overpowering sense of the Father's love and His presence. They report feeling bathed in the Father's love. Still others hear God speaking through the Holy Spirit. They hear words in their spirit such as "I was always there for you." Others primarily hear Scripture. Most amazingly, a few people to whom we have ministered did not see or sense anything specific, yet had a profound experience of God's peace replacing their feelings of hurt.

While we want to be totally open to whatever way God chooses to reveal Himself, we must confess to having a preference. We have experienced particularly significant fruitfulness when the ministry receiver directly encounters Jesus within the memory. For that reason, we always begin by having the receiver invite Jesus to be there with him. If Jesus doesn't come into the memory, we must discern whether or not there is a blockage or whether God is choosing to heal in one of His other ways.

▶ *Conduct a three-way conversation (direct guidance from the Holy Spirit).* *
For years, we have used a three-way conversation as we worked with the ministry receiver within his memory. We have talked to the ministry receiver (i.e., "Now, pour out your heart to the Lord"). We

have talked to the Lord (i.e., "Lord, would You come and heal John?"). We have asked the receiver to report what the Lord was saying or doing (i.e., "What is the Lord showing you?" "He is showing me that He wants me to forgive my mother.") God has brought tremendous fruit using this approach. Recently, Dr. Ed Smith has written about using this "three-way conversation." We appreciate his expansion and addition to this ministry. He says:

> I also talk to the Lord out loud during the process and carry on three-way conversations with Him. I ask the questions and allow the client to give response. I do not guide the moment but rather ask questions as to what the client senses Jesus is wanting him to do. I avoid leading questions that might be a subtle way of directing. I ask the Lord Jesus honest questions about my inadequacies, such as, "Lord Jesus, I don't know what it is You are wanting to do, know, see, etc. Would you give us more understanding, direction, light, etc.?" I then trust that Jesus will speak to the person.[13]

Notice the way it works. The minister asks the questions of the Lord, but is given the answer as the Lord speaks or brings revelation to the ministry receiver, who reports back to the minister. This roundabout way can be very helpful. It is another communication link to complement our direct listening to the Holy Spirit.

▶ *Have the ministry receiver release any remaining pain.* *
As we approach the end of bringing healing to a memory, we ask the ministry receiver to check whether or not he has any remaining pain. If some still remains, we direct him to give the pain to the Lord.

8. Take notes (1) on what Jesus says and does and (2) on any revealed UGBs.

Even though the ministry receiver may be tremendously affected by what Jesus says and does within the memory, we have noticed that he may quickly forget. We keep careful notes of what occurs so we can give him a record of these profoundly important events.

Jesus frequently speaks truth into the lies associated with the SSH as part of bringing the healing. This usually completely destroys the power of the UGBs that were holding the hurt in place. However, it is important to record the truth and add what Jesus says to the list of godly beliefs so that the ministry receiver can continue to meditate on it. If necessary, we lead the receiver in repentance for believing the lie or lies.

9. Test the healing by "checking the results."

Dr. Ed Smith has brought the world of Christian inner healing ministry a step farther by sharing his godly revelation through Theophostic Counseling. We are grateful for his insight of "confirming the healing,"[14] or "checking the results," once healing has taken place.[15] Checking the results allows us to determine if all of the negative emotions have been completely healed, or if there are some negative emotions still present.

The principle is to focus on whatever negative emotion the Lord has just healed, such as anger. We then ask the ministry receiver to search and see if he can find any remaining anger. In our experience, the receiver usually says, "No, Jesus has taken it all away," or something similar. There are times, however, when anger (or some other negative emotion) remains. In these cases, as Dr. Smith points out, more healing is needed. The remaining anger is most often stored in one or more additional hurtful memories. We are thus alerted to follow the anger theme into other hurtful memories until the anger is completely healed in all of the memories.

▶ *Deal with every negative feeling.*

In addition, this process of "checking the results" helps the ministry receiver locate other negative feelings that are contained in the same memory. For example, he may say, "No, there is no more anger, but I do feel a lot of bitterness." What a wonderful entrée for the next area for healing. Now bitterness becomes the focus in the same memory. Once bitterness is dealt with, we recycle and again "check the results." The approach is to continue until all negative emotions are healed.

Illustration

We were about to pray and wrap up the session with a ministry receiver when he spoke in a very irritated voice saying, "I'm feeling really angry." Although surprised, we asked the Holy Spirit to show him the root of his anger. The Holy Spirit took him back to the original memory of molestation, which we thought had been dealt with. This time, Jesus healed him of his anger from being victimized. Again we thought we were finished. Then he began to weep because Jesus was dealing with his lifelong feeling of helplessness. As the Lord flashed memory after memory before this man, He showed him how He had been his Source of strength in the many "helpless" situations of his life. Helplessness, which we had not even realized was there, was healed. We suddenly had a radiant, empowered man because Jesus had healed *all* of his negative emotions.

▶ *Follow a theme.*

A number of years ago, the Lord taught us a tremendous lesson as we ministered to a man struggling with lust. The Holy Spirit revealed to him an early experience of molestation by a neighbor. Although Jesus healed him of this, none of us felt his healing was quite complete. As soon as we said, "Holy Spirit, show us what else needs to be healed to complete the process," the man immediately had two more memories of sexual defilement come to him. We then worked through each of these memories individually. It wasn't until Jesus had brought healing in all three of the memories that this man felt free. From that experience, we learned the importance of following a theme through several memories until everyone knows freedom has come.

We also have discovered that God is efficient. So often, when He heals a memory of a particular type, for example, rejection, He heals other memories of the same type or theme simultaneously. Sometimes, however, He wants to deal with several memories individually, especially if there is significant trauma involved. We as ministers simply need to ask Him if there are related memories He wants to heal. Sometimes we will see a picture, like a map, showing several related memories connected by a timeline. We share this information with the ministry receiver and have him ask the Holy Spirit to bring the next related memory.

10. Do "clean up/follow up" of remaining healing issues.

In the soul/spirit hurt area, we have often been reminded of Jesus' raising Lazarus from the dead[16] and then His turning to His disciples and telling them to remove the grave clothes. Jesus has done the hard part. He has done the life-giving part. However, He directs His helpers to "loose him and let him go."[17] It is the same in the area of soul/spirit hurts. Jesus, the Father, or the Holy Spirit has brought life and healing. Now we as ministers need to take care of the legalities. We need to be sure our "Lazarus" is completely unbound with no grave clothes in sight! This process involves ministering to any new areas that have been exposed. Typical clean-up/follow-up jobs include making sure forgiveness is complete—especially self-forgiveness—that soul ties are broken, that newly identified ungodly beliefs are addressed and that SOFCs are broken. If the presence of additional demons becomes evident, we need either to cast them out then or add them to our list for the upcoming deliverance.

3. Hindrances that need special attention

Besides the ministry ingredients discussed in the previous section, there are two very important hindrances that may need to be dealt with.

a. Blocked emotions

Occasionally, your ministry receiver may have blocked emotions. He is simply not in touch with his own feelings (or only at a very minimal level). He is not being stoic or obstinate. During some period of his life, he experienced so much pain that he learned to block it out in order to survive. The problem is that he not only shut off his pain, he also blocked out almost all of his feelings. Ask him how he feels and he truly does not know. (An interesting note is that he may feel many emotions about what is happening to other people, just not about himself.) You, as the minister, must be careful not to shame him for being so out of touch with the feeling/emotional part of himself. Having blocked emotions is one form of dissociation. What do you do? First, begin by praying for safety and protection over his life. Allow the Holy Spirit to lead you. Do not try to push him. You may, however, want to explain why feelings are an important part of the "abundant life" that Jesus has promised him. Ask him if he is willing to access his feelings again, to help bring this part of himself back to life. If he agrees, you can continue the soul/spirit hurts session by asking, "Lord, would you please take John back to the place where he first started shutting down his emotions?" Then begin to work with the memory that the Holy Spirit brings into his awareness following the procedure discussed previously.

In our experience, there are usually three or four key memories in which the ministry receiver has made the repeated decision that it is too painful for him to feel anything. In each memory he needs God's healing. In each one, he also needs to renounce his decision/vow not to feel. Treat this decision as an ungodly belief that he vowed. Frequently the deep hurts that caused him to block his pain occurred very early in the ministry receiver's life. Besides the pain and grief of loss, there may be much anger that begins to surface. Help him to be real and to express the anger and other negative feelings contained in each memory to the Lord.

Healing blocked emotions is a process. You may see amazing things happen as Jesus heals, but also know that your ministry receiver may need time to integrate the new healing by beginning to give his emotions a valid place in his life.

b. Anger and disappointment with God

A natural result of hurt is to question God's care, or to believe that if He does care, He cares more about other people than about us. Someone who feels God has hurt, betrayed or abandoned him has a difficult time expecting to receive anything good, particularly healing, from God. The bottom line of the disappointment-with-God issue is a *trust* issue—a lack of trust in God. Why would the one who "hurt" you want to heal you? We must address the issue of anger/disappointment with God.

This is one of the most sensitive areas in which to minister. However, this delicate area is not unique to those who are severely wounded. Many devout, serious, searching Christians have struggled with these same questions, especially when they feel that God has not met their expectations or answered their prayers. They feel "He has not 'been there' for me." The serious believer has to come to terms with such unanswered questions as:

- *God, where were You?*
- *God, if You love me so much, why didn't You intervene?*
- *God, why didn't You warn me not to get involved?*
- *God, why have I had to go through this?*
- *God, why don't You answer my prayers?*
- *God, why do You seem so far away, so hidden, so silent?*

Added to these questions are the "bigger" issues:

- *Why is there so much suffering in the world?*
- *Why do people hurt and kill each other?*

The gnawing belief that a caring God has abandoned us in our time of need *must* be addressed.

Obstacles to acknowledging this problem
The problem of anger/disappointment toward God is greatly compounded in some Christian circles. Questioning God is considered sacrilegious, ungodly and yes, even dangerous. As a result, attempting

to work through real, negative feelings is seen as lack of faith, weakness or rebellion. This makes it difficult for a person to admit these feelings to himself, since he feels they are too abhorrent, too scary to look at and too shameful to acknowledge. He may fear disapproval from his pastor or other church friends. He may fear that God will be angry with him and punish him for having and expressing his real feelings. His relationship with God, however, will be greatly stifled until these feelings are exposed and resolved. Until they are, he may feel he is merely going through Christian "motions."

Ministry
As we begin to minister, we encourage the ministry receiver to follow David's example and pour out his real feelings, as we discussed previously. We frequently need to remind him that God already knows how he feels. Sometimes we read the "Anger at God" poem (see page 176) to help the ministry receiver "get with the program." It helps him put things in perspective as we discuss some or all of the following items to encourage him to unload his pain.

Encourage being real
Encourage the ministry receiver to acknowledge his true feelings toward God. It helps to be understanding rather than confrontational. If he is having trouble admitting his feelings, use softer words and a permissive tone unless the Holy Spirit leads you otherwise. This avoids defensiveness on his part. The suggestion that he is disappointed or upset with God is usually easier for him to admit than "anger." It doesn't seem so "awful."

Use scriptural examples
It is also helpful to show the ministry receiver some examples from Scripture of men who were angry or upset with God. This helps him know that he is not alone or unique in his feelings. Moses, for example, was terribly upset with God in Numbers 11:10–15. David expressed his frustration with God as he cried:

> Why do You stand afar off, O Lord?
> Why do You hide Yourself in times of trouble?
>
> Psalm 10:1, NASB
>
> How long, O Lord? Will You forget me forever?
>
> Psalm 13:1, NASB
>
> Why have You rejected me?
>
> Psalm 43:2, NASB

David asked, "Lord, where are You? What's happening in our relation-ship?" Isn't it good to know that someone who loved God as much as David did still dealt with these type of questions? Yet God continued to love David. It's reassuring to know we can come and say, "God, why?" The point is that it is *okay* to have these feelings and it is *okay* to express them. It is *not*, however, *okay* to stay stuck with these feelings.

> **"Anger at God"**
>
> I told God I was angry;
> I thought He'd be surprised.
> I thought I'd kept hostility
> quite cleverly disguised.
> I told the Lord I hate Him;
> I told Him that I hurt.
> I told Him that He isn't fair,
> He treated me like dirt.
> I told God I was angry,
> but I'm the one surprised.
> "What I've known all along," He said,
> "you've finally realized.
> "At last you have admitted
> what's really in your heart;
> Dishonesty, not anger,
> was keeping us apart.
> "Even when you hate Me,
> I don't stop loving you.
> Before you can receive that love,
> you must confess what's true.
> "In telling Me the anger
> you genuinely feel,
> it loses power over you
> permitting you to heal."
> I told God I was sorry,
> and He's forgiven me.
> The truth that I was angry
> had finally set me free.
>
> Jessica Shaver[18]

Show real sources of hurt

A turning point occurs when the ministry receiver realizes that the root cause of his hurt is sin in operation in the lives of other people and/or in his own life. Satan is always there, too, seeking whom he may devour,[19] encouraging sin to continue. A ministry receiver can often see that sin is the cause of hurt as a general principle, but he has trouble applying this truth in his own case. Sometimes we ask the ministry receiver to think about the person or people who have hurt him the most and identify the hurts operating in their lives. We pray for God's revelation of this important truth: Sin is the underlying cause. When this fact becomes clear, the ministry receiver can *stop blaming God* and begin to put the blame where it belongs. It takes the Holy Spirit to help the person see that God did not want those things to happen to him and that it wasn't His plan for him to be hurt. With some people, it may help to emphasize that God promises to be with us through the pain, the hurt, the disappointment. He promises to be with us through the things that we don't understand, as well as the grief process—not only in the past, but also in the present as we face the pain. He wants to bring comfort and to raise up beauty from ashes. Isaiah 43:2 speaks powerfully about the fact that we will experience hard, trying and hurtful times. That's a given. After all, we live in a fallen world. The good news is that we do not have to face these alone. The passage reads:

> "When you pass through the waters,
>   I will be with you;
> and when you pass through the rivers,
>   they will not sweep over you.
> When you walk through the fire,
>   you will not be burned;
>   the flames will not set you ablaze."
>
> Isaiah 43:2, NIV

Verbalize the anger/disappointment

When the ministry receiver, following David's example, pours out the deep pain of his resentment, abandonment, disappointment and anger to the Lord, the relief can be immediate, and healing can begin. We encourage him to do two things: to be very specific about his feelings and to let himself *really* feel his feelings as he expresses his heart to God. In the majority of cases, just expressing his true feelings will lead him into a place of repentance.

Another phenomenon may occur first, however. Sometimes the ministry receiver, as he is verbalizing his upset with God, will immediately see or sense the hurtful memory where his anger/disappointment is rooted. He is already "there." In this event, it is natural to lead him right into the steps/ingredients of soul/spirit healing. For some individuals, it is only *after* the healing of a specific memory that they realize that the Lord has not failed them and they can truly trust Him.

Repentance
Quite frequently, as the ministry receiver is engaged in the "Pouring Out My Complaint" to God process, he recognizes that he has been putting the blame in the wrong place. Then, on his own accord, he begins to ask God's forgiveness for blaming Him, instead of seeing the real source of his hurt. With some individuals, however, you may need to lead them in a brief prayer of repentance. Many tears have been shed as people sought God's forgiveness for misplaced blame. Repeatedly, this experience has been the turning point in being able to receive from God and beginning to trust Him again.

God redeems hurt
God can bring *good* out of our hurts.[20] God can use hurt to develop us and to mature us if we don't let ourselves get stuck in it. Think about Joseph, for example. Many were the plans and purposes of God, but, oh, what he had to go through—and the hurts that he had to endure—before he got there! God can use hurt to chisel, to make, to strengthen and to mold if we will give the hurt to Him. If we don't, the enemy uses it to keep us bound and wrapped in grave clothes, so that we can't move forward into all the Lord would have us to do and to be.

4. Case histories

The following are transcripts taken from actual ministry sessions and used with permission. Enjoy these with us as we reexperience God's loving guidance and healing in the lives of these people. We will highlight the ministry steps/ingredients as we go along.

a. Joseph's soul/spirit hurt
This portion of a soul/spirit hurts session illustrates so well the perfect way that Jesus interacts with the ministry receiver to obtain maximum trust, obedience and healing.

Ministry receiver's background
We were working with Joseph, an outstanding Christian leader who had come from a home in which both of his parents were alcoholics. In Joseph's emotional abandonment, he had developed mistrust of both

people and God. He acknowledged that he saw patterns in his own life of being aggressively controlling, self-sufficient and independent.

Ministry preparation

As we went through all the steps of preparation, Joseph became well acquainted with the format we were about to use. We decided to start with the broad, general approach, since he had hurts in many different areas. It seemed better initially not to restrict the healing to any specific focus.

Ministry

- *Minister* (Listening prayer): We are going to pray now and ask the Holy Spirit to bring into your awareness any key hurts and/or hurtful events that He wants to heal at this time. We want you to listen and then report to us any hurtful memory or impression, once it comes.

  (As we "wait upon the Lord," we pray quietly in the Spirit, and listen for revelation about what God wants to do. We also try to discern any hindrances that may attempt to block the process. In this case, we don't discern any problems.)

- *Joseph* (Receiving a memory): This memory is very clear. It was my wedding day, and I had forgotten something important I needed. I have to drive back to our house to get it before the wedding. My father begins to ridicule me about forgetting whatever it was.

- *Minister* (Wanting to help specify feelings): What are you feeling as he is ridiculing you?

- *Joseph*: I feel alone and angry. I am very angry. I immediately jump to the defensive mode. I guess I want to reject Dad before he rejects me.

- *Minister* (Feel the feelings): Let yourself feel your anger. Get more in touch with it.

- *Joseph*: I am feeling my anger now. Actually, what I feel even more is hatred. I am feeling hatred toward my father. He ridiculed me so many times. He was never there for me when I needed him.

  [Pause] I can also see Jesus over in the corner of the room. He is trying to get my attention, but I am ignoring Him. I am just too mad to listen.

  (Notice, Joseph is aware that Jesus is already there. We don't need to have Joseph ask Him to come.)

- *Minister*: Why don't you let Jesus talk to you?

- *Joseph*: He already is. He is telling me that Dad wanted to act right, but that he didn't know how. I am so mad that I am not interested in what He has to say.

    [Long pause] I am driving away from the house now. Jesus is in the back seat of my car. He is telling me He has been waiting a long time for me to acknowledge Him. He is telling me to release my dad to Him; that He will change Dad, that I can't.

    [Silence]

- *Minister* (Checking the results): What is happening to your anger?

- *Joseph*: I am still feeling it. Jesus is asking me to let Him drive the car. He wants to take me to my dad. He is showing me that my dad has this covering over him. I have never realized that before. He is showing me what is underneath the covering, who my dad really is. I see my dad as a much younger person who is really scared and very ashamed.

    [Long pause] I realize now that my dad needs my love and my support.

    [Tearful] I never saw that before.

    [Continues by describing his actions] I am going over to my dad. I want to hug him but I am thinking of all the times he smelled like alcohol, all the times that he stunk. I'm going over anyway and putting my arms around him. I can't remember hugging him. I don't know what he will do. He is starting to hug me back. We are just holding each other. I am forgiving him for all the neglect, the times he wasn't there for me. I see that I have judged him and cut him out of my life. I am asking his forgiveness, too. I thank him for being my dad.

- *Minister*: (Realizing that the Lord is healing years of Joseph's anger, stays quiet.)

- *Joseph*: Now, I see myself back in the car. Jesus is in the front seat. He is telling me that He wants to make up for the things I have lost, but that He can't do it very well when He is in the back seat— when I am leaving Him out of my life. I am asking Him what I should do. He is telling me to trust Him, to let Him get in the driver's seat, to let him drive my car.

- *Minister* (Wanting to follow the Lord's direction): Just keep letting us know what you are doing.

- *Joseph*: I'm telling the Lord that I have never been able to trust anybody. That is my problem. If I trust Him, I will have to get rid of all my crutches and strategies, all the things I have used to keep Him away and keep other people away.

  [Pause]

- *Minister* (Three-way conversation): Jesus, would You be willing to show Joseph how to let go of his mistrust?

- *Joseph*: He's telling me He wants to do an exchange. He wants to take all of my strategies and give me what will be satisfying. We are making the exchange. Now I am transferring my trust to Him. I am going to trust Him.

  [Pause] He says I am His son. He is telling me to focus on Him and that He won't walk away or leave me.

  (Joseph's once tense and tearful face looks much more peaceful.)

- *Minister* (Checking the results): Would you look within yourself and see if you can find any anger or mistrust?

- *Joseph*: There is no anger anywhere, or mistrust, but there is something left.

- *Minister*: What is left?

- *Joseph*: What is left is my concern about what others think. I have always been overly concerned. Jesus is asking me to write this fear on a card and give it to Him. He is saying that He will take care of what others think. He is taking away the card I have written on.

  (Joseph looks up and begins to laugh in amazement at what the Lord has done.)

- *Minister* (Checking the results): Can you find any fear about what people think?

- *Joseph*: No! No, Jesus has taken it all. I am at peace.

- *Minister*: Where is Jesus now?

- *Joseph* (With surprise in his voice, as if it should be obvious): Oh, He's in the driver's seat, driving the car. I'm sitting next to Him.

- *Minister*: That's wonderful. Before we stop, we need to take care of just a few more things.

Discussion

Let's discuss this segment of Joseph's healing before going on to the clean-up/follow-up ingredient.

This healing was smooth and easy from the minister's point of view. We did not need to clarify the memory Joseph received. There were no blocks or hindrances. He was very able to identify his feelings and to feel them. He recognized anger, hate and concern or fear. We did not need to have him ask for the Lord to come with him since he was already aware of Jesus' presence. If Joseph had been unable to go on at this point of the healing, we would have suspected unforgiveness to be a hindrance. Clearly, however, he remained in good contact with Jesus. We just followed what he and the Lord were doing.

We skipped the step of "Pouring Out My Complaint" to the Lord. It wasn't needed to help him get in contact with a memory or in contact with the Lord. It wasn't needed to express and release the anger, hatred and fear. Jesus took care of these directly.

Did you notice how He did it? Joseph's anger and hate left both when he forgave his dad and also when the Lord showed him his dad as he really was, ashamed and fearful. Jesus took his fear of "what others think" away on a card.

Out of Joseph's abandonment, he felt he couldn't trust God or anyone else to take care of him. As a result, he lived his life out of the ungodly belief, *I can't trust God to take care of me; I have to take care of myself.* We identified several other related ungodly beliefs, as well. He had to stay in control at all times. This problem of trust was directly dealt with as Jesus asked Joseph to trust Him and they made an exchange. The issues resulting from mistrust, control and self-sufficiency were challenged as Jesus asked Joseph to let Him sit in the driver's seat, and Joseph yielded.

In this short healing session, Jesus also touched another related area: Joseph's deep sense of not belonging. Joseph's heart was touched as he was reconciled to his father and also as Jesus said, "You are My son."

Clean up/follow up
The clean-up/follow-up ingredient was fairly simple. We ministered to the several ungodly beliefs and helped Joseph formulate new godly beliefs for each one. The anger/hate/bitterness area needed to be broken as a sin of the fathers and as a resulting curse. Lastly, we added this grouping of demons, plus unforgiveness demons, to the list of demons to be cast out in the next session.

Because of Joseph's strong commitment to becoming all that God wants him to be, he has held on to his healing and seen outstanding changes in some major lifelong patterns. It was a great privilege to be a part of God's healing of Joseph.

b. Cathy's soul/spirit hurt

Let's look now at an excerpt from a soul/spirit hurts session that includes some additional ingredients. In this session, we have to help our receiver stay focused on her memory, as well as stopping some demonic interference. Note also how we had the ministry receiver "Pouring Out My Complaint" to the Lord very early in the ministry.

Ministry receiver's background

Cathy, a strong, self-motivated leader and prayer warrior, is married to a Christian man who loves her. Over the twenty-plus years of their marriage, he has had several different periods of unfaithfulness that brought much pain to them both. Cathy and Dave have had ministry over the past year, but as they came to us, there appeared to be a subtle but real breach lingering between them, the kind that is hard to identify. We chose to go with a specific focus for the initial healing, since their problem was both current and obvious.

Ministry

- *Minister* (After Cathy has been prepared, we direct her to ask for a specific focus): Would you just wait on the Lord now and ask Him to take you to a memory that has roots causing this current separation you are experiencing?

- *Cathy*: I am seeing tons of different incidents.

- *Minister* (Clarifying the memory): Ask the Holy Spirit to highlight one of them.

- *Cathy*: I just feel so much anger at Dave.

- *Minister* (Deciding to work with the feeling, thinking it can be used to help take Cathy to an important memory): Let's start there. Just begin to pour out your complaint to the Lord. Tell Him all about your anger.

- *Cathy* (Pouring Out My Complaint): Lord, I am so mad that this stuff keeps happening. It seems like Dave doesn't do what he needs to do to get over his problem. Lord, it creates a constant inner stress in me. I'm always wondering when the other shoe is going to drop. I hate living like this.

  [Pauses] I am seeing a memory now of the early years of our marriage.

- *Minister* (Clarifying the memory): Where are you and what is happening?

- *Cathy*: We are in Kentucky. Dave has gotten into sexual trouble. I go to a pastor to get help. I come home and tell Dave what we need to do, but he won't listen. It's as if he doesn't hear me. He needs to get help. We both need help, fast, if we are going to save our marriage. I am so frustrated. Dave is looking at me and acting as if he is listening, but I know it's not penetrating.

- *Minister* (Asking for the Lord's presence): Would you ask the Lord to come be there with you?

- *Cathy*: Jesus is already here. I can see Him. He is over in the corner of the room, listening.

- *Minister*: Cathy, do you want to ask Him to help you with your frustration and anger?

- *Cathy*: (Starts to try to talk to Jesus but as soon as she starts, she comes out of the memory. She looks up and begins analyzing her past situation.)

- *Minister*: Cathy, what just happened? You left your memory just as you were beginning to talk to Jesus. Would you see if you can go back to the memory and be there again?

- *Cathy* (Takes a minute, closes her eyes): Yes, I am here with Jesus.

- *Minister*: Tell Him about your anger and frustration. Tell Him what that anger and frustration feel like to you. Tell Him what it made you want to do.

- *Cathy*: (Starts once again to talk to Jesus. She then looks up and goes into analytical mode for the second time.)

- *Minister* (Briefly explains to Cathy that there is demonic blockage hindering her contact with Jesus): We bind every antichrist demon and every demon of analysis. Cathy, now reenter the memory again, and see if you are able to talk to Jesus.

- *Cathy*: Lord, I'm so angry with my husband. I am looking to him to be my covering. Lord, he is not even aware of my pain and how much he has hurt me. I want him to see and hear how bad he has hurt me. I want to make him repent.

    [Continuing] Jesus is coming over to me. I can see this very large sword inside of myself. He is trying to pull it out of me.

    [Pause: A minute or more go by before Cathy continues] The sword is out now. Across it is written the words *Man's Justice*.

    [Another pause] Lord, I repent of the lie that I have to be the one to bring Dave to a place of repentance, rather than You convicting him. Forgive me, Lord, for all of my anger and control.

- *Minister*: What is happening to the sword? Are the words still there?
- *Cathy*: I can't see the words anymore. Jesus has put the sword into the fire. When it is tempered enough, He will give it back to me.

  (The implication here is that when Cathy is healed, she will be able to safely use the sword, this time as a weapon of spiritual warfare.)

- *Minister* (Checking the results): Cathy, would you see if you can find any anger or frustration within yourself?
- *Cathy*: There is none here, but I do see a very large void in me. That void held the anger and frustration and bitterness. It held my need to fix things myself and force my husband to repent. It is where the sword was.
- *Minister* (Three-way conversation): Jesus, would You be willing to heal this void in Cathy?
- *Cathy*: He is bathing me, washing me with His love. Jesus is just filling the void. It is going away. I also see His tears for Dave. He is hurting for my husband.

  (As she sees this, Cathy's heart is softened toward her husband.)

Discussion

We made the decision to have Cathy begin the session by pouring out her complaint because often the feeling that is poured out will take the person directly back to a major memory. This happened in Cathy's case.

When Cathy tried to talk to Jesus, she came abruptly out of her memory instead. We suspected demonic blockage, but we were not sure yet. When it happened a second time, we asked the Holy Spirit what demons were hindering and heard the words *antichrist* and *analysis*. These demons were trying to prevent Cathy from keeping contact with Jesus, her Healer. (In another ministry time, it could be different demonic forces.) The demons responded to being bound in the name of Jesus. Otherwise, we would have stopped and done deliverance.

When Cathy saw the sword with *Man's Justice* written on it, she immediately saw the connection between "man's justice" and her own sin of trying to force her husband into repentance her way. She began to repent, without our having to intervene.

Lastly, note the significance of the final "Checking the Results." It was then that Cathy saw the void within herself, left by removing the sword. Filling the void was an important step. It needed to be done. It was also during the Checking the Results that Cathy saw Jesus' care for her husband and her heart toward him was softened.

Clean up/follow up

The clean-up/follow-up part of the session included ministering to two ungodly beliefs: "I will be the one to cause Dave to see my pain and come to repentance" and "My husband will never see the depth of my pain and repent from his heart." We also sensed that bitterness was a result of SOFCs, which we hadn't previously identified, so we dealt with this using the SOFCs ministry steps. Lastly, we did deliverance of the two demonic spirits identified, antichrist and analysis, as well as bitterness and control. We were out of time, but we felt that in the next session, we would like to pursue anger and bitterness and make sure no more similar roots were hidden in other memories.

5. Summary

Our job as ministers is to work with the Lord as He leads. If we need further clarification, we pray again for the interpretation until we know what needs to be done. We may need to lead our receiver in forgiving others, receiving more ministry concerning his ancestors' sins and curses, reading certain Scriptures, etc. The key is to listen to the Holy Spirit and to draw upon our knowledge of the ministry approach/process until we know how to pray for the situation and how to lead him.

So we pray and again wait upon the Holy Spirit to minister healing to the person. He never fails to do so! We then repeat the process for the next hurt that God wants to heal.

This is an amazing process, as we truly experience the unity of colaboring[21] with God on our receiver's behalf. We pray to find out what God wants to heal, and God tells us. Then we pray for the healing, and God heals the soul/spirit hurt. God effectively does it all! What a privilege to serve a living God!

We are continually awed by the "rightness" of what God shows and/or speaks as He brings complete healing and release. He knows the best way to present the information to our receiver. He may bring a vision. Jesus may be in the vision, either as an image or as a "felt" presence, but sometimes He is not. Sometimes, the remembrance is not a vision but an impression or a "knowing." At times, the receiver experiences a profound sense of peace and well-being, and he knows that Jesus is restoring that which was lost. It is always just right, perfect and specifically for that special person. It is always far better than anything we could have thought of or prayed for. It touches the heart where it is needed and accomplishes healing that can be obtained no other way.

Let's look now at an additional example of the Lord's powerful healing work, as we return to Sandy's story.

K. Sandy's Story: Covered at Last

Sandy needed much soul/spirit healing. Her wounding started while still in the womb. The abandonment, the occult terrorizing, the fears, the betrayal, the abuse, the occult control had all contributed to the tattered state of Sandy's heart. She was in so much pain herself that she could be a "tiger" in protecting those in her care. This may be one reason she became a counselor.

Much of the healing that the Holy Spirit brought to Sandy was done in combination with other ministry, but there was one very special healing encounter she had with the Lord that we would like to share.

Waiting upon the Lord

We had done the preparation for the "Waiting upon the Lord" Listening Prayer. Sandy was usually able to hear the Holy Spirit quite well, so this approach for praying for soul/spirit hurts was working very effectively for her.

We had been praying for the wounds suffered while she was four to five years old and later at twelve to fourteen. She had felt particularly "exposed" during these periods. During early childhood, she had been frequently left alone at home at night—an experience that caused much terror and feelings of being unprotected. The early teenage period brought the betrayal by her school girl "friends." We prayed for the healing of the sensitivity of being "uncovered" (unprotected), for the shame and for the pain of betrayal. Then we became silent, quietly praying in the Spirit, "Waiting upon the Lord."

Sandy began to cry with silent tears sliding down her face. We continued to wait until the Holy Spirit signaled to us He was finished.

"You know the story of Ruth and Boaz," Sandy said, still weeping. "I have always loved that story. Well, I saw Jesus come to me. He wrapped me in a cloak and took me away. He 'covered' me with His cloak."

The Holy Spirit also spoke the word *innocence* to Sandy.

"I lost my 'innocence' during that time. Jesus is healing the grief of my lost innocence and my lost childhood. He is covering me. I have never felt protected, and I still don't feel protected by the men in my life."

Sandy began to sob as the fuller meaning of what Jesus had done for her began to sink into her spirit. No wonder the book of Ruth had always been special to her. She had yearned for the "Kinsman Redeemer"[22] to come and provide the protection that she had never felt during her life. Now Jesus had done it, and He did it with the little four-year-old girl.

L. Ministering Healing to SSHs: Specific Ingredients/Steps

Many of God's people merely plod through their Christian life. With hurts still needing the Master's touch, they lack both joy and growth. Does that describe you? If so, you may be wondering what is wrong and why you do not seem to care anymore. Do the same memories keep coming back, even though you have spoken words of forgiveness over and over? Friend, you need God's healing! It is time for your soul/spirit healing.

1. Final thoughts before ministry

Remember that we as ministers or as caring people praying for one another cannot bring healing into anyone's life. Why, then, should we be anxious or concerned about what happens during ministry? If the Lord does not show up, there will be no revelations, no deliverance, no healing. It doesn't matter what *we* do, nothing of eternal value will happen unless the Lord accomplishes it. So, we might as well relax and enjoy the session.

Our responsibility is to pray and to be obedient. God's responsibility is to be faithful to His Word (which He is) and to fulfill it. He does watch over His Word to perform it.[23] So we can let go of any burden or false sense of responsibility for what happens to the person. We can't make anything happen on our own!

Also, remember that, as we are praying, the Lord may do any of a number of things for the ministry receiver, as we have discussed throughout this chapter. Our job is simply to bring the ministry receiver to Jesus, as Andrew did,[24] and let the Lord do what He wants to do.

Exercise

We encourage you to use the "Waiting upon the Lord" Listening Prayer approach and move through the following ministry ingredients. The Holy Spirit will be faithful to bring to your awareness those hurts that He wants to heal, and then as you pray, He will heal them. You can do this in the privacy of your prayer closet. Give yourself permission to "feel" and to "be." This will free the Holy Spirit to minister to you at maximum effectiveness. May God bless you as you entrust yourself to Him!

---

2. Bind demons

As we prepare to pray, it sometimes is helpful to again bind all demonic interference, even though we did this in the opening prayer. Otherwise, the demons may still try to block the receiving of the healing. They may also attempt to masquerade as angels of light, passing themselves off as angels or the voice of God. If we sense that there is a significant amount of demonic oppression within the person, significant dissociation or a very confined range of emotions, we may "pray prophetically" or "pray chronologically," rather than relying on the person's ability to hear the Lord. We may also go ahead and do some deliverance to clear out the blockages and then proceed with SSHs ministry.

3. Submission prayer

We like to have the ministry receiver pray and submit to the healing process as we begin the actual "Waiting upon the Lord" Listening Prayer. The prayer on page 190 is typical of what we ask him to pray.

4. Ingredients/steps for ministering to soul/spirit hurts

The ingredients/steps are helpful in preparing the way and then praying so the brokenhearted person can receive the healing of Jesus. This is a list of "ingredients" rather than the precise order of events. Use them as the Holy Spirit directs. Receiving healing for the hurts of the soul/spirit takes time as we wait upon the Lord, so don't feel in a rush. Relax and enjoy, as the Lord of the universe operates on the ministry receiver while you watch from a ringside seat. Bless you as you take time to listen to the Lord with someone else or for yourself.

SSHs submission prayer

Lord, I choose to be open and submitted to You today. Like David, I cry out to You and tell You my troubles. I ask You to bring my soul out of prison so I can praise Your name. I trust You not to give me more than I can handle. I can and do trust You to be my protector, my shield and the revealer of my hurts.

Lord, only You know what lies in darkness, the deepest secrets inside me. I ask that You reveal the deep and hidden things to me and to my ministers. Search me, and show us the hurts that You want to heal today. I trust You not to reveal more than I can bear.

I give You permission to dig deep for the roots of any hidden memories that are affecting my life. I ask You to take the keys to my heart now and unlock the doors. Bypass any denial or deception that may be blocking my memory. Bypass anything that has hindered me, or is hindering me, from receiving my healing.

Lord Jesus, I ask You to bring those things to the surface that You want to heal. I ask You to be with me as I reexperience any past hurt and pain. I want to be set free by the power of the cross and Your shed blood.

In the name of Jesus Christ I pray. Amen!

Ministry steps/ingredients

1. **Wait on the Lord**: Ministry receiver "waits on the Lord," listening to the Holy Spirit to bring the memory. (The minister has already determined the scope, either general or specific. Throughout the ministry process, the minister listens as well, both for guidance and for revelation about hindrances.)

2. **Clarify memory**: If needed, encourage the receiver to work with the Holy Spirit for greater clarity of the memory/impression.

3. **Deal with hindrances**: If needed, help the receiver work through any hindrances to receiving the memory, such as unforgiveness, anger with God or demonic interference.

4. **Enter the memory**: Help the receiver enter the memory as he specifies and enters the feelings of the memory.

5. **"Pouring Out My Complaint"**: Direct the receiver to share his feelings honestly with the Lord.

6. **Invite Jesus into the memory**: Have the receiver invite Jesus into the memory. (Sometimes the receiver may not see Jesus in the memory, but he may have an awareness of God's presence.) Have the receiver keep his focus on what Jesus is saying or doing. Have him report to you. If needed, help the ministry receiver remove any further blocks to healing. (At this point in the healing process, shame or demonic oppression is the most common difficulty.)

7. **Take notes**: Record what Jesus says and does as well as the ungodly beliefs revealed within each memory.

8. **Test healing**: Check with the receiver to see if the negative emotion is truly gone/healed. If not, discern whether there is a further hindrance or whether the same negative emotion is stored in an additional memory or memories.

9. **Clean up/follow up**: Lead the ministry receiver in cleaning up any remaining healing issues from this memory or revelation. This may include:
   - leading the receiver through any remaining confession or forgiveness, including self-forgiveness
   - breaking soul ties
   - renouncing sins of the fathers and removing the resulting curses
   - breaking agreement with core ungodly beliefs (lies) embedded in the hurt and creating godly beliefs
   - removing demons associated with the memory and/or adding them to the deliverance list for the next session.

M. Thought-Provoking Questions

1. What is the benefit of the "Waiting upon the Lord" Listening Prayer?

    . . . .

    . . . .

2. Please describe two or three ways your hurts have hindered your walk with the Lord.

    . . . .

    . . . .

3. What do you think is the real source of your pain?

    . . . .

    . . . .

4. Are you able to be real about your own pain? With whom do you share it?

    . . . .

    . . . .

5. Since God already knows how you feel, why do you sometimes hide your feelings?

    . . . .

    . . . .

6. What do you think about "pouring out your complaint" to the Lord as David did in Psalm 142?

    . . . .

    . . . .

7. In the "Waiting upon the Lord" Listening Prayer, what should you do if a memory comes that you don't understand?

    . . . .

    . . . .

8. What ingredients are usually contained within a painful memory?

. . . .

. . . .

9. How do you know if your healing is complete?

. . . .

. . . .

6

Demonic Oppression (DO)

"I have given you authority to trample on snakes and scorpions
and to overcome all the power of the enemy;
nothing will harm you."
Luke 10:19, NIV

The woman lived in a constant state of fear. She had never understood why she startled so easily, why she seemed to hear sounds that no one else heard or why she would wake up at night drenched with the sweat of terror. Not even the reassurance of kindly parents, locked doors and night lights quieted her quivering discomfort. Filled with shame, the woman hid her fear from everyone. A Christian from early childhood, she had experienced precious times of God's closeness and love. She had learned many Scriptures and secretly memorized those that should directly counteract fear. Why did God's Word fail to bring peace and comfort as the evening shadows fell and night approached? She loathed her fear.

This woman's acute sense of failure resulted not from some beset-ting sin but rather from her inability to overcome her number one enemy: the paralyzing *fear*. She would ask herself, "How can I say that I trust God and still panic if the wind slams the door shut at night?" By age forty, she had become resigned to defeat and what she felt must be her "weak faith." Nothing had worked. Then something happened, something life changing. She experienced the wonderful infilling of the Holy Spirit and soon afterward was prayed for in the area of deliverance. She had never contemplated the possibility that demons might be involved in her prevailing fear. The deliverance ministers, however, with their gifts of discernment and years of experience, easily saw the connection. They prepared the way early in the session and then went right for this enemy stronghold.

As the fear demons were forced out into the open and began to leave the woman, these evil beings made one last threat: "We are going to kill you. You will choke to death, and no one will help you. They will think that you are merely manifesting, but you are going to die before they realize what is happening." Sure enough, she began coughing and choking. Fear rushed through her whole being. Panic filled her as she realized the demons were right! She was going to die. There was nothing she could do about it. She couldn't yell out, "Stop!" with all of her coughing and choking. She was doomed!

Then it was over. "Out in the name of Jesus," the ministers commanded. "Out!" Quiet filled her. The fear was gone. She was still alive! She couldn't believe it. Was she really different? Was she really free?

Betsy was that woman. The answer was and has been a resounding "YES, YES, YES!" The longstanding enemy of her soul had been defeated. She would never be the same again! The lengthening evening shadows had lost their threat. In a way she had never imagined, Betsy experienced the reality of God's promise:

> When thou liest down, thou shalt not be afraid; yea, thou shalt lie
> down, and thy sleep shall be sweet.
>
> Proverbs 3:24, KJ21

A. Christians and Demons

Many fine Christians are like Betsy. They do not realize that they can be oppressed by demons. Consequently, they do nothing to stop this oppression, leaving themselves at the mercy of the devil.

Yet he has no mercy. During the normal course of life, people are continually baffled by seemingly unexplained problems, calamities, failures, losses, interruptions, etc. It is only because of God's mercy and grace that Satan can not directly kill us during our time of immaturity.[1] In fact, none of us would probably survive childhood if not for God's grace. The longer we minister and learn more about the different ways Christians are hindered or defeated by demons, the more we are aware of the magnificence of God's grace.

God wants us to come into maturity regarding Satan and his demons. He wants us to enforce His victory over their kingdom of darkness. He wants us to "know the *truth*, and the *truth* shall make you [us] free."[2] He wants us to grow in maturity and faith and to appropriate His freedom by casting out demons.

Some Christians have concluded that the Holy Spirit will not cohabit with demons. They believe that, at the moment of salvation when we are born again, the Holy Spirit comes into us and all oppressing demons are forced to leave. Unfortunately, there is no scriptural basis for this teaching. In fact, the opposite is true. We can read in Ezekiel that the presence of God was in the temple with at least four groups of abominations. At some point, the cup of iniquity of the people became full, and God withdrew from Israel, letting them go into exile.[3]

With Christians, the opposite process occurs. As the Holy Spirit comes and sets up house, He begins His work of sanctification. In the process, He brings us to an understanding of demons, increased faith and eventual displacement and eviction of the demonic.

Derek Prince, the popular British speaker and Bible scholar, was once asked publicly, "Can a Christian have a demon?" In his crisp British humor, he is said to have replied, "Yes, Christians can have anything they want to have."

The deception inherent in the issue of whether or not Christians can have demons can easily be exposed. How? By stopping to realize that we were all sinners before God mercifully gave us grace and faith to become saved.[4] Satan had plenty of time to infiltrate and oppress us before we changed kingdoms.[5] The ancestral sins, with the resulting curses, our ungodly beliefs and ungodly attitudes and the hurts to our soul and spirit—all these have given Satan plenty of opportunity to ensnare us from the moment our earthly lives begin. Even though the Holy Spirit does come to us at the time of salvation—and even though some deliverance does frequently occur at that time—it is a mistake to conclude that we as Christians are totally free of demonic oppression.

We agree, however, with those who contend that Christians cannot be "possessed" by demons, since possession involves *ownership*. On the other hand, we would *not* agree with those who say that Christians can't "have" a demon, since this is an issue of harassment and oppression. For some people, the open door[6] for oppression is so large that the thief can easily do his stealing, killing and destroying.[7] To stop demonic oppression, the legal ground[8] must be reclaimed. Then the trespassing demons can be easily evicted.

The ministry situation is an excellent place to accomplish this liberation. We can help fellow Christians mature in this area and move into their ordained place in the army of God so they can get involved in the spiritual warfare that is so prevalent. The two major blocks that keep Christians from dealing with the demonic world are both addressed during ministry. The first issue is, "Do demons really exist?" The second is, "Do I really have authority over demons to cast them out?" These questions should not and would not be issues if we literally believed the Word of God. But we don't, and they are. After demons have been cast out of a person, however, and he experiences them leaving when "he" gives the command, these two issues are usually settled forever.

Many excellent books have been written about demons, demonology, deliverance and the subject of whether Christians can have demons, as well as the other issues touched on here. Several recommended authors are Basham,[9] Hammond[10] and Philpott.[11]

Restoring the Foundations ministry[12] is concerned with removing whatever basis (legal ground) has been allowing the demonic oppression, and then casting out the demons. This is followed by teaching the ministry receiver how to stand against further attacks by the devil. It is usually better, however, to delay the deliverance until the necessary forgiveness, repentance, renouncing, etc., has been done in the other three problem areas. In this way, we can reclaim the legal ground for holiness. Otherwise we risk setting the stage for reentry by other demons with similar natures.[13] Sometimes, though, it is necessary to do at least some deliverance before effective ministry can occur in one of the other problem areas. In this case, we always come back and "check out" the same ground again during the deliverance time to cleanse it again if necessary.

The need for the integrated approach to biblical healing ministry once again becomes relevant. Why? Because ministry to each of the four problem areas works together. Let's look at the specific ways deliverance is related to the other problem areas.

B. Understanding the Interrelationship among the Ministry Areas

Because deliverance normally comes after we have ministered to all of the other problem areas, it may appear to be the most important area. Nothing could be farther from the truth. Each area is *equally important*. Each area needs to be ministered to so that ministry to the other areas is effective and remains completed. We don't want any openings left that would allow the healing and freedom to be undermined in the future.

1. How deliverance is related to sins of the fathers and resulting curses

When a particular type of generational sin occurs in two or more consecutive generations, we can expect to find demons of that same type in the family members of each generation, including the generation that has come for ministry.

Sometimes, a generational sin pattern may seem to skip a generation. This raises two questions: "Is this sin pattern really ancestral?" and "Are demons actually involved with this sin?" Whatever the appearance may be, the answers are yes! Expect to find both the curse and the demons present and active.

Generational sin and curses are passed down a family line along with the demonic forces that help to carry them out. It does not mean, however, that every member of a particular generation will yield to any particular sin. Sometimes, godly teaching and guidance—and/or a quality decision on his part—will enable a person to resist. As a result, the curse does not manifest. The curse and the demons remain dormant, waiting for an eventual opportunity or for the next generation.

At other times, it seems that one person in a generation will receive *all* of the *evil*. His siblings may have some struggles but nothing compared to the extremes he experiences. He seems to be the *focus* of terrible demonic oppression. This seems very unfair, but perhaps we just don't understand the "setup" that has caused him to be a focus. The good news, however, is that freedom is available, regardless of the intensity of the oppression or the demon's legal rights.

Even when the power of sins of the fathers and curses is broken in a sin pattern area, it is rare that every demon will leave spontaneously. Normally some do leave, but the majority will remain and pressure the person to continue in the same sin. He is extremely vulnerable to this demonic pressure, particularly if the core ungodly beliefs and/or soul/spirit hurts have not also received ministry. To fail to do demonic deliverance would leave the ministry job unfinished. It would most likely bring confusion to the person who had anticipated freedom but instead still feels the same old pressure and temptation.

2. How deliverance is related to ungodly beliefs

Demons do not in themselves create a person's core ungodly beliefs. Their goal, however, is to help engineer circumstances that will cause the person to form the ungodly beliefs in the first place. They arrange for hurtful situations that cause the person to evaluate and make decisions about life, which then become beliefs. Then they further work to cement these untrue (based on God's Word) beliefs firmly into the core structure of the person. The demons continue to *reinforce the ungodly beliefs* by bringing them frequently to mind and by arranging experiences that verify the "truth" of the ungodly beliefs. They also try to *prevent* a person from hearing God's truth. They are ingenious and have numerous strategies. They will harass during church or Bible reading time and send all manner of distracting thoughts or even coughing spells or sleepiness. Demons will do anything to keep the Word of Truth from being planted and working in the person's life. In Mark we read:

> "And when they hear, immediately Satan comes and takes away the word which has been sown in them."
>
> Mark 4:15, NASB

If a measure of truth is able to slip in, the demons will counter with thoughts such as *That may work for some people, but it won't work for me. I am too bad. Look at all the sins I've committed.* Unfortunately, the average Christian frequently buys into these lies and believes that he is the one thinking these thoughts. He passively sinks into defeated resignation, never countering with the truth of the cross. The ungodly beliefs continue to rule and reign.

Every area of ungodly belief is actually an area of *unbelief*. When a person has an *agreement* or covenant with unbelief in his life, the demon(s) have a legal right to stay. The person, his belief system and the demon are all *in agreement*.

During one deliverance session, we actually had a demon say to a person, "I don't have to leave because you believe . . . ," and it went on to name the ungodly belief. Obviously, a person must break any and all agreements before the demon(s) can be evicted and before they will stay away. Also, the person must sincerely plant the new godly belief(s) in his heart if he is to stay free. We suspect that much deliverance, which is successful at the time, is short-lived because the person's belief system has not been changed. This leaves the door open for other demons to reenter.

3. How deliverance is related to soul/spirit hurts

The problem area of deliverance relates to soul/spirit hurts in several different ways. First, demons, which do their work primarily by putting thoughts into our minds, *remind* a person of his hurts. For example, a demon of rejection might say, "See there, *I* am left out again. *I* am always going to be a misfit." Secondly, the demons will try to *reinforce the person's continuing in the same hurtful patterns.* They will put *explicit thoughts of temptation* into a person's mind. In addition, at a crucial time when the person's flesh is being tempted, the demon will *amplify* that thought. For example, the person may be feeling lonely and his flesh is tempted to have an alcoholic drink to block out these painful feelings. "Yes, yes, that is a great idea," the demon will say. "Why don't *I* cruise on down to the local bar right now?"

Lastly, demons seem to find ways to keep a soul/spirit hurt *agitated to keep it from healing.* They will coordinate with the demons in another person to cause hurtful experiences that repeat and reinforce the existing hurts. Just as germs must be cleansed from an infected wound, the soul/spirit hurt must be "disinfected" before it can properly heal.

4. Summary

Dear reader, as we have elaborated on the intricate interconnectedness of these problem areas, has it become clear to you why the integrated approach to biblical healing ministry is both necessary and also powerful?

Let us turn our attention now to the scriptural basis for demonic oppression and deliverance.

C. Scriptural Basis for Deliverance

We want to look first at God's plan for deliverance from demonic oppression, as revealed in the second book of the Bible, Exodus. Then we will consider[14] examples of how Jesus dealt with demons. Next we will see how His ministry multiplied as He sent out the twelve and then the seventy. Then, in the book of Mark, He commissioned all believers to cast out demons. In other New Testament books, we will study Scriptures about Satan, demons and deliverance. The testimony of our early church fathers concerning demons and deliverance clearly indicates that the ministry of deliverance as Jesus did it was continued during the first several centuries of the church. This section concludes with a challenge to us, the 21st-century church.

1. God's strategy for deliverance

God used the Israelites as examples for us.[15] The things He had them do in the natural are spiritual lessons for us. For example, He first gave them the Promised Land and then enabled them to fight and conquer it. In Exodus 23:20–33, He laid out His plan. This plan is repeated in Deuteronomy 7:1–26, where additional insights are provided. As we read these passages in the context of demonic deliverance, it is evident that God's heart and plan is to deliver His people and to bless them. In the Exodus passage, we read:

> "*I will not drive them out from before thee in one year*, lest the land become desolate and the beast of the field multiply against thee. *Little by little I will drive them out* from before thee, *until thou be increased and inherit the land*. And I will set thy bounds from the Red Sea even unto the Sea of the Philistines, and from the desert unto the river; for *I will deliver* the inhabitants of the land into your hand, and *thou shalt drive them out* before thee."
>
> Exodus 23:29–31, KJ21, emphasis mine

We see several principles in these three verses. First, God doesn't drive out the inhabitants of the land in one year (or one ministry session). He does it over time, using the criteria, "until thou be increased, and inherit the land." The New International Version makes God's condition even clearer: "until you have *increased enough to take possession* of the land." As we grow in our Christian maturity, in our awareness of Satan, his schemes and his army, in our ability to wage the good warfare of faith, we are "increasing" and thus able to possess and manage more of the land. The land is "us." Each one of us is the "land." We are destined to become holy land, dedicated and sanctified unto the Lord.[16] Part of this process is to remove the inhabitants of the land. Thus, it is not uncommon to experience more than one deliverance over the course of several years, as we gain back "legal ground," deliverance after deliverance, and then learn to live in that new freedom. We are continually going deeper—going for another cycle of regaining ground followed by consolidation.

The deliverance session Betsy described at the beginning of this chapter was actually her fourth experience that included casting out demons of fear. The earlier sessions were not failures on her part or on the part of the deliverance ministers. They were "gaining ground" sessions that enabled her to mature in her Christian walk. Eventually, she was ready for the final stronghold of the "fear of death" to be broken. Today, she must merely resist periodic temptations to reopen the door to fear. If she has a moment of weakness and she does allow fear to enter, it is a simple thing to repent and clean her "house" again.

Note in Exodus 23:31 that God *delivers* the inhabitants of the land into our hand, and we *drive* them out. This is another important principle shown in the above passage. It is our "partnership with God." We are to colabor with Him. As we fulfill God's requirements concerning any *legal* rights the "inhabitants" suppose they have, their status changes from inhabitants to "trespassers," making it easy for us to drive them out. In Israel's case, the cup of iniquity of the inhabitants of the land became full[17] and God said, "That is enough. You have lost your rights to the land." In our case, we have God's provision (Jesus and the cross) to remove the legal ground by forgiveness and dealing with the first three problem areas. As we break any agreements that we have with the demonic and renounce them, God *delivers* them into our hands. Our part is to *drive* them out. This is the "casting out" process that Jesus did in His ministry and that He tells us to do in ours.

2. Jesus, our model for deliverance

Two wonderful Scriptures, 1 John 3:8 and Acts 10:38, provide summary statements about the purpose of Jesus' life and ministry. He came:

> "...to destroy the works of the devil..."
>
> 1 John 3:8, NASB

and He fulfilled what He came to do:

> "You know of Jesus of Nazareth, how God anointed Him with the Holy Spirit and with power, and how He went about doing good and healing all who were *oppressed* by the devil, for God was with Him."
>
> Acts 10:38, NASB, emphasis mine

We again see the Father's heart in these verses. God equipped Jesus to accomplish His will, "doing good" and "healing all who were oppressed by the devil." Jesus was indeed "revealing" the Father to us.

Table O on pages 203–204 lists a number of wonderful Scriptures showing Jesus' authority over demons and His willingness to deal with them. Also included are Scriptures about believers casting out or being cautioned about demons and the devil. Please refer to this table as we proceed through the following discussion.

Table O: Scriptures Concerning Deliverance

▶ *Jesus' dealing with demons*

1 John 3:8
The purpose of Jesus' life was that He might destroy the works of the devil.

Acts 10:38
Jesus healed all who were oppressed by Satan, because God was with Him.

Matthew 12:28; Luke 11:20
Jesus cast out demons by the finger of God. This brings the Kingdom near.

Luke 8:31
Jesus has authority to cast demons into the abyss.

Luke 8:28
Jesus has authority and ability to torment them.

Matthew 15:22, 28; Mark 7:26–30
Jesus cast out a spirit from a distance.

Mark 9:25
Jesus forbade any return of the demon.

Matthew 4:24; 8:16
Jesus healed all oppressed by demons.

Matthew 9:32; Luke 9:42
Jesus cast out a dumb spirit.

Matthew 12:22
Jesus cast out blind and dumb spirits.

Matthew 17:18
Jesus cast out a mental-illness demon.

Mark 1:39; 5:2–13
Jesus cast out demons.

Mark 16:19
Jesus cast seven demons out of Mary Magdalene.

Luke 4:33–35
Jesus cast out demons.

Luke 4:40–41
Jesus healed all those who were oppressed by demons.

Luke 13:12–16
Jesus freed a woman from a spirit of infirmity.

John 8:44
Satan's nature and character is that of a murderer and a liar.

John 10:10
Satan's nature and character is that of a thief.

Table O: Scriptures Concerning Deliverance (*cont.*)

▶ *Believers' dealing with demons*

Acts 5:16
Peter healed people afflicted with demons.

Acts 8:7
Philip cast out demons.

Acts 19:12
Paul cast out demons, even using cloth that had touched his body.

Matthew 10:5–8
The twelve extended the Kingdom of God.

Luke 10:17–19
Believers have power, authority and protection.

Mark 16:17, 20
Believers shall cast out demons.

James 4:7
Believers resist Satan.

Ephesians 4:27
Believers do not give place (legal ground) to Satan.

1 Peter 5:8
Believers are to be on guard.

2 Corinthians 2:11
Believers need to be aware of Satan's schemes, snares and devices.
(Read 1 Timothy and 2 Timothy for many traps, particularly 2 Timothy 2:26.)

The four gospels offer numerous examples of Jesus casting out demons. One most noteworthy account involves the Gerasene demoniac.[18] Here, an insane, untamable man is restored to his right mind. The death demons, which had dominated him, are allowed/commanded by Jesus to go into the swine who rush rapidly to their death. The insane man becomes sane. He clothes himself, and as a result of his wonderful freedom, he wants to follow Jesus.

For two thousand years, the effects of deliverance have not changed. Deliverance brings freedom from torment and restoration to normalcy: normal mental states, normal physical states and normal spiritual states. Deliverance creates a new desire in the believer to want to stay close to Jesus.

When Jesus did demonic deliverance, it was never a strange or hidden part of His ministry. He never went to the "basement" of the synagogue and closed all of the doors. He did it in broad daylight and often with a crowd looking on in amazement. It was a normal part of His ministry as He showed us the Father's desire to bring healing and wholeness.

In Luke 4:18, Jesus proclaimed that part of His ministry was to "preach deliverance to the captives" and "set at liberty them that are bruised." Did Jesus accomplish His goal? Absolutely! Nearly one-fourth of the gospel accounts of Jesus' ministry refer to His setting people free from demonic oppression.[19]

In Matthew, Jesus said:

> "But if I cast out devils by the Spirit of God, then the Kingdom of God is come unto you."
>
> Matthew 12:28, KJ21

Modern translations use the word *demons* rather than *devils*. There is only one "devil," Satan, but he has many "demons" in his fallen army.

The coming of God's kingdom includes freedom from demonic oppression. Jesus did not have merely a "deliverance ministry," but a "healing and wholeness" ministry that included teaching, preaching, salvation, freedom, healing and deliverance.[20]

3. Jesus' ministry extended

Jesus not only did deliverance Himself, but He extended His ministry first by sending out the *twelve*[21] and then the *seventy*.[22] Finally, He commissioned all "them that believe."[23] In every case, besides the general command to extend the Kingdom of God, He included the command to "cast out demons." In Mark He said:

> "These signs will accompany *those who have believed: in My name they will cast out demons.*"
>
> Mark 16:17, NASB, emphasis mine

It is clear that Jesus expects us as believers to cast out demons, along with other forms of ministry that bring healing and freedom.

4. Believers' dealing with demons

Scripture provides many examples of believers doing demonic deliverance. In Acts 5:15–16, Peter is in Jerusalem, where the people were "bringing sick folks and those who were vexed with unclean spirits; and they were healed, every one" (Acts 5:16, KJ21). Notice the connection here between demons and being healed. Acts 8:7 records the work of Philip in Samaria: "For unclean spirits, crying with a loud voice, came out of many who were possessed with them" (Acts 8:7, KJ21).

As we study the Scriptures, the major requirement for doing demonic deliverance is being a Christian believer.[24] It definitely helps to be filled with the Holy Spirit and to have the various spiritual gifts in operation, but the basic criterion is to "be a believer."

A graphic, humorous account[25] of attempted deliverance is given of the seven sons of Sceva, who was a Jewish chief priest. These sons were not believers, but they had observed the power and effectiveness of Paul's deliverance ministry. They tried to duplicate it by saying:

> "In the name of Jesus, whom Paul preaches, I command you to come out." [One day] the evil spirit answered them, "Jesus I know, and I know about Paul, *but who are you?*" Then the man who had the evil spirit jumped on them and overpowered them all. He gave them such a beating that they ran out of the house naked and bleeding.
>
> Acts 19:13, 15–16, NIV, emphasis mine

The sons got "cast out" instead of the demons! Why? Because they lacked the authority that true believers have. When the demons looked at them, they "did not know them." When demons look at us, we want them to see the Spirit of God with us, ready to drive them out.[26]

5. Additional supporting Scriptures

Additional key New Testament passages reveal the ways Satan and his legions try to oppress believers. These verses primarily give guidelines about how *not* to give him any place in one's life. Examples are this passage in James:

> Submit yourselves therefore to God. Resist the devil, and he will flee from you. . . .
>
> James 4:7, KJ21

and in 1 Peter:

> Be sober, be vigilant, because your adversary the devil walketh about as a roaring lion, seeking whom he may devour.
>
> 1 Peter 5:8, KJ21

These passages tell us to stand guard against our spiritual enemy. Although they refer to Satan and do not refer directly to demons, it would be presumptuous to think that Satan is personally and directly attacking every single Christian. He delegates his authority down through the ranks of his multi-level organization, until it gets to the demons that are assigned to us. Paul refers to this organizational hierarchy in Ephesians:

> [God] set Him at His own right hand in the heavenly places, far above all *principality and power and might and dominion, and every name that is named*, not only in this world, but also in that which is to come.
>
> Ephesians 1:20–21, KJ21, emphasis mine

> For we wrestle not against flesh and blood, but against *principalities, against powers, against the rulers of the darkness of this world, against spiritual wickedness in high places.*
>
> Ephesians 6:12, KJ21, emphasis mine

Somewhere below the top levels, we find the demons that oppress the average Christian. They are the ones who must flee when we resist the "lion" looking to chew on us[27] if we leave our "doors" open and let him into our house.

Praise God that we know something about the organization and strategy of our enemy, that we are less and less "unaware" of his schemes and that we are learning how to resist and defend ourselves. Praise God that He has given us authority and victory[28] over the devil and that we don't have to be defeated Christians. We can go on the offensive and extend the Kingdom within our lives and in others' lives. Praise God that in Revelation we know the end of the story: Satan's final defeat.[29]

While not much is written in other parts of the New Testament about demons and deliverance, there are some passing comments made. These comments, along with the gospels, indicate that the knowledge and understanding of demons, i.e., evil or unclean spirits, was common and widespread throughout all of the cultures of that region.[30] As we see in the next section, the concept of exorcism was well known.[31] As a result, the writers of the New Testament had no need to lay out the details concerning demonic deliverance for us in the 21st century. They did not know that modern Christians would "define" demons out of existence and ignore the reality of their presence.

6. Testimony of early church fathers

It is a testimony to the powerful results of deliverance by Jesus and His followers that the ministry of deliverance was continued by the early church fathers, including Justin Martyr, Origen, Cyprian, Tertullian and Hippolytus. Justin Martyr, who was martyred in 165 AD, recorded these words:

> Many of our Christian men have exorcised in the name of Jesus … numberless demoniacs throughout the whole world and in your city. When all other exorcists and specialists in incantations and drugs failed, they have healed them and still do heal, rendering the demons impotent and driving them out.[32]

The power and the practice were passed on in the first several centuries of the early Church.

7. Challenge for the 21st century

Ours is an age in which "seeing is believing." Truth has to be provable through visible, repeatable outcomes to be accepted as truth. Anything invisible is discounted as *unreal*. Demons, of course, are delighted that the modern American ignores them, helping them remain hidden. For most Christians, accepting the reality of demons is a lot like accepting the reality of divine physical healing. It is hard to believe until experienced. Once it has been seen in a close friend or experienced personally, doubt vanishes. We know that it is true. Our eyes become open. "He who has ears to hear, let him hear."[33]

The deliverance ministry of Jesus is clear. Equally obvious is the fact that He delegated His authority and name to believers to do deliverance. Why have we not gratefully embraced this ministry for the relief that it brings? Have we allowed ourselves the "privilege" of *selective reading*, somehow *discounting* or *retranslating* any Bible passages that do not fit into our established theology or our religious tradition? Well, the days of selective belief of the Gospel are over. Jesus Christ is calling His Church to become fully healed, equipped and committed to do battle at the end of the age.

Prayer
Lord, give us ears to hear, eyes to see and hearts to understand *all of Your truth*. Lord, help us become Your faithful and trustworthy soldiers.

D. Demonic Oppression: Words and Definitions

When discussing the demonic kingdom, it is important that we be clear about the meaning of several words that are used for Satan (its leader), demons and demonic oppression. Table P below gives some definitions of these frequently used words.

The English words for *Satan* and *devil* are transliterated Greek words meaning "adversary" and "accuser." Whenever we say "Satan," we are declaring his true nature of "adversary." Likewise, when we say "devil," we are stating his true nature as "accuser."

For the word *demon*, we have this excellent definition by Derek Prince, the British scholar who has studied and lectured widely about the demonic realm:

Definition
Demons are invisible spiritual entities with minds, emotions and wills of their own, in league with and under the control of Satan. They are out to do his bidding and to torment the people of God.

Table P: Kingdom of Darkness Definitions

Satan
   Adversary. Adversary of God, Christ and His people.

devil: serpent, evil one, Beelzebub, Abaddon, Belial
   Accuser. Accuses saints before God. The devil has many different names. These are only a few.

demon
   Evil spirit, unclean spirit.

"de"
   A prefix meaning to distort, deceive, take away from, denude or detract from. (This is just what demons do!)

"mon"
   A suffix meaning an entity, or "one."

daimonizomai (Greek)
   Demon influenced. (This word has been translated as "possessed," but "influenced" or "oppressed," or one of its other synonyms as shown in Table Q on page 210, is better.)

spirit (*pneuma* in the Greek)
   Breath, air or gas. This has connotations of the unseen, the invisible, the hidden.

Now read the definition again and take a moment to think about it. What does it add to your current understanding of the demonic realm? This definition is solidly biblical and has certainly been confirmed in our own experiences in dealing with demons.

The writers of the Bible did not deal directly with the issue of whether or not a believer can be "possessed" or "oppressed." In the Greek, they described people as *daimonizomai*. This is best translated "demon influenced," but "afflicted," "harassed" or "oppressed" are also correct. We could include other strong words such as *tormented, tortured, tried, worried, wronged*. These words are defined in Table Q below. We understand that the literal meaning of *daimonizomai* is "to have a demon in one's possession" with the same connotation as "having a quarter in one's pocket."

Demonic oppression is the term used to represent the pressure exerted by demons to get us to sin, or to keep us bound in limitations. Usually they have an open door to gain access to us. Open doors come from SOFCs, UGBs, SSHs and our own sin, as well as from witchcraft directed toward us.

We usually use the word *oppressed*, as we have for the name of the fourth problem area below, because it avoids the issue of "ownership" and because Acts 10:38 uses this word to summarize the ministry of Jesus.

Table Q: Demonic Oppression Definitions

afflict: to inflict upon one something hard to endure.

harass: to make a raid on.

influence: to affect or alter by indirect or intangible means, to have an effect on the condition or development of.

oppress: to lower in spirit or mood.

torment: to cause severe suffering of body or mind.

torture: to punish or coerce by inflicting excruciating pain.

try: to subject to stress.

worry: to disturb one or destroy one's peace of mind by repeated or persistent torment.

wrong: to inflict injury on another without justification.

Jesus ... went about doing good and healing all who were *oppressed* of the devil, for God was with Him.

Acts 10:38, KJ21, emphasis mine

In her testimony at the beginning of this chapter, Betsy described experiencing some, if not all, of these influences of opposition. People suffering from demonic oppression usually can relate to one or more of these synonyms in some areas of their lives.

As we mentioned in the introduction to this chapter, we agree that Christians cannot be "possessed," or "owned," by demons, since we are "owned" by Jesus Christ:[34]

You were bought at a price. Therefore honor God with your body.

1 Corinthians 6:20, NIV

However, we hope that the above definitions clearly show that we can be *daimonizomai*. We can be demon influenced or demon oppressed.

E. Operation of Demons

Let us now turn our attention to specific information about demons and how they operate. We can use the analogy of a high-fidelity (hi-fi) amplifier. Just as the amplifier takes a weak signal and magnifies it, the demons *sit* upon the places where we (or our ancestors) have given place to sin and they amplify/aggravate whatever weakness is there.

1. Important facts about demons

The Bible provides no description of demons. They are simply assumed, as if it is obvious to the reader what they are.

In Ezekiel 28:12–19, there is a description of Satan's fall. His fall is also mentioned in Revelation 12:3–10, where one third of the angels fall with him. It seems likely that demons are fallen angels; but we do not know for sure.

It is clear, however, that they, like Satan, are created beings. As such, they ultimately are subject to the authority of the Creator.[35] Since God passed His authority on to the Church, we, therefore, as believers, do indeed have authority over the demons, as well. We have authority to "cast them out."

a. Personality

Demons are entities with a personality. They hear, speak, compete with each other and have a will of their own. They are emotional, calculating, strategizing, sadistic, ruthless and proud. They seem to come with different levels of ability and with different strengths and powers.

b. Knowledge

Demons have at least some knowledge. Revelation 9:4 shows that they know the difference between the saved and the unsaved since they can sting those without God's mark (of ownership) on their forehead. The question arises as to whether or not they know our thoughts. The answer seems to be a qualified yes for demons that are on the "inside" of a person, but no for those on the outside.

c. Organization

We know from a number of Scripture passages[36] that Satan's kingdom is highly organized. The demons we usually deal with are probably the low-level peons in the hierarchy, but, nevertheless they are able to be effective in carrying out their master's purpose. The books by Frank Peretti, *This Present Darkness* and its sequel *Piercing the Darkness*,[37] have helped to bring much more awareness and understanding to the Body of Christ of the satanic kingdom.

Demons also seem to have a *region* or *home base* from which they have come and/or are assigned. In one incident, we felt the Holy Spirit impress us to cast out a witchcraft demon from Europe. So we said, "Get out, all you foul witchcraft demons from Europe." Then, speaking through the person, a demon said, "I'm not from Europe; I'm from Haiti." So we cast it out. Then the next one said, "I'm from Jakarta." So we cast it out as well. Finally, the next demon to manifest was the witchcraft demon from Europe. We had to laugh at how their arrogance and pride caused them to betray themselves as we cast out all of them.

d. Purpose

We do know that demons affect people today and that they affected people in Jesus' time. Their first goal is to *prevent someone from receiving salvation*. If that fails, they work at preventing *Christian maturity*. They try to shut us down and make us ineffective. Their chief strategy is *to try to get people to turn away from God*. They do this through many forms of *temptation*, many forms of *harassment* and many forms of challenging our trust of God and His Word.

Demons take after their leader, Satan. John 10:10 states that Satan has come to "steal, kill and destroy," and demons are the instruments through which he does much of his work. In John 8:44, Jesus stated that Satan is a murderer, a liar and the father of liars. Read what He said in a heated conversation with the Jews.

> "Ye are of your father the devil, and the lusts of your father ye will do. He was a murderer from the beginning, and abode not in the truth, because there is no truth in him. When he speaketh a lie, he speaketh of his own, for he is a liar and the father of it."
>
> John 8:44, KJ21

Demons *lie to us* and work hard to have us *lie to ourselves* (self-deception).

Another form of *harassment* is *accusation* and *criticism*. Demons, following their leader, the Accuser, interject many condemning thoughts into the minds of believers. They particularly like to stir up the past with thoughts like *You really should have . . .*, or *If only you had done . . . differently*. It is a comfort to know that the all-time great Accuser is going to come to an end. In Revelation we read:

> And I heard a loud voice saying in Heaven, "Now have come salvation and strength, and the kingdom of our God, and the power of His Christ; for the accuser of our brethren is cast down, who *accused them before our God day and night*. And they overcame him by the blood of the Lamb and by the word of their testimony, and they loved not their lives unto the death."
>
> Revelation 12:10–11, KJ21, emphasis mine

The Bible tells us that we are at war with Satan. In fighting any war, one crucial ingredient is knowing all we can about the nature of our enemy!

2. Demons affect all parts of man: body, soul and spirit

Demons are on a *"seek and destroy"* mission. They work together. They strategize. They take advantage of weaknesses. They love times when people are either physically and/or emotionally weak and vulnerable. In short, demons don't play fair. They endeavor to affect all areas of a person: *body, soul and spirit*. Table R shows us some of the typical ways that they affect us.

Table R: Typical Oppression by Demons

Body
    Appetites (lust, gluttony, sex, clothes, etc.); addictions (pornography, Internet, shopping, overeating, sports, gambling, TV, etc.); illness (cancer, arthritis, epilepsy, asthma, "incurable diseases," etc.); bodily states (sleeplessness, sleepiness, lethargy, pain, nervousness, etc.).

Soul/mind
    Torment (thoughts of accusation, temptation, distraction, terror, insanity, death, etc.); blocked memory; forgetfulness; lethargy; compulsive thoughts; blocked understanding of God's Word, etc.

Soul/will
    Weak will (a will that has no follow through); passivity.

Soul/emotions
    Exaggerated emotional states: fear, anxiety, anger, rage, shame, rejection, grief that is overextended or out of proportion, etc.

Spirit
    Attempted prevention of salvation. Spiritual lethargy, doubt of salvation experience, unbelief. Can affect, harass, prevent maturing, but not take over (in a Christian).

Demons are out to do the same things that their leader does, that is, "to steal, kill and destroy."[38] They do it at every level within the human personality that they can possibly access and through any open door that exists. Such was the case with our friend Sandy.

3. Sandy's story: captured: body, soul and spirit

As Sandy's story continued to unfold during our ministry sessions, it showed the octopus-like grip of the enemy's tentacles woven around every area of her life: *body, soul and spirit.*

Sandy's pastor, himself also a childhood victim of sexual abuse, pleaded with her to fill needs that "only she could fill." Demons of deception obtained such a grip on her *mind* that she was convinced that his lies were truth. She believed that she was doing a "good thing" by helping him feel better about himself. Soon, she thought, he would reach a place of healing and confidence and all the church would benefit from what she had done in secret.

Sandy said that at times she would come to herself and vow never to sleep with him again, but a power seemed to draw her back. Her will was defeated. *Her mind and her will, such key parts of her soul, were no longer ruled by herself,* but by demons of deception, sexual perversion and occult control.

She described her existence in this poem:

> I felt so lonely, Lord,
> And so empty.
> Finally, there was no laughter
> And happiness was a distant memory.
> Everything—even pleasant tasks—
> Became burdensome, loathsome.

Her life was tormented, devoid of joy. Since the enemy doesn't stop with one area, soon Sandy's *spirit* became clouded, like a thick cataract over an eye that longs to see. Though daily she would tell others of God's love for them, she couldn't experience it herself. She was serving water to others while she herself remained desperately thirsty.

Sandy's *body* was not immune to the demonic onslaught. In covering her secret life, she accepted the lie that if she worked harder and longer, she wouldn't feel so guilty. The demons drove her. She stayed at the church far too many hours. Exhaustion merged into numbness.

In addition, there was another strange kind of *physical* deception. For years, Sandy had endured multiple back surgeries, resulting from injuries in a car accident. She lived in constant pain. During the sexual encounters with her pastor, the demons would greatly reduce the pain. She felt enticed, and yet at the same time she felt trapped and defiled.

Sandy despaired of ever getting free, but finally her prayers were answered. Her freedom, however, came at great cost to herself, to the congregation and to her pastor.

Those who have faced the depth of the depravity of the human heart may treasure beyond measure God's merciful forgiveness and deliverance. Here are the remaining stanzas of Sandy's poem which were written near the end of her ministry.

> Now, even the most difficult exercise
> Is touched with ease, with peace.
> Joy is more than just a word.
> Music dances through my heart,
> I have a new song—a song of hope.

You exchange
My death for Your life,
My emptiness for Your fullness,
My darkness for Your light.

Rejoice, O my soul,
And sing praises to the King;
For He has set the captive free
And brought home the destitute.
His promises are true,
His love is authentic,
His mercy and loving-kindness are
From everlasting to everlasting.

I will declare His faithfulness and goodness
And follow after Him with my whole heart.
He alone satisfies the soul!

Sandy

God was setting Sandy free: *body, soul and spirit.* We will have more of Sandy's story later.

4. How demons enter: open doors

Since demons are such bullies, one might ask, "Do demons randomly pick on people, like the random checking done by the IRS on income-tax returns?" While demons do target people (particularly those who are serious about serving God and who are advancing the Kingdom of God), there are some very specific "open doors" by which demons frequently *gain entrance* into a person's life. Genesis 4:7 recounts what the Lord said to Cain after he expressed anger because his brother's offering was preferred:

> "If you do not do well, *sin is crouching at the door;* and *its desire is for you, but you must master it.*"
>
> Genesis 4:7, NASB, emphasis mine

In general, it is our opening of the door that allows sin (and the accompanying demons) to come in. The exception to this statement are the demons that come with our "inheritance"—those who have already entered while we were helpless in the womb. No one is immune unless our parents and/or other relatives knew to protect us with prayer and spiritual warfare.

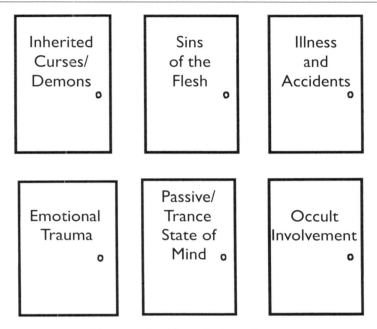

Figure 4: *Open Doors for Demonic Entry*

Let's look in some detail at six common doors through which demons enter. Figure 4 above illustrates these doors.

a. Inherited curses and accompanying demons

Some demons apparently come down the family line. They often manifest soon after birth. We suspect that they are present even as the child is being formed. This seems particularly true of demons of fear, rejection, rebellion, anger, rage, shame, sexual perversion, control and abandonment. They are able to enter at this early age because of the "legal ground" from sins of the fathers (and mothers). Because of the curses resulting from the generational sin, or because of others cursing the family line, the demons are able to pass from generation to generation to carry out the curses. The cycle continues as the demons put *pressure* on the person to *enter into* the same sins as his ancestors. As he yields to that pressure, the sin becomes his own, and he gives legal rights for the demonic oppression.

Another form of "inheritance" occurs when one or more of our ancestors have dedicated or committed their descendants to their particular god or occult guild, i.e., witchcraft or freemasonry. Here the demons claim "ownership" right from the womb and will do all within their power to prevent the person from hearing or understanding the Gospel.[39] This can be particularly severe if bloody oaths and/or sacrifices have been made. The good news is that the blood of Jesus overrides and neutralizes any other blood that has ever been shed. As a result, even people with major open doors of occult sin in their family line have the hope of freedom and healing.

In 2 Samuel we read of the example of David cursing Joab and his entire family line because Joab deceptively killed Abner after David had entered into an agreement with him. This was the *starting point*, or *entry point*, where demons were given legal right to enter a family and carry out the spoken curses. This curse, and its accompanying demons, will continue to move relentlessly down through the generations until it is finally broken and the demons are cast out.

> Now when Abner returned to Hebron, Joab took him aside into the gateway, as though to speak with him privately. And there, to avenge the blood of his brother Asahel, Joab stabbed him in the stomach, and he died. Later, when David heard about this, he said, "I and my kingdom are forever innocent before the LORD concerning the blood of Abner son of Ner. *May his blood fall upon the head of Joab and upon all his father's house! May Joab's house never be without someone who has a running sore or leprosy or who leans on a crutch or who falls by the sword or who lacks food.*"
>
> 2 Samuel 3:27–29, NIV, emphasis mine

b. Sins of the flesh

By far, sins of the flesh are the *door that we most frequently open* to invite the enemy in to destroy us. This is especially true when the sin is repeated and becomes a pattern, leading to a lifestyle of indulging the flesh. Sin does not have to be "exotic" to provide an opening for demons. The "garden-variety" sin will do the job just fine as far as the demons are concerned. Weakness of the flesh and demons *colabor together* to keep a vicious cycle going. We sin, then the demons enter and help influence us to continue to sin in the same way. They usually work by putting persistent, deceptive thoughts into our minds. "The devil made me do it, *but* my flesh sure helped him out!"

The following list contains some very common areas in which we indulge our carnal appetites.

1. **Anger:** We give ourselves permission to vent our anger on others.[40] Anger can lead to violence, adding to the legal ground.

2. **Fear**: The Bible says "fear not."[41] Fear and worry often lead to sinful ways of coping. Since there are as many types of fear as there are possible ways to be injured or killed, there are many opportunities for demonic entry.

3. **Greed/covetousness**: We are told not to covet, and we are warned about the severe consequences if we do.[42]

4. **Jealousy/envy**: Envy is rottenness to the bones. It will make us sick.[43] James speaks of lusting to envy.[44] Lust and envy can work together.

5. **Rebellion**: Ephesians speaks of walking in disobedience (rebellion).[45] First Samuel states that rebellion is "as the sin of witchcraft," abhorrent to God.[46]

6. **Pride**: This, the original sin of Satan, leads to many wrong actions. It is often the sin most hidden from us. Important Scriptures about pride are: 1 John 2:16, 1 Timothy 3:6–7, Isaiah 14:12–17 and Ezekiel 28:12–19.

7. **Lust**: Satan tries to arouse us to lust. His strategies are subtle. Samson provides us with a sad example: "Get her for me, for she pleaseth me well."[47]

8. **Gluttony**: *Aim* magazine reported that as much as 73 percent of the American population is overweight.[48] This is a serious national health problem. (Note: We must be careful, however, not to be judgmental in this area since there are *many reasons* for weight problems.)

9. **Gossip**: This sin gives Satan rich opportunity to work.[49]

10. **Strife**: James states that where there is envying and strife, there is confusion and every evil work.[50] God hates those who sow strife/discord.[51]

11. **Bitterness**: In the book of Hebrews, God commands us to allow no root of bitterness in our lives.[52]

12. **Self-righteousness**: "I am right and everyone else is wrong." This sin distances us from others in the Church, as well as from God.

13. **Criticizing, blaming, judging**: In this sin, we often hold up our own lives as the standard of rightness. Others are put down or seen as the cause/reason for everything being wrong.

14. **Unforgiveness**: God makes it very clear that forgiveness is an absolute requirement for freedom. The story of the unjust servant shows that if we do not forgive, God allows the tormentors (demons included) access to us.[53]

It's sobering to realize that any of these "ordinary" sins may provide an entrance for Satan's demons.

c. Illness and accidents

Illness provides an opportunity for demons to enter. In these two forms of physical trauma—illness and accidents—defenses are lowered, the will is weakened, and the ability to pray for oneself is lessened. As previously pointed out, demons love to take advantage of our vulnerability and to kick us while we are down. With illness, we have the added liability of medical drug use. We have personally cast out many demons by the names of different drugs—even simple over-the-counter drugs such as *aspirin*—and seen amazing results. *Anything* that we are in bondage to is a potential open door for demonic oppression.

In accidents, during the time of shock and trauma, demons take advantage of our weakened defenses to "swarm" into our soul realm. Demons of "shock," "trauma," "depression," "accident," etc., will move right in, ignoring the fact that "it isn't fair." They sometimes are able to set up additional accidents, starting a cycle of "accident proneness."

d. Emotional trauma

Emotional trauma is another common, yet unrealized, potential open door. A traumatic emotional or physical experience fractures the defenses that normally keep demons out. Many of us experience, at one time or another in our lives, the emotional trauma of loss. Common examples are the breakup of a relationship, divorce, unexpected death, job loss and abuse. Other more severe forms of emotional and physical trauma include violence, rape and ritual sexual abuse.

When any of these occur in our childhood, it can lead to fractured or multiple personalities as part of our "coping" mechanism for survival. Any or all of these personalities may also be oppressed by demons. This can complicate the job of ministering to these people considerably, as the minister needs the wisdom of the Holy Spirit to discern when he is dealing with a part of the personality and when it is a demonic entity.[54]

e. Passive or trance state of mind

Under normal circumstances, the mind has a protective wall around it, provided by the will—which is man's ability to say no to what is wrong and yes to what is right. When one gives up his will in a passive or trance state of mind, the door is opened for demons to invade. The person may become partially or even completely controlled by the demonic.[55]

There are three main ways that we allow our minds to enter the passive state that makes us so vulnerable to demons:

- **Trances**: when the mind is neutral, open and unguarded (i.e., hypnosis).

- **Induced mental states**: voluntarily letting go, usually through drugs, chants, music (rock and roll), meditation (yoga or TM [mantra]), watching TV (yes, this can produce a trance).

- **Anesthesia**: when used during operations.

The experience of being anesthetized—though different from either self-induced passivity or a trance state—is similar in that it leaves the mind unguarded. In reality, it is a "drug-induced" passivity or trance. We expect that much of the depression following surgery is caused by demonic oppression. Betsy experienced a severe depression following surgery in 1983. This ended dramatically as a result of deliverance. When our minds are passive because of anesthesia, a strong prayer covering can be very helpful, if not essential.

f. Occult involvement

The last open door through which demons enter that we want to discuss is the occult area. Occult involvement is the major form of idolatry.[56] The word *occult* means "hidden." Occult involvement means looking for knowledge and/or power in "hidden" sources, sources other than the true and living God. This eventually leads to allegiance to or worship of those other sources.

Participation in occult activities amounts to rebellion against God. It is frequently driven by a *lust for power* through knowledge and control.

Occult involvement, like drug use or sexual sin, *is progressive*. It takes more and more to be satisfied. People start out with something mild, such as astrology, and progress to something more serious and eventually end up in witchcraft. This level of involvement puts a person into contact with demons.

Biblical Healing and Deliverance

Demons can enter even when we dabble in the occult areas in *ignorance*. Unfortunately, ignorance of the law is no excuse. Some of these activities are relatively minor and are done as "harmless fun." Yet, if an ancestral sin or curse is in operation, it takes very little "harmless fun," particularly in the occult area, to provide an opportunity for demon entry.

God hates the occult. This is clear through many Scriptures, in which God strictly forbids the following activities.

Deuteronomy 4:19—Astrology and worshiping the stars

Deuteronomy 18:10–12—Many things detestable (an abomination) to the Lord are listed, such as sacrificing one's children, practicing divination, sorcery, interpreting omens, witchcraft, casting spells, mediumship or consulting the dead.

Leviticus 20:2–5—Sacrificing children to false gods

Leviticus 20:6—Consulting familiar spirits (mediums, witches and wizards)

Leviticus 20:27—Being a medium, witch or wizard

Galatians 5:20—Paul lists the occult among the works of the flesh: idolatry, witchcraft.

Revelation 21:8—Occult practitioners (sorcerers and idolaters) are headed for the lake of fire.

The demons of occult power are unusually strong when people have been involved in occult activities, or when the person is a generational "focus" for witchcraft or occult sin done in past generations. These demons can bring a wide variety of demonic gifts and oppressions. ESP gifts and psychic powers provided by these demons are frequently seen in these people. It is important that the person renounce all desire for psychic (demonic) gifts and abilities and affirm that he wants only the giftings of the Holy Spirit to operate through him.

In addition to "special giftings" in a person, we can identify the presence of occult influence if the person has *several* of the following: *accident proneness* or *illness, sexual sins, strong fears* and/or *strong control*.

As we mentioned earlier in the inherited curses section, one frequently observed entry point for demons occurs when a person's *ancestors dedicate their descendants* to their particular god. We have seen this repeatedly with occult and/or secret organizations, such as the Mason's bloody oaths, Indian ancestor dedications and witchcraft.

We use an Ancestral Open Doors form (on page 273) to provide the ministry receiver an opportunity to list all occult activities in which he or his ancestors have participated. Often, a prospective ministry receiver will begin to do some family research as he prepares for ministry, and in the process he will find some very significant information. During the ministry session, the Holy Spirit also will show occult activities and other open doors of which the ministry receiver and RTF ministers have no previous knowledge.

Note

Reading occult books does not automatically produce demonization, but unless the Holy Spirit directs you to absorb this kind of literature for the purpose of advancing the Kingdom of God, you are taking a risk. Studying occult material does begin to produce a mindset (a set of ungodly beliefs) that makes one more and more prone to be drawn into the occult/demonic. Unless it is a part of the ministry into which God has called you, we suggest that you remain ignorant in this area.[57]

---

g. Summary

While the six doors of demonic entry we have just discussed are not the only ways that demons infiltrate our personhood, they do appear to be the major ways. It is important to be aware of them as we each become better equipped to minister to the Body of Christ.

Exercise

Think about the six doors of entry we have just discussed and whether one or more may be in operation in your life. Also, pray and ask the Holy Spirit to reveal to you any open doors that you are not aware of, either in your own life or in the lives of your ancestors. We suggest that you jot down some notes so that when we come to the ministry steps section, you can either do some self-deliverance and/or enlist the help of a mature Christian.

---

5. Test your understanding

As ministers, when we hear descriptions of these open doors in a ministry receiver's life, we want to check out whether the doors have been used for *demonic entry* and *influence*. So, to help you practice your increased knowledge and understanding of this important subject, consider the following situations to determine whether or not demonic activity may be involved.

a. Situation 1

David, a man in his early thirties, moved away from his lover, whose life was becoming more erratic and more eccentric. He found out later that she had gotten a frightening message from her Ouija board about their future together, and she had basically given up on him. The following year, David was led to salvation by a street evangelist and shortly thereafter married a Christian girl. Over the next five-year period, David, whose job involved much travel, was in three rear-end collisions. One required extensive hospitalization and follow-up chiropractic treatment. He came to us as he was trying to decide whether or not to take a job with less travel. "My life just seems to be jinxed," he said.

- Is demonic activity indicated?
  . . . .
- If your answer was yes, what was the probable door of entrance?
  . . . .
- Is David's problem primarily a problem of his undisciplined flesh?
  . . . .
- Is this a case in which both flesh and demons may be involved?
  . . . .
- Is there enough information to determine a clear answer?
  . . . .

b. Situation 2

Sam and Jenny were having marital difficulties. Both had grown up in single-parent families and had been given much responsibility early in life. They both liked things to be neat and orderly. The trouble was that they both had their own definition of what "neat and orderly" was, and each wanted things their own way. They both felt more in control when they were "running the show." Sometimes what started as a simple conversation erupted into violence when they disagreed and ended with Jenny throwing kitchen utensils and Sam pushing her against the wall. A friend jokingly said he was going to report them to the police if they didn't learn to calm down.

- Is demonic activity indicated?

  ....

- If your answer was yes, what was the probable door of entrance?

  ....

- Is Sam and Jenny's problem primarily a problem of their undisciplined flesh?

  ....

- Is this a case in which both flesh and demons may be involved?

  ....

- Is there enough information to determine a clear answer?

  ....

c. Situation 3

The Browns lived with Mr. Brown's father, a melancholy man who had lost everything in the Depression. Though he had been able to start a business again and make a go of it, somehow he had never been able to relax or enjoy his work. The Browns also had been through years of tumult, with their little upholstery business humming along some years, and then barely making it others. "I guess we are just doomed not to get ahead," Mr. Brown said after looking at their accounts. They didn't really mind not having a lot, but what really puzzled them was that their son, who had been the valedictorian of his high-school class, was having one business failure after another.

- Is demonic activity indicated?

  ....

- If your answer was yes, what was the probable door of entrance?

  ....

- Is Mr. Brown's problem primarily a problem of his undisciplined flesh?

  ....

- Is this a case in which both flesh and demons may be involved?

  ....

- Is there enough information to determine a clear answer?

  ....

As we listen to our ministry receiver's life story, we as ministers want to begin to learn to "tune in" to possible open doors to demonic oppression. As we practice listening to them and to the Holy Spirit, our spiritual discernment will increase.[58]

6. Behavioral indicators of demonic operation

As a child, did you ever go on a treasure hunt in which you had *clues* to follow in order to find the treasure? Well, many demons leave "clues" in the form of behavioral manifestations, which are an easy giveaway if you know how to recognize them. This section should help you become a "demon detector," as well as helping you learn to use the wonderful gift of discernment. This list of behavioral indicators was originally developed by Ernest Rockstad.[59] We have confirmed and expanded it here. Table S on page 227 shows the listing (a "Who's Who" in the demonic-manifestation world). Following is a discussion of some of the less obvious items.

a. Incapacity for normal living
This symptom manifests in a variety of ways. Some examples are:

- The *inability to feel joy* or satisfaction in life. A person experiences ongoing feelings of confusion, heaviness or depression, similar to dragging an anchor. This occurs at times when there is no particular external situation causing stress.

- *Agitation at gospel meetings* that keep one from truly entering in or from receiving the message. Demonic strategy can often be seen in causing restlessness, irritation, sleepiness or even physical attacks or coughing, especially as the main truths of the Gospel are being read or preached.

- In the *yo-yo effect*, a person goes from *one extreme to another*. For example, he is not happy in a crowd and not happy alone. He may yo-yo between exuberance and depression, between being very disciplined and undisciplined, between having much sexual passion and being frigid.

b. Extreme bondage to sin
The person is *unable to stop the sin* even when trying very hard. He becomes hopeless and defeated. This is the case in some besetting sin.[60] Examples might include a person who can't stop abusing his own children, can't stop temper tantrums, can't stop shoplifting, can't stop involvement with pornography, etc.

c. Deception about normal personality
Demons masquerade as part of our personality. They hide within our personhood. The person thinks, *This is just the way I am. This is part of*

Table 5: Behavioral Indicators of Demonic Oppression

- Incapacity for normal living
- Extreme bondage to sin
- Deception about normal personality
- Abnormal emotions
- Breakdown of marriage and family
- Tragic happenings and accident proneness
- Financial insufficiency
- Inner anguish
- Restlessness and/or insomnia
- Abnormal sex life
- Trances
- Violence, super-human strength
- Demonic torment
- Self-inflicted injury
- Functional sickness
- Unidentified foul odors
- Rapidly changing personality

---

my personality or a normal *part of my family characteristics.* (The Smiths have always been hot tempered; the women in this family have always been bossy, controlling, etc.) When the demons are cast out, the person frequently experiences a transitional time of loss and instability as he becomes familiar with his real personality.

d. Abnormal emotions
Demons can cause a person's emotions to become exaggerated, intense, out of control or all-consuming. This is particularly true with fear, anger, jealousy, grief, shame, resentment and unforgiveness. Betsy's past fear of death is an example.

e. Breakdown of marriage and family
We believe demons are at work in the breakdown of family life and, in many cases, of divorce. We know some people whose control demons continually battle each other.

f. Tragic happenings and accident proneness
There are individuals and families in which tragic happenings and accidents occur on a frequent and ongoing basis.

g. Financial insufficiency

Demonic infestation is particularly indicated in situations where there is an adequate supply of income and there "should be enough," but there isn't.

h. Inner anguish

This anguish takes many forms, such as pressure on the inside, turmoil, depression, despair, mental lapses and the inability to concentrate. The anguish exists even when there are no obvious pressures from the external environment.

i. Restlessness and/or insomnia

One strategy demons use is: "Let's wear him out." Demons may be present when a person can't slow down. He will overexert himself and then go to bed and not be able to sleep.

j. Abnormal sex life

Demons may cause a person to have abnormal sexual patterns, demanding too much or not wanting any. They can also cause spouses to have the opposite desires.

k. Trances

A person may be demonized if he goes into a trance-like state even when there is no apparent reason, i.e., hypnosis. The mediumistic trance is the ultimate form of demonization—a state in which the demon is in complete control and the person has willed to yield totally to his "spirit guide."

l. Violence, superhuman strength

Demons can cause people to have super-human strength. We have the scriptural example of the Gerasene demoniac[61] who could not be bound.

m. Demonic torment

Examples of demonic torment include people having doors slam when there is no wind, having their bed lift a foot or more off of the floor, hearing voices when there is no one present or even having the lights go on or off by themselves. People with sexual perversion or occult involvement in their family lines may experience being sexually violated by demons.

n. Self-inflicted injury

Demons, like their leader, are working to kill us. If they can cause a person to harm himself, they are accomplishing their mission. Scratching one's arms, cutting and other forms of mutilation are signs of demonic mental anguish and pain. Both suicidal fantasies and suicidal attempts can be caused by demons.

o. Functional sickness

Functional sickness includes pain or sickness at inopportune times (such as at church or in ministry sessions) and undefined pains that move around the body. It seems very likely that demons are involved with many, if not all, of the "incurable" illnesses, such as MS, cancer, AIDS, arthritis, ringing in the ears, etc. They may not always be the root cause, but they certainly make the illness worse.

p. Unidentified foul odors

On rare occasions, people will emit a strong, unpleasant odor which has no physical cause. One possibility is that the source of the odor is a demon. Occasionally, we have experienced a brief, intense stench during deliverance. This may be the smell of a demon that is leaving.

q. Rapidly changing personality

Sometimes very rapid changes of personality occur for no external reason. Demonic oppression is one possible cause. (Chemical and hormonal imbalances and multiple personalities are other possible causes.)

This is a long, but important, list of behavioral indicators which we learn to observe as we grow in our ability to recognize demonic oppression and the resulting manifestations.

7. Demonic oppression groupings

Like many other people involved in deliverance, we have benefited from the early work of Frank and Ida Mae Hammond.[62] Over the years, we have adapted their "groupings" list to match what we were finding with the people coming to us for ministry. This list will be different with each group of people, i.e., different in different churches because of the principalities that have "place" over each church. We have provided a list of ancestral open doors groupings in the appendix that you may use as a starting point for deliverance.

8. Demonic interconnectedness

We can take the demonic grouping concept a step farther and construct a simplified diagram showing the interconnectedness, mutual support and protection that the various demonic groupings provide for each other. While it is true that demons are very competitive, cutthroat and ruthless, they will work together in their mission to destroy the person they inhabit.

Figure 5 below shows an example diagram that applies to a particular individual with abandonment as the root/foundational problem in his life. (Remember, we are trying to show the main functions, not all of the detail that is actually present.) During the ministry, we observed that abandonment interconnected to and supported shame, fear and rejection/rebellion. Shame also fed into fear, which gave place to control and the victim groupings.[63] Anger and violence came out of the victim, fear and control groupings. The occult both drew from the rest of the demonic groupings and fed power and support into every other grouping through the control grouping. In actuality, the occult probably interconnected into every other grouping directly, but the control group was its main partner in oppressing the person. With this diagram, we had a better grasp of how to do the deliverance for this person, i.e., in what order we should attack and disassemble the demonic groupings.

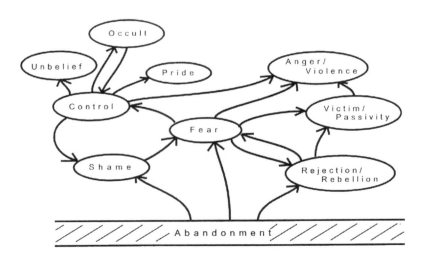

Figure 5: *Demonic Grouping Interconnectedness and Support Diagram*

Sometimes the Holy Spirit directs us to start at the outer fringes of the demonic oppression. Then we work through the "weak" groupings first and move toward the root grouping(s) last. In this approach, we are undercutting the support from the "mutual-aid society" that the demonic groupings provide for each other. As we approach the final groupings, even though they are strong in themselves, they have lost the support of the other groupings and are more easily removed.

Other times the Holy Spirit directs us to "go for the jugular," and we penetrate into the center of the enemy's camp and cast out the foundational demonic grouping(s) first. We usually have to command a separation of the groupings in this case by isolating the main ones from each other. Then we pick off these "strong men," casting them and their associated demons out. This is followed by moving out to the weaker and weaker groups. The diagram helps us understand how to separate groupings and move from one group to the next as we demolish the demonic strongholds within the person.

Some of you may be asking, "Where do these diagrams come from?" Well, they come partly from experience, but mostly from praying through the notes taken throughout the ministry sessions. We ask the Holy Spirit to show us the structure of the enemies' camp, i.e., how all of the different parts are connected. The components of the structure have been assembled from the sins of the fathers and the resulting curses, and from the place(s) given by the ungodly beliefs and soul/spirit hurts. Then, as the Holy Spirit shows us, we sketch the diagram. We try not to have too much detail but just the right amount. Then we can see how the major demon groupings are cooperating so as not to lose their "house," keep the person captive and carry out their work of "stealing, killing, and destroying."[64]

F. Background Information for Deliverance

Here is some significant background information we need to understand before we minister deliverance.

1. Deliverance in the integrated approach context

Doing deliverance in the context of the Restoring the Foundations integrated approach to biblical healing ministry has tremendous advantages that make the deliverance process so much simpler. Because trust has already been built, repentance and forgiveness largely completed, curses broken, hurts healed and ungodly beliefs dealt with, much, if not all, of the legal ground has been cleared before we move into deliverance. Although demons may try to resist, there is usually little or no legal ground left for them to stand on.

2. Commanding

The minister's attitude is one of commanding. He needs to be firm and prepared to press in. He does not need to be loud. (Demons are not deaf.) The ministers' commanding attitude resembles that of a person speaking to a little "yappy" dog, commanding him to go home and stop barking. We also want the ministry receiver to set his will to resist and then command the particular demon or grouping of demons to leave him, in Jesus' name. This is repeated until the demons are gone.

3. Affirming

It is usually good to have the ministry receiver affirm that he is serving God, that all of him belongs to Jesus Christ and that he is a child of the living God. He is no longer in the kingdom of darkness but is in the Kingdom of light.[65] The prayer of submission at the end of this chapter contains these elements.

4. Equipping

During the initial phase of the deliverance, we take the lead and guide the ministry receiver through the ministry steps. This way, he learns what to do while we are dealing with the stronger demonic groupings. Then we gradually shift the lead over to the person as we move more into a supporting role. This helps him learn to do self-deliverance, an "equipping" that he will use for the rest of his life.

5. Dealing with manifestations

We have full authority to allow or not allow the demons to manifest as they are leaving.[66] We usually allow manifestations because they help the ministry receiver accept the reality of demons and their oppression. Manifestations also clearly show Christ's victory over the forces of darkness and the authority that Jesus has given to us, His Church. On the other hand, we command the demons to stop the manifestations if they become excessive, harmful or distracting to the person.

6. Sending demons to Jesus

We are frequently asked what to do with the demons after we cast them out. Scripture is not specific about this issue; however, we have been given a hint in Luke.

> And they besought Him that He would not command them to go out into the deep [abyss].
>
> Luke 8:31, KJ21

Our suggestion is simply to say, "I command you to go to where Jesus sends you." This is scripturally safe. However, as we sought the Lord about this issue, we felt He was saying He does indeed "send them to the abyss," which is the same as the "outer darkness" and "dry places."

7. Preventing demons from returning

Jesus, our model, told the epileptic demon never to come back:

> Jesus . . . rebuked the evil spirit. "You deaf and mute spirit," he said, "I command you, come out of him and never enter him again."
>
> Mark 9:25, NIV

By forbidding the demons to return and turning them over to Jesus to go wherever He sends them, the demons being cast out of the person are essentially removed from our planet. Thus, their ability to oppress the ministry receiver, or anyone else for that matter, comes to an end.

However, plenty of other demons of "like nature" (i.e., having the same function, such as anger) are waiting in the wings ready to tempt the delivered person as they strive to find a home. If the recently delivered ministry receiver yields to the temptation, the door may be reopened. The "replacement" demons can then set up housekeeping, drawing the person back into bondage.[67] So while we need not fear the "previous" demons reentering, we do want to warn our ministry receiver to be on the alert against counterattacks from replacement demons trying to infiltrate.

G. What to Do with Obstinate Demons

When eviction day arrives, the demons are not excited. Their bags are not packed and they have not bought their airline tickets in advance. Rather, they will do everything within their power to hinder and block their departure. They will continue to resist right up to the very last moment.[68] They may claim "squatters' rights," saying, "I have been here a long time, and I don't have to leave." They may say, "He [the ministry receiver] doesn't want us to leave." They may even have a group meeting and strategize how to interfere, confuse, sidetrack and even prevent the deliverance. Sometimes the "strongman" will force the weaker demons to be "sacrificed," hoping that the ministers will think that they have evicted the "big guy," who will actually attempt to remain in hiding and not be cast out. This is why we need the gifts of the Holy Spirit in operation so we are not deceived.

This section centers around what to do when you meet the enemy face to face and he says, "I'm not leaving." In principle we could "force" him to leave because of the authority given to us by God. In practice, however, the ministry receiver is usually (unknowingly) giving "legal ground" to the demon(s). Thus, rather than fighting against the demon (and the receiver), it is much better to take care of the "legalities." Then we can easily cast the demon out and a replacement demon of "like nature" won't be able to find an open door for reentry.

1. Blocking demons

Sometimes deliverance resembles an old West *log jam.* As the logs came down the river, maybe first one and then another would get stuck and cause other logs to begin to pile up around them. These might block other logs, until the entire flow of logs was brought to a stop. The loggers, using long poles, would poke and prod and pry to find the "key" log. When the key log was loosed and set free, the entire jam would release and move on down the river. Getting demons out can be very similar to breaking up a log jam, particularly when we are dealing with a demonic stronghold.[69] Like the loggers, we poke around, prying a little here, pushing a little there, following the leading of the Holy Spirit as we recover legal ground. When we get things loosened up, and we find and remove the "key" log (the strongman demon), the remaining demons generally leave quite easily.

At other times, the enemy may have a definite plan to stop the deliverance process. His tactics, however, are all doomed to failure since the victory has already been won. All we have to do is to follow the Holy Spirit's leading to remove the various obstacles that the demons erect until all blocks are gone.

a. Mental-blocking demons

Mental-blocking demons strategize to prevent deliverance of other demons. They whisper messages to the person's mind such as: *Demons are not real. This is an outdated concept. My problems are really psychological.* They may say, *This is not going to work. It works for other people, but it is not going to work for me.* They have even been known to say, "I'm not here," as the deliverance minister called their names. These demons work to affect the person's belief system and, thus, his will. The most common blocking demons are *doubt, unbelief, skepticism, rationalism* and *pride*. Pride, of course, attempts to keep the person from admitting that he could "have" such a thing as a demon.

This demonic strategy needs to be met with a strong biblical offensive. Share Scriptures about demons, illustrations of Jesus doing deliverance and stories of deliverance in your experience. Also specifically bind the blocking demons, or proceed with their deliverance. Go through the usual forgiveness, renouncing and casting-out process. Forgiveness, in this case, includes having the ministry receiver ask forgiveness for giving place to the blocking demons and agreeing with their lies.

b. Other commonly occurring blocking demons

Many other types of blocking demons exist, but these are the more common ones:

- **Fear** demons may try to block through threats. They may say, "I'll kill you" or "I'll kill your family" or "You can't make it without me."

- **Control** demons try all sorts of tactics and will do anything to stay in control and not have to come out. They may have the ministry receiver talk incessantly and/or change the subject away from deliverance. The minister must stay alert and retain "legitimate" control.

- **Passivity** demons try to keep the ministry receiver from exerting his will and choosing to get rid of his (passivity) demons.

- **Pain and distraction** demons cause various kinds of pains and distractions. These pains can move rapidly from one part of the body to another.

We bind all these blocking, hindering and distracting demons. The ministry receiver is often not even aware that he is being demonically influenced. We tell him to stay in control and explain that Jesus gives him power to resist. If necessary, we have him begin to quote Scripture verses about the defeat of Satan and his demons. (We will have more about this later.)

c. Remaining legalities

Sometimes certain legalities have not yet come to our attention. Demons may claim these as justification for remaining. Thus, they are effectively "blocking demons." These legalities usually fall into the following categories.

Unconfessed "secret" sin and/or vow
In the ministry receiver's mind, shame magnifies the past sin into the "untellable," unpardonable deed. Sexual sins particularly fall into this category. Sometimes a long-forgotten vow, brought to light by the Holy Spirit, will need to be nullified.

Open doors from generational sin
It is common for the ministry receiver to have a specific ancestral sin that a demon is using for legal ground. Here we need the Holy Spirit's revelation gifts to show us what the legal ground is and how to minister so that the demon(s) lose all "rights."

Occult/witchcraft
Open doors from past, generational sins frequently reside in the occult/witchcraft areas. Sin in these areas seems to particularly empower curses to propagate down the family line, as well as strengthening other demons and strongholds. These curses, however, are broken by confession and the power of the cross as readily as curses from any other source.

Agreement
Every ungodly belief is a potential agreement with the forces of darkness that provides legal ground for demonic oppression. The most severe agreement is the identity UGB, that is, a belief about who I am as a person. Examples might be, *I am an angry person, I am ashamed* or *I am depressed*. Notice the "I am" identity phrase. This type of identity agreement is generally hidden from us because it is buried so deeply within our personhood. While it is expected that we will have normal human emotions of anger, shame or depression, an identity UGB may give place to demons that magnify and manifest anger, shame or depression. When we provide this legal ground to

demons, they won't leave until we exert our free will and cancel (renounce) the agreement on the basis of the cross and the lordship of Jesus Christ. Of course, any needed forgiveness should also be accomplished.

Since God doesn't violate our free will, we, likewise, cannot override the free will of our ministry receiver. However, our job is to help him become aware of the lies (UGBs) he has believed about who he is. The demons, of course, don't want to lose their place and so they try to prevent the person from becoming aware of his identity UGBs. If he does become aware, the demons try to fool him into believing that he and the demonic stronghold are the same. They deny that a "false" identity is at work as well as the real one. It often takes time for the person to become aware of the deception and to become hopeful of being freed from the old, destructive patterns. He must become determined to be free from the false demonic identity.

In the Old Testament, God expressly forbade agreements (covenants) with the Canaanite inhabitants of the land. Joshua and the Israelites, however, formed a covenant with the Gibeonites.[70] Although it was done through deception and without the Israelites "asking counsel at the mouth of the Lord," God expected the Israelites to honor their commitment. In fact, it was Saul's breaking of this covenant that provided the final straw and lost him his kingship.[71] We are truly blessed that our covenant with Jesus Christ can be used to override and cancel all agreements with the demonic "inhabitants" of our land. We need to apply this covenant and remove all false identity demons.

2. What demons hate

Demons hate many things. At the top of their list are God, His Word and humans. We can make use of this when we are casting them out. We can "stir them up" with things they hate, forcing them out of hiding and maybe even pressuring them to leave.

Demons really hate Bible Scriptures like the ones in Table T (see pages 238–239). Read these out loud to magnify God and minimize Satan. Taunt the demons with Scriptures about the fall and the defeat of Satan. They will reveal themselves as they cry out in defense of Satan and their position in his kingdom. Reading these Scriptures to the demons (and to the ministry receiver and ministers) during deliverance is guaranteed to bring *good* results.

We encourage you to read through these Scriptures for yourself. Let the *truth* of God expressed in these verses penetrate your heart. These

Table T: Scriptures That Demons Hate

1 John 3:8
"For this *purpose* the Son of God was manifested, that He *might destroy* the works of the devil" (KJ21, emphasis mine).

Acts 10:38
"*God anointed* Jesus of Nazareth with the Holy Ghost and with power, and . . . He went about *doing good* and *healing all* who were *oppressed* by the devil, for God was with Him" (KJ21, emphasis mine).

Colossians 2:13–15
"God made you *alive* with Christ. He forgave us all our sins [NIV, emphasis mine] . . . having *canceled out the certificate of debt* consisting of decrees against us, *which was hostile to us*; and He has taken it out of the way, having *nailed it to the cross*. When He had *disarmed the rulers and authorities*, He made a public display of them, having *triumphed over them* through Him [by the cross]" (NASB, emphasis mine).

Hebrews 2:14–15
"He also Himself likewise took part of the same [flesh], that *through death* He *might destroy him that had the power of death*—that is, *the devil*—and *deliver those* who all their lifetime were *subject to bondage* through *fear of death*" (KJ21, emphasis mine).

Luke 10:18–19
"I beheld *Satan as lightning fall from heaven*. Behold, I give unto you *power to tread on serpents and scorpions* and *over all the power of the enemy*, and *nothing shall by any means hurt you*" (KJ21, emphasis mine).

Luke 11:20
"But if I with the *finger of God cast out devils*, doubt not the *Kingdom of God is come upon you*" (KJ21, emphasis mine).

Mark 16:17
"And these signs shall *follow them that believe: In My name* shall they *cast out devils.*" (KJ21, emphasis mine).

Isaiah 14:12–17
"How art *thou fallen from heaven*, O *Lucifer*, son of the morning! How art *thou cut down to the ground* . . . For *thou hast said in thine heart, 'I will ascend* into heaven, *I will exalt* my throne above the stars of God; *I will sit* also upon the mount of the congregation, in the sides of the north. *I will ascend* above the heights of the clouds *I will be like the Most High.'* Yet *thou shalt be brought down to hell*, to the sides of the pit. They that see thee shall narrowly look upon thee and consider thee, saying, *'Is this the man that made the earth to tremble, that did shake kingdoms, that made the world as a wilderness* and *destroyed the cities thereof, that opened not the house of his prisoners?'* " (KJ21, emphasis mine).

Table T: Scriptures That Demons Hate (*cont.*)

Ezekiel 28:17–19
"Your heart became proud on account of your beauty, and *you corrupted your wisdom* because of your splendor. So I *threw you to the earth; I made a spectacle* of you before kings. By your many sins and dishonest trade you have desecrated your sanctuaries. So I made a fire come out from you, and it consumed you, and I reduced you to ashes on the ground in the sight of all who were watching. All the nations who knew you are appalled at you; *you have come to a horrible end and will be no more"* (NIV, emphasis mine).

Revelation 12:10–11
"Now have come salvation and strength, and the Kingdom of our God, and the power of His Christ; for the *accuser of our brethren is cast down,* who accused them before our God day and night. And *they overcame him by the blood of the Lamb* and *by the word of their testimony*, and *they loved not their lives unto the death"* (KJ21, emphasis mine).

Revelation 20:9–10
"And fire came down from God out of heaven, and devoured them. And *the devil* who had deceived them *was cast into the lake of fire and brimstone"* (KJ21, emphasis mine).

---

are *godly beliefs* that will set you free from fear and concern about the devil and enable you to minister freedom to others.

Please particularly note the last phrase of Isaiah 14:17 (in the table). The Scripture contends that Lucifer (the devil) would open "not the house of his prisoners." When we cast out demons, we are *forcefully* going into the prisons of the kingdom of darkness and *forcefully* opening the house of Satan's prisoners and setting them free. It is good work. It is what Jesus said would be happening.

> "From the days of John the Baptist until now, the kingdom of heaven has been forcefully advancing, and forceful men lay hold of it."
> Matthew 11:12, NIV, emphasis mine

Demons also hate praise and worship of God. The importance and power of adoration of God the Father and the Lord Jesus Christ during the deliverance session cannot be underestimated, particularly if any resistance arises. Demons hate any talk about the name of Jesus, the blood, the cross, the resurrection, Satan's defeat and the lake of fire. Songs about the blood of Jesus will definitely stir them up and force them to reveal themselves. Speaking in tongues will also aggravate them nicely. Use the weapons God has provided us to maximum advantage when dealing with obstinate demons.

3. Additional considerations in removing a resisting demon

If you still have an obstinate demon (or stronghold) after employment of the previously discussed items, completing the removal of legal ground may require one or more of the following tactical maneuvers. We use these when the Holy Spirit indicates in order to complete the deliverance.

- **Sever** ancestral ties. Affirm and declare that all ties are broken—from the time of conception in the womb right up to the present.

- **Speak forgiveness** to any ground that the demon(s) may be standing on (using), and/or to any agreements that the ministry receiver may have with the demon(s). Lastly, speak forgiveness[72] to the person for his putting up with, entertaining, catering to and/or giving place to the demon(s).

- **Break** any agreements/lies/contracts/covenants still remaining between the ministry receiver and the demon(s).

- **Appropriate the blood of Jesus** over any legal ground the demons think they have and nullify all agreements. Declare that every part of the ministry receiver's life, all of his "land," is holy ground, dedicated and consecrated unto the Lord.

- **Taunt the demons**, continuing to stir them up as discussed earlier. Remind them that they are losers who are working for, and in league with, a loser.[73] Tell them that Satan and all his demons were defeated at Calvary. Remind them that Jesus went into hell and defeated them all and made an "open show" of Satan as Jesus disarmed and triumphed over him.[74] Remind the demons that all certificates of debt[75] have been nailed to the cross. Tell them that they do not have any legal ground remaining. *So leave!*

4. How to know when the demon is gone

The minister usually has a sense or a "witness" in his spirit when the demon(s) are gone. His spirit feels at peace again. Also, the gift of the discernment of spirits is most helpful. While this gift may manifest in any of the ways that we can hear God's voice, frequently the Holy Spirit will give us visual, symbolic images showing what is going on in the spirit realm as the demons are leaving.

In addition, the ministry receiver may report a change, a release, a sense of peace and/or an end to whatever manifestations he was experiencing. However, the most reliable guide is the "fruit." Does the ministry receiver report a changed life in the days and weeks following the deliverance? For example, he may report that his temper is now under his, and not the demon's, control. He may indicate that he no longer has lustful thoughts, or that he is no longer riddled with insecurity.

Having removed the demons, the next step is to keep the "house" in such condition that other demons of like nature have no opportunity to come in.

H. Post-Deliverance: Keeping the House Cleansed

No one wants to go through deliverance only to have seven more demons worse than the original ones come take their place.[76] As the demonic oppression session comes to an end, we pray for the Holy Spirit to fill all of the places that have been vacated by demons. Yes, the battle was won, and the demons are out, but the war is not over! We can be assured that Satan and his army will do their best to launch a counterattack. So the smart thing to do is to anticipate the counterattack and attack first. As they say in the military, "The best defense is an offense." If we have the ministry receiver immediately begin the following activities, there will be no opportunity for Satan's counterattack. The person, whose "house" the demons were in, *must go on the offensive* and take a number of assertive steps to guard his victory. He is to live in a way that is actually a counterattack against the demonic. This lifestyle should be the normal Christian life.

> Be not overcome by evil, but overcome evil with good.
>
> Romans 12:21, KJ21

What is involved in keeping one's deliverance? The following suggestions are a combination of our own insights plus those of Frank and Ida Mae Hammond[77] and Chris Cobb.[78]

1. Put on the whole armor of God

Ephesians 6:10–18 commands us to be properly *clothed* in the whole armor of God as we walk through this life. This is even more critical as the ministry receiver begins to walk in the newfound freedom and healing from several ministry sessions. If necessary, we teach the ministry receiver how to put on his armor and stop any counterattacks before they can occur.[79]

2. Guard our minds

You know the saying that we have no control over whether a bird flies over our head, but we do have control over whether he builds a nest in our hair! Replacement demons most often try to reenter the same way they got in originally: through our thoughts. God's Word tells us to take control of our thoughts: "bringing into captivity every thought to the obedience of Christ" (2 Corinthians 10:5, KJ21).

Think about what you are thinking. You do not have to be a victim of your own thoughts. Chester says there is an area of weakness in his life where a demon tries to gain entry occasionally. The demon usually suggests something like, *I am really too tired to deal with this. I think I will just give in.* Then Chester realizes what is happening and he counters with, "No, I'm not too tired. Get away from me and stop your harassing."

If you start hearing critical, condemning thoughts such as, *I am no good,* you should be able to recognize the source. (Hint: It isn't you or the Holy Spirit!) Determine to put ungodly thoughts out of your mind. Stop what you are doing and read, pray or sing the Word. Replace the wrong thoughts (UGBs) with pure ones (GBs). Change what you allow to be "center stage" in your mind. If needed, change activities or locations.

Most of us have at least one or two important weak areas where the flesh has habitually ruled and/or been pampered. Be on guard in these areas. Attacks on the flesh always start in the mind, so stay on *double guard* in those vulnerable areas. Don't give in an inch. Each victory we win in the thought realm strengthens us for the next victory. It is an upward trend. We must be walking in James 4:7 on a continual basis.

> Submit yourselves therefore to God. Resist the devil and he will flee from you.
>
> James 4:7, KJ21

3. Guard our mouth

In the book of Psalms we read:

> Set a guard over my mouth, O LORD;
>   keep watch over the door of my lips.
>
> Psalm 141:3, NIV

Life and death are in our tongues.[80] We can speak life or death over ourselves. We need to make a decision *not* to confess doubt, unbelief or whatever is negative (ungodly) about ourselves or anyone else. Rather, we should seriously follow Paul's admonishment:

> Finally, brothers, whatever is true, whatever is noble, whatever is right, whatever is pure, whatever is lovely, whatever is admirable—if anything is excellent or praiseworthy—think about such things. Whatever you have learned or received or heard from me, or seen in me—put it into practice. And the God of peace will be with you.
>
> Philippians 4:8–9, NIV

4. Crucify/control the flesh

Don't give in to the lusts of the flesh. Crucify/control the flesh. It will always try to act as if it is ruling and reigning instead of our spirit man. Submit the flesh to the lordship of Jesus Christ and the discipline of the Holy Spirit.[81]

5. Overcome by the word of our testimony

Our testimony about the victories God has accomplished in our lives and the stability He has brought brings a strengthening to our spirit.[82] It builds up our faith. It provides a strong force against the enemy.

6. Resist the devil

A basic Scripture that applies here is:

> Submit yourselves therefore to God. Resist the devil, and he will flee from you.
>
> James 4:7, KJ21

This resistance involves the strategies listed above, as well as doing further self-deliverance, if needed. Also, it is important to cover (pray for and bind Satan out of) our households, which includes all that God has given us and all for which we are responsible.

7. Move into and stay in fellowship, and be accountable

We are instructed not to forsake gathering together[83] because we are built up and strengthened, as well as confronted, by God's people and hearing His Word.

8. Be totally committed to Christ

This can only happen when we have an active prayer life, study the Word, continually submit our plans to Him and listen for Him to guide our steps. As we yield ourselves to Christ, He will speak to us about all areas of our lives: relationships, places to go, things to do, what to let ourselves see and experience, etc.

9. Praise God in the middle of the battle

God is ever present with us and, therefore, He is our strength and protection as we praise Him.[84] Demons flee as we celebrate God's victory over our enemies.[85]

Now let's turn our attention to deliverance as it occurred in Sandy's life.

I. Sandy's Story: "Evil Core" Stronghold (continued)

As we continue with Sandy's story, we want to share with you how we disassembled the demonic aspect of the "evil core" stronghold. (A diagram of this stronghold is shown in Figure 6 below.) We started

Figure 6: *Sandy's "Evil Core" Stronghold*

this part of Sandy's story, the "evil core" saga, in the ungodly belief chapter (see chapter 4). The ministry pattern we used is a good example of the integrated approach to biblical healing ministry.

As we shared earlier, we led Sandy through forgiveness and then ministered to the SOFCs. We then had Sandy break her agreement with the two primary UGBs that held the "evil core" stronghold in place. They were:

1. *I am basically evil, rotten at the core.*

2. *God, You can't save me out of this mess. I am so evil that Your cross can't save me. This is too big for You, and I will never be free.*

Now as we continued, we asked Sandy to renounce the demons promoting the lies in the "evil core." She renounced deception, unbelief, hopelessness, confusion and others, as well.

We then began to cast out different demonic groupings that made up Sandy's entire "evil core" stronghold. The diagram shows how we visualized this stronghold as the Holy Spirit revealed it to us and how the various groups "held on" to and reinforced each other. The Holy Spirit had us start with the group occult control, which included control. After casting them out, we moved on to deception.

"I've not known who I was," Sandy said, looking up sadly. "I've been too busy being what I thought others wanted me to be!"

After that, Sandy reported that a thought went through her awareness. "Time to wrap this up. This is enough ministry!" We all chuckled, knowing the source of the thought, and continued on.

Next, we proceeded to cast out demons of distraction, mind control and interference.

At that point, the Holy Spirit gave Sandy an inner vision.[86] "I see a column of blackness that is shooting out of me!" she exclaimed. We realized that she was seeing the demons leaving. Rejoicing over the confirmation of our progress, we kept up the attack.

We commanded fear to leave, especially the fear of "never being free of evil" and the fear of "always being bad." Then, we commanded a whole legion of fears to go. Sandy continued to see the demons leave. "I knew they were real," she said, almost awed, "but I had no idea I had so many." Energized, she was "on a roll." Altogether we came against many of the accusing spirits: self-condemnation, false guilt and even a spirit that accused her of being selfish, when in actuality, she wasn't. We knew that we were working our way in toward the center and getting closer to the "big guns." Death and antichrist were sent to the same place as the previous demons.

As we were proceeding to the next grouping, Sandy suddenly saw the strategy of the mind-tormenting demons. She saw that they would distract her and then condemn her for being distracted.[87] "I see it," she said jubilantly. "I see their strategy, and I'm not going to let them do that to me anymore!"

As the Holy Spirit led, we asked Sandy to forgive the three spiritual authority figures (the evangelist and the two pastors) who had hypnotically controlled her, abused her, promoted error, and then abandoned her. For the first time, drops of sweat lined her forehead. Slowly, painfully, she forgave each one. Then she broke all soul ties[88] with each of them.

Suddenly, she saw another inner vision. She saw three crowns fall off the three men and onto the ground. She knew what each crown represented. With no further prompting, she broke the power of all sins and curses of idolatry of authority, of servitude and of temple prostitution. She was seeing a symbolic representation of the dethroning of powers that had ruled her life.

A voice said to her, "You don't have to do that!"

"Oh, yes I do!" she spoke back. Then we cast out the demons behind the crowns.

Pride, arrogance and perfection ("be perfect") were next. She gave and asked forgiveness and then broke the curse of "having to be perfect."

She heard the Holy Spirit say, "How much better it is to be free than 'good!'"

We moved on to inferiority and worthlessness ("I have to try harder to overcome my inadequacies").

We could tell that the innermost groupings of demons were getting worried. It was clear that they had thought they were more than adequately surrounded and protected by outer layers of demons, plus Sandy's agreements with their lies. They had been confident that we would never get anywhere close to them. But we were burrowing our way in, continually having Sandy cycle through forgiveness, renouncing, casting out, etc., as needed. We would do what the Holy Spirit directed us to do to remove the next layer of obstacles and then press in farther.

The intensity was building. Finally, we were closing in on the roots of this stronghold. We got rid of idle chatter and words, and then attacked the center.

"Out, 'Core of Evil,' and all remaining demons! Out in the name of Jesus!" The manifestations rose to a peak. Now all that was left was "bad girl: unacceptable, unwanted bad girl."

"No mercy, you foul thing, that has tormented the real Sandy all of her life. Get out now, 'unwanted, unacceptable bad girl.'" Things quieted down. Peace filled the room. "Unwanted bad girl," the demon that had lied to Sandy since she was five or six years old, was gone. "Thank You, Lord!"

It's over

The "evil core" stronghold had been made up of many demonic forces that intertwined with, and lived next to, the real, God-given personality of Sandy. Once the "evil core" was exposed and cast out, the real Sandy was left.

After the demolishing of the "evil core" stronghold, Sandy was amazed that her basic, core feeling about herself changed almost immediately. She stopped "feeling bad" about herself and began to feel "clean" on the inside and "loved by God." Even more amazing, the good feelings continued day after day. They did not go away!

If she herself had not experienced the change from one day to the next, she would not have believed that "just" casting out a "few" demons could make such a difference. Of course, it was not "just" casting out the demons that brought the freedom. Healing came from applying the integrated approach to biblical healing ministry to her life: breaking the sins of her fathers and resulting curses; breaking soul ties; renewing her mind regarding her value and identity; healing her hurts and then casting out the demonic forces. Major freedom was gained by the eviction of the demons that had deceived her into believing the lie that *I am uniquely bad!*

Aftermath

Several weeks later, Sandy reported to us,

> The farther I get away from it (the "evil core" stronghold), and the more I see how totally deceived and defiled I was, the more evil it looks. The "evil core" seems real close to the truth; therefore, it's hard to separate out the real evil from the flesh (evil).

Sandy's victory was not without its counterattacks. Demons were still able to affect her dreams. She would wake up from an occult dream feeling defiled and ugly. "This is who you really are!" Evil-core demons were shouting lies at her. "It is just a matter of time. You will fall and we will get in." Their intent was to make Sandy feel violated, ashamed and angry so she would give up and admit defeat. They wanted to convince her that it was hopeless and they had been right all along: she was "evil, evil to the core."

"I rejected deception," she said. "I don't want to go back. I won't go back!"

She struggled from day to day. She knew how to identify with "evil" or "bad," but who was she, really? What was "normal"? One day, God said to her in her quiet time, *I am teaching you what "normal" is.*

Sandy's "walking it out" took time. The bouts with occult dreams full of lies and terrors continued. We continued, too! We continued to pray for God to show us the remaining open doors. Renewed, we would work through the SOFCs and the UGBs and pray for SSHs associated with each area of wounding. Then we would do the deliverance with the relevant demons. Slowly the intensity and frequency of the attacks decreased.

As you might expect, Sandy had several periods of grieving. She still felt stupid and deceived about having been drawn into the adulterous affair with her pastor. "The loss, the number of prime years wasted! I can never get them back." The extent of the feeling of loss was often overwhelming.

We cautioned her, "Don't let your guard down even during legitimate grieving periods. This, too, shall pass."

"Evil core" was defeated. Although it tried, it has never regained a toehold. True victory was hers.

J. Preparation for Ministering Deliverance

We have seen the greatest fruit when both ministry receiver and minister are rightly prepared for the deliverance.

1. Preparation of the ministry receiver

How can the ministry receiver be best prepared for deliverance? We like to cover the following items.

a. Requirement: salvation, seriousness

First, it is highly preferable—shall we say "essential"—that the ministry receiver be saved. We verify his salvation condition in the first ministry session as part of reviewing his application form. We proceed with introducing him to Jesus if he isn't saved. Of course, in a church setting, it is unlikely that anyone will come for Christian ministry unless he is saved, but it doesn't hurt to check.

In addition to being saved, it is important for the ministry receiver to be serious in wanting deliverance. After all, it is his house that needs the cleansing. He should want to cooperate with the process and actively engage in setting his will and joining in with the deliverance process. Also, since he is the one who must "walk it out," he needs to be serious about appropriating God's provision so he can be successful in maintaining lasting victory.

The balancing word for the previous paragraph is that someone severely oppressed by curses and demons may need help before he can come into a condition of seriousness. There are times when it is the minister's faith and determination, his "standing in the gap,"[89] that brings that measure of freedom and healing that enables the person's own will and faith to begin to operate. Once again we are "forced" to rely on the Holy Spirit in these situations to see what we need to do. Do we confront the ministry receiver's passivity and encourage him to "get determined"? Do we press ahead and confront the demons on his behalf? Or do we do both?

One additional measure of a ministry receiver's seriousness is his willingness to enter into praying and fasting before he comes for deliverance. We do not make a rule about the fasting part of this, but usually leave it to the ministry receiver to do as he desires and God directs. We personally do not generally fast before a deliverance session because we would not eat very often if we did. When, however, we are coming against major occult strongholds, we are very likely to fast beforehand. We also enlist intercessory support, which has proven to be vital at times.

b. Specific information for the ministry receiver

As it seems relevant for a particular ministry receiver, we may cover some or all of the following points with him. In addition, we review the ministry steps at the end of this chapter so that he will be familiar with the process. Obviously what we discuss depends on his maturity level, his understanding of the demonic kingdom and his previous experiences with demonic deliverance.

Some ministry receivers may be fearful and anxious before the first deliverance session. Fear of the unknown, particularly of the spiritual realms, can be extremely unnerving. Some of the ministry receiver's anxiety may be alleviated by instruction on what to expect and how to participate constructively.

Unconfessed sin/need for forgiveness

Demons will cling to any hidden or *unconfessed sin* so it is very important to make sure that repentance and the forgiveness of others is as complete as possible. This is especially true in the occult area, so double check! It is better to be too thorough than not thorough enough. What's not already covered will become apparent during the "casting-out" phase if and when strong resistance is encountered.

Occult objects

If the ministry receiver still possesses *occult books* on magic, fortune telling, astrology, sexual perversion, witchcraft, psychic gifts, etc., he needs to agree to get rid of them. This is also true of trinkets or jewelry with magical and/or idolatrous significance. Use of the occult section on the Ancestral Open Doors form in the appendix can be helpful in bringing items to the person's remembrance.

The truth that sets us free

By the time we start deliverance, the ministry receiver's UGBs should be "on the way out" and being replaced with God's truth as expressed in his GBs. In addition, it may be helpful to ensure that the ministry receiver *knows* the truths that Jesus has defeated, disarmed and triumphed over all the power of the enemy.[90] Demons have to leave because He has given us authority over them and we are releasing the word of truth. It is the truth that sets people free and not the volume of our voices nor the force of our will. The lies contained in the UGBs gave demons "place," and these have been exposed and dealt with. We can proclaim the truth by using Scripture and praise as part of the deliverance, if necessary.

Set his will

Once the legal ground has been recovered by ministering to the first three problem areas, the determination and setting of the ministry receiver's will becomes the critical factor regarding long-term freedom. In fact, the degree of his desire and persistence to be free is the deciding factor between an easy versus a difficult deliverance. When he has purposed in his heart that the demons have to leave, and he stands on the truth and authority that Jesus has given him, there is no contest. The demons are in his house, and he needs to insist that they go. The last thing we want is a passive ministry receiver. If necessary, we help him be active and involved.

Speak in English, and keep eyes open

Normally, we ask the ministry receiver to speak in English and not in tongues during the "casting-out" process. There is some indication that "tongues" hinders the demons' departure through the mouth. We don't make a "federal case" out of this, however. If the person repeatedly switches back to tongues without realizing what he is doing, we drop the matter. Of course, the tongues stir them up and encourage the demons to leave, but then, so does English.

It also helps us (and the ministry receiver) if he keeps his eyes open. This helps him stay in control and not go into a trancelike or passive state. In addition, the minister will sometimes see a demonic presence through the eyes of the person. Occasionally his eyes change as a demon manifests, so it is another indicator of how the deliverance is going.

Laying on of hands

Often our discernment is increased if we lay hands on the ministry receiver during the deliverance. Before touching him, we are careful to ask for his permission. We, of course, use discretion about where we place our hands, particularly for members of the opposite sex. We recommend touching the person's shoulders only, which is generally safe.

The presence of hands with the anointing of the Holy Spirit often further agitates the demons, which can make the receiver upset. When that is the case, we need the Holy Spirit's wisdom to determine whether the stirring of the demons is more beneficial than any confusion to the person.

Joint effort

Instruct the receiver that we will all be commanding and putting pressure on the demon(s) at the same time. This is no time for polite conversation, not even in the South!

Reporting

Let the ministry receiver know that he can help by reporting any negative experiences such as thoughts tempting him to withdraw from the deliverance process, strong negative feelings and/or any physical symptoms (i.e., moving pains, dizziness, confusion, etc.).

Expect hindrances

Demons will try to block the deliverance. That is just part of the warfare. We may explain to the ministry receiver the "log jam" concept used by "blocking demons" to hinder us. We also inform him of strategies we will use if we run into hindrances. (See the previous section on what to do with obstinate demons on page 233.)

Use of Scripture, praise

Demons hate any talk or songs about the name of Jesus, the blood, the cross, certificates of debt,[91] the resurrection, Satan's defeat, their defeat, the lake of fire, etc. They get stirred up, agitated in different ways, and have a hard time remaining hidden. They particularly hate Scripture, especially verses about the fall or the defeat of Satan. The ministry receiver should be ready to say or read Scripture and to join the ministers in praise. (See the previous section on what demons hate on page 237.)

Possible manifestations

Let the ministry receiver know that there may be manifestations, both of resistance and as the demons leave. The most common signs of resistance are thoughts such as *This won't work* or *Demons aren't real*. The receiver may experience sharp pains that move about his body, sleepiness, changing body temperature and/or tightness somewhere in his body. Sometimes demons mock the process.

At these times, the receiver may appear to be sarcastic, sneering and/or uncooperative. Demons generally manifest according to their type or function. For example, a demon of anger will cause a person to feel angry; a demon of shame, shameful, etc. Occasionally, the demon will manifest in a physical struggle. Also, somewhat occasionally, the demons may speak through the person. Be prepared for whatever form the manifestations may take. Assure the ministry receiver that you will limit the extent of the manifestations if they become distracting or potentially harmful.

Explain how demons leave

Demons usually leave with the breath, through a yawn, a cough, a sigh, a burp, a hiccup, deep exhalation, laughter, crying or a scream. Sometimes, as an act of the will, it is helpful to have the person breathe deeply and then to forcibly breathe out, even to cough. This seems to help encourage the demons to leave, especially if they are already close to leaving. While the breath or cough does not cause the demons to leave, it provides the receiver an opportunity to exercise faith that the demons are leaving.

Screams may occur, but this happens infrequently and usually when related to occult, witchcraft or death demons. Demons may also leave through gas expulsion, but we usually don't mention this manifestation until it occurs!

Sometimes there are no manifestations

Sometimes we see no manifestation when the demons are leaving, but the ministry receiver experiences a release of tension and/or a greater degree of peace or clearheadedness. It is helpful for the receiver to know how he manifests, even if only internally. Of course, we are doing our best to exercise the gift of the discernment of spirits so we know where we are in the "casting out" process. We want to be able to verify when a particular demon (or grouping) is gone.

2. Preparation of the minister

Any minister doing deliverance needs to be thoroughly convinced of two things: (1) demons really exist and (2) Jesus has given us authority over them.[92] This will occur as he experiences deliverance himself and/or works with an experienced deliverance minister.

The minister needs to know that even while he is pursuing the ministry and issuing the commands, that Jesus is the actual deliverer.[93] During the deliverance, he will be relying strongly on the Holy Spirit for the gift of discernment and for words of knowledge concerning each stronghold he addresses.

The last part of the minister's preparation is to develop a list of the specific demons (demonic groupings) and demonic strongholds to be cast out. We start by looking back over the Ancestral Open Doors form and noting the SOFCs groupings we ministered to earlier. We also prayerfully go back over notes of the previous sessions, noting the person's main problem areas.

Usually, God will show which category/group of demons or which demonic stronghold[94] to deal with first. At times, He has given a strategy that appears to be analogous to the disarming and dis-assembly of an armed fortress. He will reveal a plan of attack if it is needed.

It is wise to *always cover* the areas of the occult, control, sexual sin, fears and physical ailments. Even though the ministry receiver may have never sinned in any of these areas, it is almost a certainty that some of his ancestors have, resulting in curses of defeat, failure and entrapment in these areas.

In summary, the minister needs to approach the time of deliverance spiritually prepared and mentally set in his knowledge and focus.

K. Ministering Deliverance: General Process

In the usual flow of the ministry process, deliverance comes after the other three problem areas. At times, however, it is necessary to accomplish some deliverance before effective ministry is possible in the first three problem areas. Sometimes the ministry receiver's ability to forgive is hindered, or he is not able to pray to receive a godly belief after renouncing the ungodly one. Perhaps he is unable to receive God's healing in the area of soul/spirit hurts. Demons can block any of these ministry areas. Remember, there is no rigid structure to the ministry process. There is only a guiding framework. We want the Holy Spirit to be in charge of the ministry session. Whenever the Holy Spirit impresses upon us that we need to alter the "normal" process in order to continue effective ministry, we do so, including the casting out of demons.

1. Starting the ministry

Once you have led the ministry receiver through the DO Submission Prayer (see page 257), you may explain the ministry steps outlined at the end of this chapter. Because the other three problem areas have already been ministered to, the forgiveness step will usually have been completed and therefore you can skip this step. Now, with a list of demonic groupings in your hand, you are ready to proceed using the strategy that the Holy Spirit has given.

Remember that the two most common strategies the Holy Spirit seems to give are (1) to start with the less important groupings and progress toward the strongest ones or (2) to dismantle the strongest ones first and work toward the less important ones. You may refer back to the demonic interconnectedness section on page 230 for a discussion of these strategies.

2. Casting out demons

Starting with the primary demon/strongman, the minister will address it until both he and the ministry receiver sense that it is gone.

Then he will address the associated demons in that same grouping, focusing on them *one by one*. He will command each one out. He and the ministry receiver will continue commanding until they both sense that the particular demon is gone. Try to avoid addressing more than one demon at a time in order to avoid confusion as to which demon has or has not left.

3. Identifying additional demons

It is normal to identify additional demons during the actual session. This occurs through the discerning of spirits either by the ministers or the ministry receiver. Sometimes the person's behavior reveals the presence of a demon. During the ministry session, the demon may speak through the person in a recognizable way, try to put the person to sleep, etc. Sometimes as the demon is stirred up, the type of manifestation exhibited by the person reveals the demon's identity. Be alert to changes in the receiver's emotions, physical actions, appearance and voice pitch or level. For example, on one occasion as we were ministering deliverance to a young woman, she raised her arms and began "pumping iron" as her voice dropped to a much deeper pitch. We immediately asked, "Who are you?" The demon replied, "Workout." Needless to say, "Workout" was commanded to go where Jesus wanted him to go, where he could continue building up his own muscles!

Note: It is important to be alert. You may think that the ministry receiver is speaking when it is actually a demon. Demons sometimes tell the truth, but mostly they don't, so it is risky to put much stock in what they say. They are so arrogant, however, that they frequently reveal significant information that allows you to get a firmer "grip" on them. As they reveal more of their legal ground, you can do what is necessary to reclaim the ground, making it easier for you to cast them out.

---

4. Continuing the deliverance

We continue the "casting out" process until one of the following occurs:

- All identified demons and all those revealed by the Holy Spirit are removed from the person.
- We have done enough for a particular session.
- The Holy Spirit indicates that we are to stop. Usually, this means that we need to allow the person to "increase and possess the reclaimed land."[95]

As we "wrap up" the deliverance session, we:

- bind the remaining demons;
- command the demons to stay separated and isolated, and forbid any manifestations, particularly the interjecting of thoughts into the person's mind;
- cancel the assignments of all demons assigned to replace the evicted demons;
- pray for the Holy Spirit to fill all of the vacated areas; and
- pray for restoration of the areas affected by the demons, including physical healing.

We are now ready to bring the deliverance ministry to a specific individual. We can use the following specific steps.

L. Ministering Deliverance: Specific Steps

Caution

If this is your first experience with deliverance, we highly recommend that you enlist the help of a mature saint experienced in deliverance. It is not that you can't do self-deliverance by yourself. Rather, because this is your first time, you don't know what type of manifestations, degree of resistance or demons/strongholds you might encounter. When you are both the "ministry receiver" and the "minister," it is harder to deal with these potential problems. This is a time for godly wisdom. Have someone help you the first time. Later, you will know what to expect and so can judge when self-deliverance is appropriate.

> ### Exercise
> If you have worked through the ministry of the other three problem areas, then you are ready for the final cleansing. Collect your Ancestral Open Doors form with the demonic groupings and review them. Then ask the Holy Spirit to give you a strategy for the order of deliverance, i.e., which demonic grouping to cast out first, second, etc. Use the following prayer of submission to position yourself properly and then proceed through the ministry steps to evict the trespassers from your land! God bless you as you receive more fully the freedom for which Christ paid so dearly.

1. Prayer of submission

We are ready to help our ministry receiver pray and submit to God's deliverance process. This is very important. It is good for the demons to clearly hear the receiver's determination and commitment to freedom.

> ### DO Prayer of Submission
> Lord Jesus Christ, I believe that You died on the cross for my sins and rose again from the dead. You redeemed me by Your blood, and I belong to You. I thank You, Lord Jesus, for Your shed blood, which cleanses me from all sin. I want to live for You. I come to You as my Deliverer.
>
> I now confess all of my sins, known and unknown. I repent of them and ask You to forgive me. I renounce them all. I forgive others as I want You to forgive me. Forgive me now and cleanse me with Your blood. I repent of any way I have given place to the enemy.
>
> You know my special need: to obtain freedom from things that bind me, torment me and defile me. I need freedom from every evil and unclean spirit. I claim the promise of Your Word: "Whoever calls upon the name of the Lord Jesus Christ shall be delivered."
>
> I call upon You now, Lord Jesus. Deliver me and set me free. I renounce Satan, all his works and all of his workers. I loose myself from Satan in the name of Jesus Christ. I command you, Satan, you and your demons, to leave me now. All this I do in the name, and on the authority, of Jesus Christ of Nazareth. Thank You, Lord Jesus. Amen!

2. Steps in ministering to demonic oppression

The steps for ministering are listed below. As with ungodly beliefs, the post-ministry follow-up is very important for maintaining one's deliverance.

Ministry steps

1. **Listen**: Identify likely groupings of demons and any sins that provide open doors for demonic oppression. (Generally, you will have these well in hand before the time of the deliverance session.)

2. **Forgive**: Have the ministry receiver forgive any people, events or situations that have not already been forgiven while ministering to the other three problem areas. (It is not uncommon during a deliverance session for additional areas to come up that require forgiveness. Have the receiver forgive as needed. This is *the* major step in removing any excuse [legal ground] that a demon may use to avoid being cast out.)

3. **Repent**: Have the receiver ask God's forgiveness for "putting up with," for "entertaining" and for "agreeing with" demons by catering to their demands and desires. (If there is any sin in the receiver's life that has not already been confessed, repented of and forgiven, have him do so at this time.)

4. **Forgive**: Have the receiver forgive himself.

5. **Renounce**: Have the receiver renounce any more involvement in the sins associated with a demonic grouping. (He renounces all agreements that he has made with demons and renounces giving power or control to the demons or Satan.)

6. **Command**: Have the receiver set his will to "push out" the demon(s) and then command the particular grouping of demons to leave him. After commanding the group to leave, proceed to cast out one demon at a time to avoid confusion as to which demons have left and which ones are still present. Continue until the entire group is removed. (If necessary, the commanding should be repeated until the demon[s] are gone. The minister adds his faith and authority in Jesus Christ in agreement with the receiver.)

Repeat the above steps until all demon groupings have been cast out.

7. **Restore**: Pray for a new infilling of the Holy Spirit into all of the newly cleared-out regions of the receiver. Pray for physical, soul and/or spirit healing of any damage done by the demons. Pray that the Holy Spirit would make the receiver very sensitive to falling back into old thought patterns or sinful habits that would begin to reopen any doors.[96]

Post-ministry: "walking out the new freedom"

Once deliverance has taken place, the minister should discuss the following areas with the ministry receiver to prepare him for the "walking-it-out" phase of deliverance. This begins immediately after the first demon has been cast out! These items are based on the previous section "post-deliverance: keeping the house cleansed."

1. **Assure** him that the *power* of the demons *is broken* but that the devil will present new opportunities to sin, especially in the areas where he has had strongholds and in the past given in to his flesh. Temptations frequently occur right after the victory of deliverance. Temptation, however, will now come from the "outside" rather than the "inside." This form of temptation really has much less power, and he will be able to resist if he *wills to resist*. He will have to keep the doors shut to the old fleshly ways. The Holy Spirit will provide all of the grace and power necessary if he wills to call on the Lord.

2. **Inform** him that *active warfare* will likely continue until the demons assigned by Satan become convinced that he is indeed firm in his resolve. The stronger he sets his will (the will of his spirit as well as the will of his soul), the sooner the battle will be over.

3. **Instruct** him *to take the offense and bind* daily any and all demons that are still "on the inside" and those "on the outside" assigned to tempt him back into the old ways. Render them inactive.

4. **Encourage** him to move into *active mode and give no place to the enemy* by guarding his mind, his mouth and his activities. Discuss possible changes that may need to be made in his lifestyle and/or friends, in order for him to keep his deliverance.

5. **Instruct** him to *quickly repent* if he sins. Remind him how to do *self-deliverance* so he can cast out demons in the future as needed.

6. **Encourage** him to be *daily in the Word*, to pray, to commune with God. Remind him that it is only those who do the will of God and whom Jesus "knows" who will enter the Kingdom of God.[97]

7. **Remind** him to *praise God* for his victory. Also in times of temptation, praise God as a way of defeating the enemy.

8. **Charge** him to *be in a place where he is accountable, where he can receive prayer support and encouragement.* It may also be helpful for him to have a one-on-one relationship for accountability with someone other than yourself.

M. Thought-Provoking Questions

1. During the last 2000 years, what has been the legal status and authority of Satan and his demons?

   . . . .

   . . . .

2. As a Christian believer, what is your status and authority over demons? How did you get it?

   . . . .

   . . . .

3. What do demons want you to do (in terms of deliverance)?

   . . . .

   . . . .

4. Why can't we cast out all of the demons oppressing a person at one time?

   . . . .

   . . . .

5. What is the enemy's strategy against Christians?

   . . . .

   . . . .

6. If Satan has been defeated, why does God allow demons to war against Christians?

. . . .

. . . .

7. Can you name some open doors in your life that may give entry to demons?

. . . .

. . . .

8. What things might you do to protect yourself after a successful deliverance? Why do you need to do these things?

. . . .

. . . .

7

Getting Free and Staying Free!

"I will be a Father to you,
and you will be my sons and daughters,"
says the Lord Almighty.
2 Corinthians 6:18, NIV

There you have it! You have learned and, we hope, received the revelation of the integrated approach to biblical healing ministry. You have learned about the four problem areas and how to minister to them. This revelation brings a unified understanding to the four problem areas so that deep and permanent healing can be achieved.

As we mentioned at the beginning of this book, we no longer have to be among those trapped, wounded and helpless. We can apply the keys God has given us to obtain His healing and freedom. We can go through the straightforward process of confessing and humbling ourselves, of forgiving and releasing judgments and then appropriating the incredible gift of what Jesus Christ did for us on the cross. God has given us a simple but profound revelation that enables us to cast off the chains that have bound us and become mature sons and daughters of a very loving Father.

In one way or another, the four problem areas of sins of the fathers and resulting curses, ungodly beliefs, soul/spirit hurts and demonic oppression underlie all of the afflictions of mankind. However, rather than looking for a different ministry approach for each and every problem, we can use the "principle-based" integrated approach to biblical healing ministry revelation. As we apply the ministry steps for the four problem areas, we have the potential to bring healing and deliverance to each and every type of problem without having to learn beforehand a special technique for each problem.

How do we apply what we have learned? Besides the many examples we have already shared, we want to present briefly two ministry applications demonstrating the integrated approach to biblical healing ministry. We will start by looking at soul ties. The other important application of this powerful approach is to demonic strongholds. These are particularly "strong" or "vicious" structures made of intertwined and interconnected SOFCs, UGBs, SSHs and DO all associated around a main theme.

We will also have some final comments after the conclusion of Sandy's story.

A. Soul Ties—
The Ties That Bind

Many people are bound by ungodly soul ties to another person without any awareness of the significance of their bondage. As we progress through the four problem areas, it may become necessary at any time also to minister to the invisible cords binding the ministry receiver to another. We have included this section in this final chapter to insure that you are able to minister the applicable parts of the integrated approach to biblical healing ministry to help the ministry receiver obtain freedom in this vital area.

1. Definition

Soul ties are an ungodly covenant with another person (organization or thing) based on an unhealthy emotional and/or sexual relationship. This covenant binds the two people together. God "honors," or recognizes, these covenants. He leaves each of us free to decide when and if we will appropriate His provisions to break/cut the ties and release ourselves and the other person.

2. Ministry to ungodly soul ties

Here is a sample prayer that you can use to break soul ties and help yourself, as well as others, to be free. We suggest you repeat the fourth paragraph for each relationship/attachment with which you have an ungodly soul tie.

Prayer

Father, in the name of Jesus, I submit myself completely to You. I confess all of my emotional and sexual sins, as well as my ungodly soul ties. [*If your soul tie is with an ancestor, or if you see this sin and curse in your family line, also include:* I confess my ancestor's sin of maintaining ungodly soul ties.] I choose to forgive my ancestors and each person with whom I have an ungodly soul tie [*be specific*].

I ask You, Lord, to forgive me for my sin that resulted in ungodly soul ties. Lord, I receive Your forgiveness. Thank You for forgiving me and for cleansing me.

I choose to forgive myself for this involvement. I will no longer be angry at myself, hate myself or punish myself.

[*Repeat the following paragraph for each soul tie*]

Lord, I break my ungodly soul ties with [*insert name*]. I release myself from him/her/it and I release him/her/it from me. As I do this, Lord, I pray that You would cause him/her/it to be all that You want him/her/it to be and that You would cause me to be all that You want me to be.

Lord, please cleanse my mind from all memories of ungodly unions so I am totally free to give myself to You and to my spouse.

I renounce and cancel the assignments of all evil spirits attempting to maintain these ungodly soul ties.

Lord, thank You for restoring my soul to wholeness. I choose to walk in holiness by Your grace. In the name of Jesus Christ, I pray. Amen!

B. Demonic Strongholds

Another important application of the integrated approach to biblical healing ministry is the concept and understanding of "demonic strongholds." This concept extends the understandings of demonic oppression groupings (page 229) and demonic interconnectedness (page 230) into a distinct, more complex structure.

1. Definition

A demonic stronghold is a structure composed of a foundation provided by SOFCs and walls/towers/rooms/etc. made from self-sins, UGBs, SSHs and DO groupings. The complexity of this structure can range from relatively simple to quite complex, with many different parts and interconnections. Picture a castle as a good illustration of this complexity.

This structure must be identified, disassembled and demolished one part at a time, following a *strategy* given by the Holy Spirit. This *strategy* involves repetitive application of the ministry steps for the four problem areas to each part of the structure until complete removal of the stronghold is accomplished.

2. Why there is a need for a strategy

In a significant stronghold, a great multiplicity of reinforcing and intertwining of the various problem areas make up the stronghold. The "normal" ministry procedure/approach of dealing with, first, sins of the fathers and resulting curses and self-sins, then ungodly beliefs, next soul/spirit hurts and finally demonic oppression, is not adequate to demolish the stronghold. The normal process only lets us deal with the "surface" of the stronghold. We are not able to penetrate into the depths of it. We are blocked by "what hasn't already been dealt with."

For example, we may deal with forgiveness at the outer layer, but more forgiveness is needed deeper within. We may break all of the ancestral curses at the boundary, but more curses may exist farther inside. In fact, ancestral dedications and commitments may need to be broken. After we expose and deal with ungodly beliefs at the surface, more will be deep within. We have to repeatedly break ungodly agreements between the ministry receiver and the demonic, regardless of how deep and how many layers we must remove.

We pray for God to touch the hurts accessible near the outer wall. Other hurts, however, are covered by demons, lies, curses and layers of negative emotions such as anger and rage. We may cast out the demons clinging to the castle wall, but the powerful "strong men" are barricaded behind layers of other demons, curses, lies and sins. Following the normal procedure for deliverance may not be adequate to do severe damage to a major stronghold. We may not be able to demolish and remove it completely.

In order to work our way into and throughout the stronghold, we need a strategy—a definite sequence of Holy-Spirit-led steps involving repeated ministry in each of the four problem areas.

We appreciate that God has given us a number of examples in the Bible where He provided the strategy.[1] When we analyze these examples, we see that:

- God gives the strategy and battle instructions.
- God generally has men carry out the plan.
- It is not the same strategy every time.
- The strategy is usually not logical, nor satisfying to the rational mind.
- The strategy may involve confusion and/or surprise for the enemy.
- Strongholds are generally defeated one at a time.
- It takes time to clear the land completely.
- Occasionally God does everything by Himself without man's help.

As we come against the more complex strongholds in people's lives, we find that the above principles are still valid. Sometimes we start at the outside and work our way in. Other times, God will have us "jump" into the middle of the stronghold and we work our way out. In other situations, He does the majority of the "clearing out" and we mostly observe the destruction of the stronghold. On other occasions, He leads us step by step as if we are recapturing a city, room by room, house by house, block by block.

Working with the Holy Spirit at this level of warfare is very exciting. It takes a close "colaboring" with Him and a consistent flowing in all of the gifts to bring this degree of freedom into a person's life. We feel as if we are an extension of the Kingdom of God here on the earth. Needless to say, it is very satisfying work.

C. Sandy's Story: Years Later

As we come to the end of this book, we want to share with you how Sandy is doing a number of years later.

Five years later

Approximately five years after Sandy went through the integrated approach to biblical healing ministry, we asked her if she would be willing to share with us (and you) how she is doing. These are some excerpts from her letter.

> It would be untrue and even unkind to suggest that I am living a "Tinker Bell existence," flying gaily through each day in a sort of

Christian fantasy land. No, Christ has called me to reality, and reality is not always easy. I have found that becoming who I am, and relating to God and others in a healthy way, is totally foreign to me. Every day I am learning how to do it "right." It isn't comfortable to go around without any makeup when I have worn a mask all my life. It isn't easy to simply let Christ clothe me when I have spent a lifetime sewing fig leaves to cover myself. And it doesn't always feel safe to walk around in the harsh world with no protection except that which the Lord has promised to provide as we need it.

Sandy is living in a world of God-centered reality rather than her old world of pretense and fantasy. She is quick to say that complete and lasting change is a slow process.

Sometimes I feel as if the person I was is completely gone—not even any fingerprints left for identification. The challenge is to discover who I am in Christ. Each new step, each new challenge, is painfully difficult, like a child learning to walk. But it is also lovely to begin to discover who I really am.

Sandy talks about how difficult it has been to get totally rid of the old lies and enter into Christ's truth.

In a recent, particularly hurtful situation, I found myself slipping back into the lie that controlled me for so long, that *I am so flawed that I am without hope.* It's such an absurd lie for anyone to believe (even for a moment), especially for anyone who walks with such a continual realization of God's love and acceptance as I do now. I'm amazed at the powerful effect it had on me. On the other hand, having embraced this lie as "truth" for fifty years, isn't it incredible that I was able to see the deception so quickly and walk away from it? (I can almost hear a chorus singing in the background, "Oh Love, that will not let me go...").

Throughout her ministry, Sandy was ardent about getting rid of all demonic influence, particularly those in the "evil core" stronghold.[2] At the same time, she shares the reality that deliverance has a challenging, "walking-it-out" aspect.

While the demons have been forced to release their grip on my life, I was left to deal with a lifetime of patterns of behavior which *were* my life for so long. One cannot release such patterns instantly, nor without struggle. The old *is* passed away, but the new *must be entered into*. The old was deadly, but familiar; the new is life-giving, but unfamiliar. Daily I have been confronted with choices.

Sandy goes on to describe the tremendous extent to which her guilt and shame have been healed. She says that before her ministry, "I never could go fast enough to outrun my shame, nor could I perform well enough to overcome my guilt." Then she adds:

> While I do retain a sense of shame about what I became and for what I have done, I am no longer haunted by the *shame* that defined my life prior to my healing. I wanted to move to a new place and start a new life; instead, I have stayed in the same place and have a redeemed life. I have done all that I know to do based on the Scripture to be reconciled to those I hurt. I can never forget the pain that my sin brought to them. I know the cost to my family and to the Body of Christ that my actions incurred, and I am forever available to be part of their restoration, whenever they desire my help. I know the boundless grace that is mine through Christ and I am confident that the One who heals me is able to heal those I've offended. I trust Him with my life and with theirs.

Sandy writes that while she once struggled to "perform" in order to achieve perfection for approval (especially in ministry), God has released her from that struggle and even redefined the meaning of ministry. Although she now teaches weekly at the county jail, it is no longer a performance for her but rather a ministry from her heart. She writes,

> God has shown me that "ministry" is running errands for my mother, seeing a movie with my granddaughter or reading and eating popcorn with my husband in the evening, just as much as it is teaching Bible in the jail.

For the first time in her life, Sandy is free from the fear of not being accepted, i.e., *abandonment*. She has taken painting classes and is becoming a gifted painter. "It's the first time I have wanted to do well but been unafraid for others to see my imperfection. It's a delight for me to paint, and my performance is irrelevant."

Sandy is a gracious person and very easy to love. Her deep appreciation for us and all that God did through us was tenderly expressed in her letter.

> The writers of this book, Chester and Betsy Kylstra, were sent to me in a most miraculous way. They were God's choice to be trustworthy instruments in His hands. Less tender hearts or loving spirits would have destroyed me. Conversely, their determined commitment to nothing less than complete deliverance for me was equally essential. God alone knows the depth of my gratitude to these beloved ones.

We want to close by sharing a few more powerful paragraphs from Sandy's letter.

> Out of the ashes beauty has emerged. Because my husband's love for God and commitment to His will was greater than his own pain, I have not had to walk alone. His love and forgiveness have enabled the Lord to use our marriage as the primary (ongoing) forum for my healing. Together, we are learning to lay down our lives for one another, thus enabling God to give us His life. Our children, my mother and other family members have been selfless in their love and support of me. They suffered deeply because of my sin and have had to endure the pain of my disclosure. But, they have also been beneficiaries of the healing touch of Christ as He has extended it into their lives, as well. Our family is restored and blessed, precious friends have remained in our lives, new ones have been added, and we are seeing foundations restored in other lives as God's healing touch continues to be extended.
>
> Since I was a child, the Word of God has been the one source of truth to which I have returned. Its power has been, and continues to be, a source of sustenance throughout the healing process. Through it, God gives direction, imparts hope, builds faith and reveals the truth that sets me free. We can discover a lot about ourselves by the Scriptures He sets before us. For as long as I can remember, He has brought Isaiah 30:15 (NIV) to me. It says this: "In repentance and rest is your salvation, in quietness and trust is your strength."
>
> How hard it has been for me to walk in those words until now; they seemed difficult for me to even comprehend. Every time I read rest and quietness and trust, my heart yearned to experience them. Such beautiful, wonderful words, but for me they were as unknowable as the stars. Today, they are a part of my life, and the reality with which I live. God has fulfilled His word to me.
>
> Sandy

Nine years later

As we worked on the second edition of the *Restoring the Foundations* book, we again asked Sandy how she was doing. We are happy to report that Sandy continues to gain in peace and rest in the Lord. All of the past striving for recognition and control is gone. While she is grateful to do and to share as the Lord provides opportunities, she doesn't "need" to do anything but fellowship with Jesus. Many people envy (in a godly way, of course) her peace.

D. Final Comments

Where do you go from here? The answer depends on what you want and to what God has called you to do.

Wanting healing and deliverance

The promise of the Lord Jesus is healing and deliverance for all of God's children. The Restoring the Foundations (RTF) integrated approach to biblical healing ministry is a powerful vehicle to receive this healing and deliverance. We especially feel all Christian leaders owe it to themselves and to those they serve to partake of this type of ministry.

There are several ways to obtain healing through the RTF ministry. One can do self-ministry by reading, praying and following the ministry steps in this book. Better would be to work with a trusted prayer partner. Spouses ministering to each other can be especially effective if unity exists in the marriage. (This can be a great way to bring unity back into the marriage.)

The next level of help can come from local church leaders trained in the RTF issue-focused format. This "one-evening" format allows a person to work on one problem at a time. Problem by problem, issue by issue, this approach can bring revolutionary change into a person's life. The local church may also have trained RTF lay ministry teams that provide a "thorough" ministry format. In fifteen hours (five three-hour sessions), a broad and deep sweep can be made to bring radical permanent healing.

The final level of RTF ministry is provided by healing house network teams. These are five-fold, fully trained and experienced teams serving the entire Body of Christ with the "thorough" ministry format. You may visit the website, call or email if you desire to know more about receiving RTF ministry from one of these teams.[3]

Wanting to be trained to bring this ministry to others

Within the local church, church and cell/small group leaders can be trained via two seminars to bring the issue-focused form of this ministry to their members. We also train RTF lay ministry teams to bring this ministry to church members using the "thorough" format.

Then there are those called to the Body of Christ as a five-fold minister. After an extensive time of training and experience gaining, many of these teams have applied for and been accepted as Healing House Network qualified teams. These teams bring RTF ministry to leaders, lead seminars, train teams and help establish local church RTF lay programs. You may visit the website, call or email the network if you desire to know more about being trained as an RTF minister.[4] We would love to help train you to be the most effective minister you can be.

Prayer of blessing

We pray God's best for you as you walk the road of sanctification with the Holy Spirit. We encourage you to set your heart to cooperate with the Holy Spirit. Then ask Him to move you as rapidly as possible through the healing process because you want to enter much more fully into the sonship relationship that Father God has and wants with you. It is time to get rid of the hindrances and blocks to this full relationship.

E. Thought-Provoking Questions

1. What is the basis of a soul tie?

   ....

   ....

2. What will happen if a soul tie is not broken?

   ....

   ....

3. What helps hold soul ties in place?

   ....

   ....

4. What makes up the structure of a demonic stronghold?

   ....

   ....

5. How is dealing with a demonic stronghold different from casting out a demon?

    . . . .

    . . . .

6. Why do you need a strategy to deal with a demonic stronghold? Name two common strategies.

    . . . .

    . . . .

7. What impressed you the most about Sandy's story?

    . . . .

    . . . .

8. Besides doing self-ministry, you can be trained to use the Restoring the Foundations integrated approach to biblical healing ministry. What two formats could you be trained to use?

    . . . .

    . . . .

9. Explain the RTF integrated approach to biblical healing ministry. Explain how it is different from other ministry approaches that you have learned.

    . . . .

    . . . .

Appendix

The following ministry form will help you determine the SOFCs and DO groupings in your life or the ministry receiver's life. You may copy this form "as is," or adjust it to suit your purposes. You are granted permission to use it for your own use but not to sell or incorporate it into another publication. We hope that this form will be a blessing for you.

Ancestral Open Doors (Genesis 4:7)

Please put a check under the A (Ancestors) category if you know about, or have observed, any of these characteristics, events or involvement in your immediate or extended family. If any of these is (or was) also true for you, put a "C" for current or a "P" for past in the S (Self) category.

A S

Abandonment
__ __ Abdication
__ __ Blocked intimacy
__ __ Desertion
__ __ Divorce
__ __ Isolation
__ __ Loneliness
__ __ Neglect
__ __ Rejection
__ __ Separation
__ __ Self-pity
__ __ Victimization
....

Rejection
__ __ Expected rejection
__ __ Perceived rejection
__ __ Self-rejection
....

Finances
__ __ Bankruptcy
__ __ Cheating
__ __ Covetousness
__ __ Debt

A S
__ __ Deception
__ __ Delinquency
__ __ Dishonesty
__ __ Failure
__ __ Greed
__ __ Idolatry of possessions
__ __ Irresponsible spending
__ __ Job failures
__ __ Job losses
__ __ Lack
__ __ Neglect
__ __ Poverty
__ __ Robbery
__ __ Robbing God (not tithing)
__ __ Stealing
__ __ Stinginess
....

Religion
__ __ Antichrist
__ __ Betrayal
__ __ Denominationalism
__ __ Division

A S
__ __ Hypocrisy
__ __ Injustice
__ __ Legalism
__ __ Liberalism
__ __ New Age practices
__ __ Religiosity
__ __ Rules, excessive
__ __ Spiritual pride
__ __ Traditionalism
__ __ Unforgiveness
....

Performance
__ __ Competition
__ __ Driving
__ __ Envy
__ __ Jealousy
__ __ People pleasing
__ __ Perfectionism
__ __ Possessiveness
__ __ Rivalry
__ __ Striving
__ __ Workaholism
....

<u>A</u> <u>S</u>

Anxiety
_ _ Burden
_ _ False responsibility
_ _ Fatigue
_ _ Heaviness
_ _ Nervousness
_ _ Restlessness
_ _ Weariness
_ _ Worry
....

Deception
_ _ Blindness
_ _ Cheating/stealing
_ _ Confusion
_ _ Denial
_ _ Fraudulence
_ _ Infidelity
_ _ Lying
_ _ Secretiveness
_ _ Self-deception
_ _ Treachery
_ _ Treason
_ _ Trickery
_ _ Untrustworthiness
....

Mental Problems
_ _ Craziness
_ _ Compulsions
_ _ Confusion
_ _ Distraction
_ _ Forgetfulness
_ _ Hallucinations
_ _ Hysteria
_ _ Insanity
_ _ Mind binding
_ _ Mind blocking
_ _ Mind racing
_ _ Paranoia
_ _ Schizophrenia
_ _ Senility
....

Unbelief
_ _ Apprehension
_ _ Double-mindedness
_ _ Doubt
_ _ Fear of being wrong
_ _ Mind blocking
_ _ Mistrust
_ _ Rationalism
_ _ Skepticism
_ _ Suspicion
_ _ Uncertainty
....
....

<u>A</u> <u>S</u>

Mocking
_ _ Blaspheming
_ _ Cursing
_ _ Laughing
_ _ Profanity
_ _ Ridicule
_ _ Sarcasm
_ _ Scorn
....

Addictions/ Dependencies/Escape
_ _ Cocaine
_ _ Downers/uppers
_ _ Marijuana
_ _ Non-prescription drugs
_ _ Prescription drugs
_ _ Street drugs
_ _ Tranquilizers
....
_ _ Alcohol
_ _ Caffeine
_ _ Cigarettes
_ _ Computers
_ _ Food
_ _ Gambling
_ _ Internet
_ _ Overspending
_ _ Pornography
_ _ Sex
_ _ Sports
_ _ Television
_ _ Video games
....

Escape
_ _ Daydreaming
_ _ Fantasy
_ _ Forgetfulness
_ _ Hopelessness
_ _ Isolation
_ _ Laziness
_ _ Passivity
_ _ Procrastination
_ _ Sleep/slumber/ oversleeping
_ _ Trance
_ _ Withdrawal
....

Unmotivated
_ _ Irresponsibility
_ _ Laziness
_ _ Procrastination
_ _ Undisciplined
....
....

<u>A</u> <u>S</u>

Pride
_ _ Arrogance
_ _ Conceit
_ _ Controlling
_ _ Egotistical
_ _ Haughtiness
_ _ Leviathan
_ _ Prejudice
_ _ Self-centeredness
_ _ Self-importance
_ _ Vanity
....

Rebellion
_ _ Contempt
_ _ Deception
_ _ Defiance
_ _ Disobedience
_ _ Independence
_ _ Insubordination
_ _ Resistance
_ _ Self-sufficiency
_ _ Self-will
_ _ Stubbornness
_ _ Undermining
....

Anger
_ _ Abandonment
_ _ Feuding
_ _ Frustration
_ _ Hatred
_ _ Hostility
_ _ Murder
_ _ Punishment
_ _ Rage
_ _ Resentment
_ _ Retaliation
_ _ Revenge
_ _ Spoiled little boy/girl
_ _ Temper tantrums
_ _ Violence
....

Bitterness
_ _ Accusation
_ _ Blaming
_ _ Complaining
_ _ Condemnation
_ _ Criticalness
_ _ Gossip
_ _ Judging
_ _ Murmuring
_ _ Ridicule
_ _ Slander
_ _ Unforgiveness
....

A S
Violence
__ __ Abuse
__ __ Arguing
__ __ Bickering
__ __ Cruelty
__ __ Cursing
__ __ Death
__ __ Destruction
__ __ Feuding
__ __ Hate
__ __ Mocking
__ __ Murder/abortion
__ __ Retaliation
__ __ Strife
__ __ Torture/mutilation
. . . .

Depression
__ __ Dejection
__ __ Discouragement
__ __ Despair
__ __ Despondency
__ __ Gloominess
__ __ Hopelessness
__ __ Insomnia
__ __ Misery
__ __ Oversleeping
__ __ Sadness
__ __ Self-pity
__ __ Suicide attempt
__ __ Suicide fantasies
__ __ Withdrawal
. . . .

Trauma
__ __ Abuse—emotional
__ __ Abuse—mental
__ __ Abuse—physical
__ __ Abuse—sexual
__ __ Abuse—spiritual
__ __ Abuse—verbal
__ __ Accident
__ __ Loss
__ __ Imprisoned
__ __ Rape
__ __ Torture
__ __ Violence
. . . .

Grief
__ __ Agony
__ __ Anguish
__ __ Crying
__ __ Despair
__ __ Heartbreak
__ __ Loss
__ __ Pain

A S
__ __ Sadness
__ __ Sorrow
__ __ Torment
__ __ Weeping
. . . .

Shame
__ __ Abandonment
__ __ Anger
__ __ Bad boy/girl
__ __ Condemnation
__ __ Defilement
__ __ Different
__ __ Disgrace
__ __ Embarrassment
__ __ Guilt
__ __ Hatred
__ __ Illegitimacy
__ __ Inferiority
__ __ Occult involvment
__ __ Self-accusation
__ __ Self-hate
__ __ Self-pity
. . . .

Unworthiness
__ __ Inadequacy
__ __ Inferiority
__ __ Insecurity
__ __ Self-accusation
__ __ Self-condemnation
__ __ Self-hate
__ __ Self-punishment
. . . .

Victim
__ __ Appeasement
__ __ Betrayal
__ __ Deportation
__ __ Entrapped
__ __ Helplessness
__ __ Hopelessness
__ __ Mistrust
__ __ Passivity
__ __ Self-pity
__ __ Suspicion
__ __ Trauma
__ __ Unfaithfulness
. . . .

Failure
__ __ Boom/bust cycle
__ __ Defeat
__ __ Loss
__ __ Performance
__ __ Pressure to succeed
__ __ Striving
. . . .

A S
Infirmities/Disease
__ __ Accidents (falls, cars, etc.)
__ __ Anorexia/bulimia
__ __ Arthritis
__ __ Asthma
__ __ Barrenness/miscarriage
__ __ Bone/joint problems
__ __ Cancer
__ __ Congestion (in lungs)
__ __ Diabetes
__ __ Fatigue
__ __ Female problems
__ __ Heart/circulatory problems
__ __ Lung problems
__ __ Mental illness
__ __ MS
__ __ Migraines/mind binding
__ __ Physical abnormalities
__ __ Premature death
. . . .

Control
__ __ Appeasement
__ __ Denial
__ __ Domineering
__ __ Double binding
__ __ Enabling
__ __ False responsibility
__ __ Female control
__ __ Jealousy
__ __ Manipulation
__ __ Male control
__ __ Occult control/Jezebel
__ __ Passive aggression
__ __ Passivity/Ahab
__ __ Possessiveness
__ __ Pride (I know best)
__ __ Witchcraft
. . . .

Fears
__ __ Anxiety
__ __ Bewilderment
__ __ Burden
__ __ Dread
__ __ Harassment
__ __ Heaviness
__ __ Horror movies
__ __ Intimidation
__ __ Mental torment
__ __ Over-sensitivity
__ __ Paranoia
__ __ Phobia
__ __ Superstition
__ __ Worry

A S

Fears (cont.)
___ Fear of authorities
___ Fear of being abused
___ Fear of being attacked
___ Fear of being a victim
___ Fear of being wrong
___ Fear of cancer
___ Fear of death
___ Fear of demons
___ Fear of diabetes
___ Fear of exposure
___ Fear of failure
___ Fear of heart attack
___ Fear of inadequacy
___ Fear of infirmities
___ Fear of loss
___ Fear of man
___ Fear of performing
___ Fear of poverty
___ Fear of public singing
___ Fear of punishment
___ Fear of rejection
___ Fear of sexual
        inadequacy
___ Fear of sexual perversion
___ Fear of success
___ Fear of violence
        ....

Sexual sins
___ Abortion
___ Adultery
___ Bestiality
___ Demonic sex
___ Defilement/uncleanness
___ Exposure
___ Fantasy lust
___ Fornication
___ Frigidity
___ Homosexuality
___ Illegitimacy
___ Incest
___ Incubus

A S
___ Lesbianism
___ Lust/fantasy lust
___ Masturbation
___ Pornography
___ Premarital sex
___ Prostitution/harlotry
___ Rape
___ Seduction/alluring
___ Sexual abuse
___ Succubus
....
....

Occult
___ Abortion (Molech)
___ Accident proneness
___ Ahab
___ Animal spirits
___ Antichrist
___ Astral projection
___ Astrology
___ Automatic writing
___ Behemoth
___ Black magic
___ Books—occult/
        witchcraft
___ Clairvoyance
___ Conjuration
___ Control—occult/
        witchcraft
___ Crystal ball
___ Death—suicide
___ Demons—dispatching
___ Demon worship
___ Divination
___ Eight ball
___ Evil eye
___ ESP
___ False gifts (occult)
___ Fortune-telling
___ Handwriting analysis
___ Hexing
___ Horoscopes

A S
___ Hypnosis
___ I Ching
___ Idolatry (of . . . .)
___ Incantations
___ Jezebel
___ Levitation
___ Leviathan
___ Meditation—Eastern
___ Mediumship
___ Mental telepathy
___ Necromancy
___ Non-Christian exorcism
___ Ouija board
___ Palm reading
___ Past-life readings
___ Pendulum readings
___ Psychic readings
___ Psychic healing
___ Python
___ Reincarnation
___ Satanic worship
___ Séances
___ Slavery—occult
___ Sorcery
___ Spells
___ Spirit guide(s)
___ Spiritism
___ Superstition
___ Table tipping
___ Tarot cards
___ Tea leaves—reading
___ Third eye—using
___ Trance
___ TM
___ Vampire
___ Victim—occult
___ Voodoo
___ Water witching
___ Werewolf
___ White magic
___ Wicca
___ Witchcraft
....

About the Authors

God called Chester and Betsy in mid-life from careers in aerospace software engineering and mental-health counseling to new careers as teachers and ministers in the Body of Christ. During their preparation time at Liberty Bible College,[1] God began both to heal them and to reveal the elements of Restoring the Foundations integrated approach to biblical healing ministry. They started to minister, teach, and train other couples to function as Restoring the Foundations (RTF) ministry teams to help bring healing and deliverance to church members.

Since 1990, when they entered fulltime ministry, God has continued to expand their vision. In addition to being RTF ministers themselves, they have established RTF ministry programs within churches, conducted healing/deliverance, activation and training seminars and trained RTF ministry teams throughout the United States and in other nations. Many times they have been asked to come to a local church and minister to the entire leadership team. They have also made numerous overseas and mission trips taking the Restoring the Foundations integrated approach to biblical healing ministry revelation to other nations.

They founded Proclaiming His Word (PHW) Ministries, Inc., in 1992. God had said that others would be joining them, and that they were to prepare a covering organization for them. This did occur, as over the years a number of top-quality RTF ministry teams joined PHW and ministered within the CI/PHW Healing House and throughout the nation.

In January 2001, the Kylstras launched the Healing House Network as a covering membership organization for the many qualified RTF Ministry Teams ministering at the Healing House level of professionalism. This network is providing quality training and oversight, as well as providing national and international referrals to the member teams.

Chester and Betsy are ordained with Christian International (CI) Ministries. They serve on Bishop Bill Hamon's Board of Governors and on C. Peter Wagner's Apostolic Roundtable of Deliverance Ministries.

They are faculty members in the CI School of Theology and Ministry Training College, Wagner Leadership Institute, Vision International University and Christian Life School of Theology.

They have developed a number of resources to help train Restoring the Foundations ministers. Besides *Restoring the Foundations* and *Biblical Healing and Deliverance*, they, along with Dorothy Ferguson Railey, have written a reference manual for RTF ministers to take into the ministry room. It is entitled *Ministry Tools for Restoring the Foundations*. This book is what its title indicates, a manual with "tools" to increase the effectiveness of the ministering process.

Another important training and ministry set of publications are the *Issue-Focused Ministry* publications. Using them, any Christian leader can increase his effectiveness in bringing God's healing touch to one specific problem or issue in a person's life.

Betsy and Chester have four adult children: James, Lewis, Eric and Pam.

You may contact Chester and Betsy at:

Proclaiming His Word Ministries
P.O. Box 2339
Santa Rosa Beach, FL 32459
Voice/Fax: 877-214-8076
Email: office@phw.org

You may learn more about them and their ministry on the Internet by going to the Proclaiming His Word Ministries, Healing House Network and/or Issue-Focused Ministry web pages at:

www.phw.org
www.healinghouse.org
www.issuefocused.org or www.cellgroups.org

If you want to contact the Healing House Network to discuss receiving Restoring the Foundations ministry for yourself or another, or to arrange for seminars and training, you may call or email the office at:

Voice/Fax: 800-291-4706
Email: office@healinghouse.org

Notes

Preface

1. See Ephesians 5:27.
2. Romans 15:16; 1 Corinthians 6:11; 1 Thessalonians 4:3.
3. Bill Hamon, *Prophets and the Prophetic Movement* (Shippensburg, Penn.: Destiny Image, 1990); and Bill Hamon, *Apostles, Prophets, and the Coming Moves of God* (Shippensburg, Penn.: Destiny Image, 1997).
4. See Ephesians 4:8, 11–12.
5. See Acts 3:21.
6. See Isaiah 40:3; Malachi 3:1.
7. See page 278 for contact information to learn about these programs.

Chapter 1

1. See Isaiah 22:22; Matthew 16:19; Luke 11:52; Revelation 1:18.
2. The most direct Scriptures are 2 Corinthians 3:18; Romans 8:29. However, see also Galatians 4:19; Ephesians 4:13, 15, 23; 2 Peter 1:4; 1 John 2:6.
3. See Luke 10:19; John 16:32; Romans 12:21; 1 John 2:13–14; 4:4; 5:4–5; Revelation 2:7, 11, 17, 26; 3:5, 12, 21; 21:7 for wonderful Scriptures about "overcoming."
4. These truths are the subject of several chapters in our book *Restoring the Foundations* where we explore them in much more detail than is possible in this book. If you are interested, you may learn how to obtain the book by referring to the contact information on page 278. You may also refer to the books referenced in the endnotes.
5. One of the most outstanding books exploring the fullness of the cross is *Cross of Christ* by John Stott, InterVarsity Press, Downers Grove, IL 60515. Pages 133–163 are particularly noteworthy regarding substitution.
6. See John 14:6.
7. See 1 Samuel 3:4, 6, 10–14.
8. See 1 Kings 19:13, 15–18.
9. See Matthew 17:2–5.
10. See note 7 above.
11. See Hebrews 5:14.
12. See Ephesians 4:26–27.
13. See Ephesians 6:10–18.
14. See Hebrews 1:14.
15. Originally recorded in 2 Samuel 22:31–51.
16. Sandy's story, with her testimony about God's freedom, cleansing and healing, is woven throughout this book.

17 Sandy (not her real name) and her husband have given us full permission to use their story, with the sincere prayer and hope that it will help others gain freedom from Satan's bondages.

18 Please note that the phrases *integrated approach to biblical healing ministry* and *Restoring the Foundations ministry* are used interchangeably. The ministry teams that conduct this ministry are identified as Restoring the Foundations ministers. This terminology is based on the title of the book *Restoring the Foundations* that presents God's revelation for the integrated approach to biblical healing ministry in great depth.

19 In the first session, after a little conversation, we like to start with an opening prayer. Then we go through an application form, giving background information that the person has filled out prior to our meeting. Then we are ready to move on into the interviewing process.

20 The RTF ministry formats are discussed in Chapter XV in *Restoring the Foundations*.

21 See John 10:10.

Chapter 2

1 See Matthew 6:14–15; Mark 11:26.

2 See Matthew 18:35.

3 See Chapter 5, "Soul/Spirit Hurts."

4 See Luke 23:34.

5 Sandra D. Wilson, *Hurt People Hurt People* (Nashville, Tenn.: Thomas Nelson Publishers, 1993).

6 Story recounted by Jim Darnel, Liberty Church Westside, Pensacola, Fla., 1985.

7 See Hebrews 12:1.

8 Note that the only condition is not blaspheming the Holy Spirit (Matthew 12:31–32).

9 See 1 Peter 5:8–9.

10 See Revelation 13:8.

11 See Leviticus 26:40. We have more to say about this in the next chapter.

Chapter 3

1 See Genesis 15:7–8, 16; Exodus 12:40–41; Acts 7:5–6; 13:20; Galatians 3:16–17.

2 See Numbers 14:18; Isaiah 14:21; Lamentations 5:7; Daniel 9:4–19.

3 See Revelation 13:8.

4 This Scripture is discussed a little later in the section, "Scriptural Basis for Freedom from Sins of the Fathers and Resulting Curses" in this chapter.

5 See Matthew 25:32–33.

6 See Genesis 1:26–27.

7 See Romans 5:9–10; Ephesians 2:5; 1 Thessalonians 5:9.

8 See the story of the sower in Mark 4:3–20. The good soil *received* the Word.

9 See Hebrews 11:6.

10 This statute is acted upon in 2 Chronicles 25:3–4 and reaffirmed in Jeremiah 31:29–30.

11 The phrase "identification repentance" is a modern term used by various intercessory organizations—i.e., Generals of Intercession—to represent "standing

in the gap" and "making up the hedge" as we identify with, and repent for, other people and their sin.

12 This passage is repeated in Deuteronomy 5:9–10.

13 See Matthew 6:21, KJ21.

14 The entire passage of Romans 1:18–32 is significant. Please note specifically 1:25.

15 See Genesis 2:16–17.

16 Please read this sad story in Genesis 3:1–7.

17 See Romans 5:6; Ephesians 2:12.

18 See 2 Kings 17:6–23.

19 "The Lamb, slain from the foundation of the world" (Revelation 13:8, KJ21).

20 See 2 Timothy 1:7.

21 When we minister, we like to move in a logical and orderly way from SOFCs to UGBs to SSHs to DO, progressively reclaiming the lost ground or "place." Because the problem areas were so interconnected, the procedure we used in ministering to Sandy was atypical and, consequently, not a good training model. We did what was necessary, however, to gain her freedom and healing as the Holy Spirit led us. In actuality, it is not uncommon for the "stereotype" training model to be "customized" by the Holy Spirit for each ministry receiver.

22 *The Interpreter's Dictionary of the Bible* (Nashville: Abingdon Press, 1985).

23 Gordon D. Fee and Douglas Stuart, *How to Read the Bible for All It's Worth* (Grand Rapids: Zondervan Publishing House, 1982), 136. Fee and Stuart provide a powerful correlation between God's covenant and "suzerain" covenants, common in Old Testament times, given by "an all-powerful overlord to a weaker, dependent vassal (servant)."

24 The first blood was shed by God Himself on behalf of Adam and Eve (see Genesis 3:21).

25 Kenneth Copeland of Kenneth Copeland Ministries, Fort Worth, TX, public communication at a conference, 1986.

26 Derek Prince, *Curses: Cause and Cure*, Tape series no. 6011, Derek Prince Ministries, Fort Lauderdale, Fla., 1983. Also see his book *Blessings and Cursings*.

27 The Bible contains prophecy declaring that there shall be only two exiles. Then the root of Jesse will come and the animals will be at peace. See Isaiah 11, particularly verse 11.

28 See James 1:17.

29 See Genesis 6:7, 13.

30 See Exodus 7–12.

31 See Deuteronomy 7:11. Similar statements are repeated many times throughout Leviticus and Deuteronomy.

32 Fee and Stuart, *How to Read the Bible for All It's Worth*, 136.

33 See Genesis 3.

34 See Galatians 3:13.

35 See Mark 11:23.

36 See 1 Corinthians 6:12; 10:23.

37 See Philippians 4:11–12.

38 See Galatians 3:13.

39 See Matthew 5:43–44.

40 See Romans 12:14.

41 See Matthew 7:1.

42 See Revelation 22:20.
43 See 2 Samuel 11:4.
44 See 2 Samuel 11:8, 12–13.
45 See 2 Samuel 11:14–15.
46 See 2 Samuel 11:16–17.
47 See 2 Samuel 12:10–14.
48 See 2 Samuel 12:15–19. God spared David, but the penalty for adultery (death by stoning) fell onto the son. Is this fair, or consistent, with the previously mentioned Scriptures about each one dying for his own sin?
49 See 2 Samuel 13:1–18.
50 See 2 Samuel 13:28–29.
51 See 2 Samuel 15.
52 See 2 Samuel 18:14.
53 See 1 Kings 11:4, 6.
54 The names *Coniah* and *Jeconiah* are also used for Jehoiachin.
55 See Jeremiah 22:24–30.
56 See 1 Chronicles 3:5; Luke 3:31.
57 See Luke 3:23.
58 See Ruth 1:22 and Matthew 1:5.
59 See Matthew 1:5.
60 See Genesis 32:22–31.
61 See Genesis 27:12–13.
62 See Genesis 31:30–35 (NIV).
63 See Genesis 35:16–20.
64 See Genesis 20:2; 26:7.
65 In Ezekiel 13:5 and 22:30, God was looking for a man to "stand in for" another.
66 See Daniel 9; Nehemiah 1, 9; Ezra 9.
67 See Jeremiah 25:11–12; 29:10.
68 See Nehemiah 1:5–11; 9:5–37.
69 George Otis Jr., *Transformations*, a video produced by Sentinel Group, Inc., Wash., 1999.
70 See 2 Corinthians 3:6.
71 See John 20:23.
72 See 1 John 1:9.
73 See Galatians 3:13.
74 See Colossians 1:13.
75 See 1 John 3:1–2.

Chapter 4

1 See 2 Thessalonians 2:13.
2 See Romans 8:29.
3 See 2 Corinthians 7:1.
4 The redemption of our body is yet to occur. See Romans 8:23.
5 See Romans 12:2.
6 See Jeremiah 1:12.
7 See John 10:10.
8 See 1 Corinthians 1:17–18.
9 See Leviticus 26:40–42.

[10] See 2 Corinthians 10:5.

[11] See Romans 12:2.

Chapter 5

[1] John 14 provides us with many examples of Jesus showing us the Father.

[2] See Matthew 8:2–4; Mark 1:40–44; Luke 17:12–17.

[3] See John 4:17–29.

[4] See John 8:11.

[5] See Mark 7:24–30; 9:17–29.

[6] Peter's betrayal is recorded in all four gospels: Matthew 26:31–35, 69–75; Mark 14:27–31, 66–72; Luke 22:31–34, 54–62; John 13:37–38; 18:15–18, 25–27.

[7] Max Lucado, *He Still Moves Stones* (Dallas: Word, 1993), 200.

[8] Note: Not all depression is rooted in hurts; nor does all depression have a spiritual basis. Some depression has physical roots, such as a chemical/hormonal imbalance. If this is the case, the ministry receiver will need medication until his physical condition is adequately treated.

[9] We do this using the steps at the end of this chapter.

[10] See Numbers 11:10.

[11] See Matthew 26:38.

[12] See Deuteronomy 31:6; Matthew 28:20; Hebrews 13:5.

[13] Ed. M. Smith, *Beyond Tolerable Recovery, Basic Training Seminar* (Campbellsville, Ken.: Family Care Publishing, 1999), 140.

[14] Ibid., 148.

[15] Note: Here we utilize the same principle of confirming but use the Restoring the Foundations integrated approach to biblical healing ministry approach. It is not intended to represent the methodology of Theophostic Counseling.

[16] See John 11:1–45.

[17] See John 11:44.

[18] Excerpt from *Under His Wing* by Patsy Claremont.

[19] See 1 Peter 5:8.

[20] See Romans 8:28.

[21] See 1 Corinthians 3:9.

[22] See Ruth 3:9.

[23] See Jeremiah 1:12.

[24] See John 1:40–42.

Chapter 6

[1] See 1 John 2:12–14.

[2] See John 8:31–32.

[3] See Ezekiel 8–10.

[4] See Ephesians 2:8–10.

[5] See Colossians 1:12–13.

[6] See Genesis 4:7.

[7] See John 10:10.

[8] See Ephesians 4:27.

[9] Don Basham, "Deliver Us from Evil," *New Wine Magazine*, 1978.

[10] Frank Hammond and Ida Mae, *Pigs in the Parlor* (Kirkwood, Mo.: Impact Books, 1973).

[11] Kent Philpott and R.L. Hymers, *The Deliverance Book* (Van Nyes, Calif.: Bible Voice, Inc., 1977).

[12] Restoring the Foundations (RTF) ministry and the integrated approach to biblical healing ministry are phrases used interchangeably to represent harmonious ministry to the four problem areas afflicting us all.

[13] See Luke 11:24–26.

[14] See Hebrews 12:3.

[15] See 1 Corinthians 10:6, 11 and neighboring verses.

[16] See 1 Thessalonians 4:3–4; 2 Timothy 2:20–21.

[17] See Genesis 15:16.

[18] See Matthew 8:28–34; parallel passage Luke 8:26–39.

[19] Please note as examples Matthew 4:24; 8:16; 31–32; 9:32–33; 12:22; 17:18; Mark 1:27; 3:10–11; 5:8–13; 7:26; Luke 6:18; 7:21; 11:14; 13:11–17; 13:32.

[20] Based on Luke 4:18.

[21] See Matthew 10:1, 8; parallel passages in Mark 3:15; Luke 9:1–2.

[22] See Luke 10:1, 9, 17.

[23] See Mark 16:15–20.

[24] See Mark 16:17.

[25] See Acts 19:12–17.

[26] See Matthew 12:28.

[27] See 1 Peter 5:8.

[28] See Colossians 2:15.

[29] See Revelation 20:10.

[30] See as examples Matthew 12:24–27; 14:26; Luke 24:37–39; John 7:20; 8:48–49, 52; 10:20–21; Acts 5:16; 8:7; 16:16–18; 19:12.

[31] See Matthew 12:27; Mark 9:38; Luke 9:49; Acts 19:13–16.

[32] Chris Cobb, *Deliverance: The Children's Bread*, a training manual, 1993, 8, quoting from these early Christians and their writings.

[33] This admonishment is found in Matthew 11:15; 13:9, 16; Mark 4:9, 23; Luke 8:8; 14:35.

[34] Other Scriptures of interest relating to this issue include : Mark 9:41; Romans 1:6; 7:4; 8:9; 14:8; 1 Corinthians 15:23; 2 Corinthians 10:7; Galatians 3:28–29; 5:24.

[35] See Job 1:12; 2:6; Luke 22:31; Ephesians 1:20–21.

[36] See Ephesians 1:21; 6:12; Colossians 1:16; 2:15; 1 Peter 3:22; Daniel 10:13.

[37] Frank Peretti, *This Present Darkness* (Westchester, Ill.: Crossway Books, 1989); Frank Peretti, *Piercing the Darkness* (Westchester, Ill.: Crossway Books, 1989).

[38] See John 10:10.

[39] This is analogous to the seed sown on the path in Matthew 13:4, 19.

[40] See Ephesians 4:26–32; Colossians 3:8; James 1:19–20.

[41] See Luke 12:32; John 12:15; 2 Timothy 1:7.

[42] See Exodus 20:17; 1 Timothy 6:9–10.

[43] See Proverbs 14:30.

[44] See James 4:1–5.

[45] See Ephesians 2:2.

[46] See 1 Samuel 15:22–23.

[47] See Judges 14:3; 1 John 2:15–16.

[48] *Aim*, January 1994, 9.

[49] See 1 Timothy 5:13.

[50] See James 3:16.

[51] See Proverbs 6:19.

[52] See Hebrews 12:15.

[53] See Matthew 18:21–35.

[54] The book by James G. Friesen, *Uncovering the Mystery of MPD* (San Bernardino, Calif.: Here's Life Publishers, Inc., 1991), presents an enlightened Christian approach to ministering to multiple personality disorder.

[55] Philpott and Hymers, *The Deliverance Book.*

[56] See Exodus 20:3–6.

[57] See 1 Corinthians 14:20.

[58] See Hebrews 5:14.

[59] Ernest B. Rockstad, *Enlightening Studies in Spiritual Warfare* (Andover, Kan.: Faith and Life Publications, 1985). Also an earlier tape series on *The Christian Life and Studies in Demonic Deliverance.*

[60] See Hebrews 12:1.

[61] See Matthew 8:28–34; Luke 8:26–39.

[62] Hammond, *Pigs in the Parlor.*

[63] The Shame-Fear-Control Stronghold resource may be obtained from Proclaiming His Word Ministries.

[64] See John 10:10.

[65] See Colossians 1:13.

[66] See Matthew 16:19; 18:18.

[67] See Matthew 12:43–45.

[68] This occurred in Betsy's deliverance, described at the beginning of this chapter.

[69] See Chapter 7 for a discussion of demonic strongholds.

[70] See Joshua 9:3–27.

[71] See 2 Samuel 21:1–2.

[72] See John 22:23.

[73] See Ezekiel 28:19.

[74] See Colossians 2:15.

[75] See Colossians 2:14 (NASB).

[76] See Matthew 12:43–45.

[77] Hammond, *Pigs in the Parlor.*

[78] Cobb, *Deliverance: The Children's Bread.*

[79] We have much more to say about this topic in Chapter V, "God's Weapons for Spiritual Warfare," in the book *Restoring the Foundations.*

[80] See Proverbs 18:21; James 3:2–12.

[81] See Romans 6:6–7; Galatians 2:20; 5:24.

[82] See Revelation 12:11–12.

[83] See Hebrews 10:25.

[84] See Psalm 22:3; Psalm 5:11–12.

[85] See Psalm 27:6; Psalm 149:6–9.

[86] This is one of the ways God "speaks."

[87] We call this type of demonic tactic a "lose-lose" or a "double-binding" strategy. Demons do their best to always keep us on the losing, failing, guilty side.

[88] We discuss soul ties in Chapter 7.

[89] See Ezekiel 22:30; Mark 2:3–5.

90 See Colossians 2:13–15.
91 See Colossians 2:14 (NASB).
92 See Mark 16:17; Luke 10:19.
93 See 1 Corinthians 3:9.
94 Some schools of deliverance ministry have developed lists of "The Proper Names of Demons." These have been gleaned from what the minister has heard in the spirit realm and what he has experienced in the response of demons. This knowledge may prove helpful in some instances but generally is not essential for deliverance once the legal ground of the first three problem areas has been recovered. Please see books by Win Worley if you desire to learn more in this area.
95 See Exodus 23:29–31.
96 See John 5:14, 8:11.
97 See Matthew 7:21–23.

Chapter 7

1 See examples in Joshua 6:2–24; 8:1–26; Judges 6:33–35; 7:1–8:12; 2 Chronicles 20:15–17, 20–27.
2 Sandy's testimony about getting free from this stronghold can be found in the chapters on ungodly beliefs and demonic oppression.
3 See page 278 for contact information.
4 See page 278 for contact information.

About the authors

1 Betsy has degrees in counselor education (M.A., Ed.S.), and Chester has degrees in mechanical (B.S.) and nuclear engineering (M.S., Ph.D.). They both earned their master's degrees in theology at Liberty Bible College in Pensacola, Florida.